Download Forms on Nolo.com

You can download the forms in this book at:

 www.nolo.com/back-of-book/SPNT.html

We'll also post updates whenever there's an important change to the law affecting this book—as well as articles and other related materials.

More Resources
from Nolo.com

 Legal Forms, Books, & Software
Hundreds of do-it-yourself products—all written in plain English, approved, and updated by our in-house legal editors.

 Legal Articles
Get informed with thousands of free articles on everyday legal topics. Our articles are accurate, up to date, and reader friendly.

 Find a Lawyer
Want to talk to a lawyer? Use Nolo to find a lawyer who can help you with your case.

NOLO
LAW for ALL

⚖ NOLO   The Trusted Name
(but don't take our word for it)

"In Nolo you can trust."
THE NEW YORK TIMES

"Nolo is always there in a jam as the nation's premier publisher of do-it-yourself legal books."
NEWSWEEK

"Nolo publications…guide people simply through the how, when, where and why of the law."
THE WASHINGTON POST

"[Nolo's]…material is developed by experienced attorneys who have a knack for making complicated material accessible."
LIBRARY JOURNAL

"When it comes to self-help legal stuff, nobody does a better job than Nolo…"
USA TODAY

"The most prominent U.S. publisher of self-help legal aids."
TIME MAGAZINE

"Nolo is a pioneer in both consumer and business self-help books and software."
LOS ANGELES TIMES

9th Edition

Special Needs Trusts

Protect Your Child's Financial Future

Kevin Urbatsch & Jessica Farinas Jones

NINTH EDITION	OCTOBER 2021
Editor	JANET PORTMAN
Cover Design	SUSAN PUTNEY
Book Design	SUSAN PUTNEY
Proofreading	SUSAN CARLSON GREENE
Index	VICTORIA BAKER
Printing	BANG PRINTING

ISSN: 2167-5716 (print)
ISSN: 2325-4920 (online)

ISBN: 978-1-4133-2901-8 (pbk)
ISBN: 978-1-4133-2902-5 (ebook)

Please note

Accurate, plain-English legal information can help you solve many of your own legal problems. But this text is not a substitute for personalized advice from a knowledgeable lawyer. If you want the help of a trained professional—and we'll always point out situations in which we think that's a good idea—consult an attorney licensed to practice in your state.

About the Authors

Kevin Urbatsch is a principal of the boutique estate planning firm, The Urbatsch Law Firm P.C. in Berkeley, California. He is a nationally recognized expert in the unique planning needs of individuals with disabilities and their families. Mr. Urbatsch is the National Director of the Academy of Special Needs Planners. He writes and is a frequent lecturer both locally and nationally on planning for persons with disabilities, primarily concerning special needs trust drafting and administration.

Jessica Farinas Jones is an attorney at the special needs and settlement planning law firm, The Urbatsch Law Firm P.C., located in Berkeley, California. Jessica is a frequent presenter on special needs planning, including first-party and third-party topics such as settlement planning and third-party special needs trusts. She is a California Continuing Education of the Bar (CEB) update author and has coauthored articles in the 2018 California Trusts and Estates Quarterly as well as the CEB Estate Planning Reporter, both covering Achieving a Better Life Experience (ABLE) accounts. Jessica is a member of the Academy of Special Needs Planners (ASNP) and served on the Planning Committee for their 2018 National Meeting in Las Vegas, Nevada. She has been a member of the California Bar since 2016.

Table of Contents

Appendixes

Your Legal Companion for Special Needs Trusts

I f you have been providing care for a child or another loved one with special needs, you've no doubt thought about what will happen when you're no longer able to give that care. Of course, you can leave property to your loved one, but—as you are probably aware—doing so without some careful planning will almost certainly jeopardize his or her ability to receive benefits under the Supplemental Security Income (SSI) and Medicaid programs. Unless you make the right legal arrangements, benefits that your loved one is relying on to meet his or her basic needs simply won't be available again until the inheritance is used up. Losing access to public benefits for months or even years while the inheritance burns down can have serious negative consequences (a small inheritance might not compensate for the public benefits that the recipient would otherwise receive). With a little forethought and planning, beneficiaries can access their inheritance to enhance their quality of life *and* maintain essential public benefits.

A special needs trust protects your loved one's government benefits and supplements his or her needs. This book explains how special needs trusts work and how you can set one up yourself. We give you the documents you need, with plenty of explanations, examples, and easy-to-understand instructions. It will take a little time and concentration, but you can do it. When you're done, you will know that your loved one's benefits will be protected when you're gone.

Step by step, this book:

- explains how special needs trusts protect the government benefits of your loved one (the trust's beneficiary)
- describes the role of the trustee (the person who disburses the funds in the trust) and helps you figure out who should serve as trustee (during your lifetime) and successor trustees (after your lifetime)

- explains who can contribute to the special needs trust, as well as the types of assets that can be added to the trust and any associated special laws or rules pertaining to those assets
- shows you how to draft a special needs trust and make it legally valid
- tells you how to set up a trust bank account and how to modify your estate plan to leave money to the trust at your death
- shows you how to leave a detailed letter or diary about the beneficiary's needs
- explains how to keep up on SSI and Medicaid rules, file taxes, keep track of successor trustees, and make sure that the trust continues to meet your loved one's needs
- details the duties of the trustees who will serve when you're gone, and
- provides a detailed explanation on an alternative option, a "pooled trust" (a trust for many beneficiaries, managed by a professional) if you don't want to set up your own special needs trust.

This book also shows you how to work with experts to make the most of your trust. For example, at times you may want to consult a lawyer, an accountant, a tax professional, or a financial planner. We suggest when that might be a good idea, and help you find the support you need. And because you'll have a solid understanding of the important issues, you'll be able to work confidently with professionals.

Before proceeding, understand that the trust we discuss here cannot be set up in the following circumstances:

- by the special needs person him- or herself. For example, someone with special needs who receives an inheritance or other money cannot use our trust to hold the money and protect that person's eligibility for government benefits. This scenario would require a different, more complex type of special needs trust and the person with a disability will likely need to hire a lawyer to help, and
- by readers who have or will have an estate plan of their own, such as a will or living trust. These readers should work with an estate planning attorney (perhaps the one who drafted their documents) to set up a special needs trust within that framework.

This Book's Special Needs Trust Will Not Protect Assets Owned by a Person With a Disability

This book will not help to protect assets that belong to a person with a disability. Rather, it helps you protect that person's eligibility for government benefits when you give that person assets as a gift or an inheritance.

When a person with a disability already owns assets—perhaps from a personal injury award, retirement plan, life insurance policy, or an unplanned-for inheritance—the owner can take steps to protect those assets, but not through the type of trust described in this book. Trusts that can help protect the assets that already belong to a person with a disability are "first-party" trusts that go by a variety of names, such as "first-party special needs trust," "payback special needs trust," "litigation special needs trust," "Miller Trust," "pooled SNT," "(d)(4)(A) SNT," and "(d)(4)(C) SNT." All of these first-party trusts must meet federal and state rules designed to keep applicants from sheltering their property in a trust in order to meet program eligibility requirements. These trusts are also generally subject to "payback" rules that require that the state be reimbursed for medical expenses after the trust beneficiary dies. Because each state has very specific rules that constantly change, if you want to establish one of these trusts, you'll need the help of an experienced special needs planning lawyer in your state. See Chapter 11 for information about finding and working with such a lawyer.

This book is designed to help families leave money to a loved one with a disability in a "third-party" special needs trust, or a trust funded with the assets of anyone other than the person with a disability. The rules are a lot easier to follow in third-party planning than in first-party planning, simply because the government wants to encourage people to leave money for the benefit of their loved ones with disabilities. By contrast, it does not want people to stash their own money in a trust in order to stay eligible for public benefits. To discourage this, the rules for first-party trust planning are more restrictive than those for third-party planning.

Chapter 1 gives you more information on the limitations of who can use the trust in this book, and options for these readers.

Finally, even if you don't make the trust provided in our book, you'll find that simply reading it will give you a wealth of information. You'll be prepared for an informed discussion with a lawyer whom you consult to set up a special needs trust.

Get Updates and Forms at This Book's Companion Page on Nolo.com

You can download the special needs trust document, the letter to trustee, the sample letter of intent, and the form, the Florida witness statement, and the worksheet, Questions to Ask a Potential Private Professional Trustee, at:

www.nolo.com/back-of-book/SPNT.html

When we have important changes to the information in this book, we'll post updates on this dedicated web page (we call it the book's companion page).

Be sure to check out the Wills, Trusts, and Probate section on Nolo.com for a wide variety of articles on estate planning.

RESOURCE

Consult the glossary for help with legalese. In Nolo's usual plain-English style, we explain a complicated legal topic with a minimum of legalese. However, when you interact with lawyers, banks, accountants, and other professionals in the course of establishing and running your trust, you'll find that these folks use legal terms frequently. So that you're not left scratching your head, you'll need to be familiar with the lingo. In addition to defining legal terms as they come up in the text, we provide a glossary of legal terms for your reference. You'll find the Glossary after Chapter 11.

> **CAUTION**
>
> **Do not use the trust document in this book in Louisiana.** While Louisiana residents will find the discussions in this book useful for understanding how special needs trusts work, the trust provided by this book was not designed to be used in Louisiana. If you are a Louisiana resident and want to make a special needs trust, see an experienced attorney.

We hope that this book will give you not only the legal documents you need, but also peace of mind from knowing that you've taken steps to protect your loved one after you're gone. ●

People Who Can Benefit From a Special Needs Trust

Special needs trusts enhance the quality of life for people with a disability, by maximizing the resources available to them. It preserves their eligibility for Supplementary Security Income (SSI) and Medicaid (which together pay for food, shelter, and medical care, but little else). The special needs trust can pay for additional things that make life better.

The following sections explain in detail which groups of people will benefit from a special needs trust. If you're unfamiliar with how Medicare and Medicaid work, or need a refresher, take a look at our brief summary of these programs, which includes the Affordable Care Act (Obamacare), at the end of this chapter.

People With a Permanent or Severe Disability Who Are Unable to Earn a Living

Special needs trusts are most commonly used for people who have permanent or severe disabling conditions. These people likely will qualify for government assistance from the SSI and Medicaid programs their entire lives.

It's important to understand that a person with a disability, as that term is commonly understood (in the context of fair housing and fair employment), won't necessarily qualify for SSI or Medicaid. For purposes of these assistance programs, the government defines "disability" as the inability to do any "substantial gainful activity" (SGA) by reason of any medically determinable physical or mental impairment. This condition must be expected to result in death or has lasted or can be expected to last for a continuous period of not less than 12 months.

So, in order to qualify for SSI or Medicaid, the two qualifications are: The person has a disability that will last at least a year or is expected to result in death; and the person must be unable to engage in SGA.

But we aren't done yet. How, exactly, does the government measure SGA? SGA is a dollar amount, a maximum amount that a person with a disability may earn each month while maintaining eligibility for benefits. In 2021, the SGA figure is $1,310 per month. The Social Security Administration reasons that an individual who is able to earn at least this amount per month is able to engage in competitive employment in the national economy. (Of course, this is contrary to what many people would view as a reasonable figure.)

Keep in mind that the Social Security Administration's definition of "disability" for benefit purposes is not the same as you will encounter in other contexts. For example, the federal Fair Housing and Amendments Act forbids discrimination against tenants who have a disability, but the definition of disabled has nothing to do with the tenant's earning capacity. (Instead, the fair housing act focuses on being substantially impaired with respect to major life activities, being regarded as such, or having a history of this condition.)

Only United States citizens automatically qualify for SSI benefits when they meet these qualifications. Noncitizens can qualify for SSI if they are legally in the country and meet some additional qualifications.

Low-income people 65 or older are also eligible for SSI (this group must meet asset and income requirements, but not the disability test). When someone *under* the age of 65 applies for SSI or Medicaid benefits, the Social Security Administration makes a determination as to whether the person is disabled. (Chapter 11 lists references to the rules and other sources of law regarding SSI and Medicaid rules that affect special needs trusts.)

People with blindness, developmental disabilities, Down syndrome, organic brain damage, chronic mental illness, physical paralysis (para-plegia), or congenital disabling afflictions, such as cerebral palsy or cystic fibrosis, have been the most common automatic beneficiaries of government benefits for persons with disabilities. But many other physical and mental conditions meet the Social Security Administration's definition of a disability that is likely to last a lifetime. Some of them are listed below.

Conditions That Can Cause Permanent Disability: A Partial List

agoraphobia	hemophilia	organic brain syndrome (OBS)
Alzheimer's disease	HIV	
amputations	Huntington's chorea	Parkinson's disease
bipolar disorder	kidney malfunction	phenylketonuria (PKU)
cancer (many types)	leukemia	severe autistic disorder
congenital heart disease	lupus	sickle cell anemia
diabetes mellitus (Type 2)	multiple chemical sensitivity	spina bifida
		Tay-Sachs disease
emphysema	multiple sclerosis	thalassemia
fetal alcohol syndrome	muscular dystrophy	traumatic spine damage
	obsessive-compulsive disorder	Turner's syndrome
fragile X syndrome		

Someone Who Might Get Better

Many disabling conditions are not permanent. For example, many combat veterans suffer from posttraumatic stress disorder, which produces a combination of mental, emotional, and physical symptoms, making it impossible to work for years, but not necessarily for a lifetime. Even then, however, it might make a lot of sense to create a special needs trust because it's impossible to tell just how long the disability will last.

How the Definition of "Disabled" Is Changing

Many factors make it hard to predict whether someone who currently has a disability will always need to rely on SSI and Medicaid.

Changes in the workplace. For SSI eligibility purposes, someone who can't work is disabled. But, as the workplace changes, so does the definition of disabled. For instance, when most people worked on farms, someone with a developmental disorder might not have been considered disabled for the purposes of an SSI-type program, because formal learning wasn't necessary to heft a pitchfork, milk cows, plant corn, or do housework. In 21st-century high-tech America, however, a pronounced difficulty in learning makes it difficult to find a job. On the other hand, technological advances in the medical field have made it possible for people with paraplegia or severe visual impairment to perform a large range of productive work. People with disabilities who are able to work and earn a certain amount of money will not meet the SSA definition of "disabled."

New treatments for old disabilities. Modern medical techniques and discoveries in areas such as gene therapy, stem cells, and neurotransmitters (molecules that facilitate nerve impulse transmissions) offer the possibility of cures for a broad range of conditions that currently are incurable. Parkinson's and Alzheimer's disease are two devastating conditions that might be amenable to treatment in ten or 20 years.

Similarly, techniques to regenerate damaged or severed nerve cells might someday offer relief to people who cannot move their limbs because of a spinal injury. Mentally disabling conditions also are reaping the benefits of modern medical technology. The pharmaceutical industry has developed drugs that let people with a large range of formerly incapacitating mental and mood conditions, such as schizoaffective disorder or bipolar disorder, engage in productive activity.

Technological advances. Profound changes in technology have ameliorated some physically disabling conditions. For example, hearing aids or surgery largely eliminate the disability of deafness for many Americans. More change is on the way in fields such as robotics and nanotechnology. For instance, research is underway to help people whose arms or legs have been amputated to regain near-full functionality with the help of "intelligent" prostheses, and to develop a computerized interface that helps blind people experience visual feedback from the environment.

Planning With Recovery in Mind

The SSI and Medicaid programs have not, by and large, taken medical and technological advances into account when determining disability. A condition that prevented employment in 1950 is often assumed to do so today. However, this could change at any time. Your loved one might not always be eligible for SSI and Medicaid, either because disabilities are defined differently or because of a dramatic recovery.

There's no way to know whether someone's disability will improve with time, either naturally or through medical and technological intervention. But even so, you can create a special needs trust without worrying that you will needlessly tie up your loved one's inheritance. The trust document takes into account the possibility that the trust, for whatever reason, might not always be necessary, and allows the trustee to terminate the trust.

> **EXAMPLE:** Jeanne leaves $100,000 in her will to a special needs trust she created for the benefit of her daughter Cassie, who is ten and has been diagnosed with schizophrenia. Jeanne named Joanne, Cassie's aunt, to take over as trustee when Jeanne dies. The trust gives the trustee complete discretion as to how the funds may be spent for Cassie's benefit, provided that disbursements do not disqualify Cassie for SSI and Medicaid.
>
> The trust document also states that if someday Cassie does not need or does not qualify for SSI or Medicaid, the person serving as trustee may terminate the trust and distribute the remaining trust money to Cassie outright.
>
> Twenty years later, when Jeanne dies, the $100,000 passes to the trust. Cassie is now 30 years old and the Social Security Administration's guidelines no longer consider her disabled for purposes of SSI and Medicaid. Joanne, the person serving as trustee, terminates the trust and distributes the property to Cassie outright.

If you are certain that a loved one with a disability is likely to get better, another option is to leave the funds to that person outright, with the expectation that the recipient will create a first-party special needs trust if needed. (A first-party special needs trust is one funded with the beneficiary's own money—unlike the trust you make with this book, which is funded with your money or someone else's.) Remember though, a first-party special needs trust is more expensive to set up than the special needs trust covered in this book, can only be set up for someone under the age of 65, must be for the "sole benefit" of the beneficiary, and requires payback to the state's Medicaid agency on the termination of the trust (which results from the death of the beneficiary). You will need an attorney's help to make sure that the trust complies with the Medicaid eligibility rules of your state.

Many people find the first-party special needs trust unattractive, because the Medicaid payback often exhausts the remaining funds in the trust upon termination of the trust, leaving nothing left over for other family members to inherit. Consult with an experienced estate planning attorney before deciding to forego a special needs trust now in anticipation of your loved one's setting up a first-party trust when you pass away.

Someone Who Might Need a Special Needs Trust Later

A special needs trust may also be useful for people who have conditions that are likely to get worse. Although they might not need help now, as the condition progresses, they might need to receive financial assistance from SSI or Medicaid.

But how do we know that a person's condition is likely to get worse? This issue often comes up in families with young children, who are beginning to show symptoms of a disability. In young children, it is difficult to know how the disability will develop over the years. Will the child be able to go to college? Will the child be able to join the work force? No magic ball can show us whether the child will grow into an adult so affected by a disability that the adult needs the added level of support that a special needs trust would provide.

In this situation, creating a special needs trust involves some guess-work. But if you think it's more likely than not that a loved one will need help either managing finances or government assistance for a significant length of time, it makes sense to set up a special needs trust. There's really no risk. The trust in this book includes a clause that allows the person serving as trustee to terminate the trust if changes in the beneficiary's disability make a special needs trust unnecessary. If it turns out that the trust is needed, however, the trustee can use trust funds to pay for all kinds of useful things, such as tuition, travel, tools, cultural events, and companion services. (See Chapter 2 for a complete list.) And because the trustee has complete control over how funds are used, you don't need to worry about the beneficiary's spending it in ways that are not acceptable to you.

Someone Who Is Eligible for Medicare or SSDI

A loved one who receives Medicare or Social Security Disability Insurance (SSDI) might not need a special needs trust because these programs do not base eligibility on the amount of money or assets an applicant has. There's no need to keep an inheritance in trust; your loved one can own it outright without losing SSDI or Medicare benefits.

If, however, the SSDI payment is low, SSI may be a valuable way to supplement your loved one's income. In addition, Medicaid might be necessary to provide benefits not included in the Medicare program— for instance, long-term nursing home care or in-home care. In other words, someone can start off with only Medicare and SSDI, but progress to Medicaid and even SSI. Once that transition happens, it makes sense to consider a special needs trust to preserve these benefits and provide a source of added income.

Put another way, suppose your loved one, Peter, suffers from a degenerative mental illness that almost certainly will require long-term care in a nursing facility. Establishing a special needs trust might make sense even if he is, at the time, eligible only for Medicare. However, if you *don't* expect Peter to need long-term nursing care, you might prefer to not tie up his inheritance in a special needs trust (assuming that you don't have concerns about Peter's ability to spend the inheritance wisely and you're not worried about the possibility that he will become the victim of predators). Instead, you can leave the property directly to Peter, who can continue to receive Medicare and SSDI.

TIP

Medicaid goes by different names in different states. Medicaid is a combined federal and state program, and is known by a different name in some states. For example, in California it's called Medi-Cal, and in Massachusetts, MassHealth.

Sources of Support and Medical Care for People With Disabilities

	Who Qualifies	Benefits
SSI	People with limited income and few resources; if a noncitizen, must meet certain criteria	Monthly cash payments (amount depends on living arrangement, marital status, and disability)
Medicaid	People who qualify for SSI People who have too much income for SSI but might still independently qualify People who qualify by Medicaid waiver People who are in a state that has enacted "expanded" Medicaid and have income below 138% of the federal poverty level (FPL)	Most medical services, including long-term nursing home care and pharmaceuticals
SSDI & Social Security	People who have paid enough Social Security taxes, without regard to resources or income People who become disabled before age 22, if their parents qualify for either SSDI or Social Security retirement benefits	Monthly cash payments
Medicare	People who are eligible for Social Security disability benefits because of their work history or that of an eligible parent	Most medical services, but not long-term care

For more information, see www.ssa.gov.

Someone Who Needs Assistance Managing an Inheritance

Even if a person is never eligible for SSI or Medicaid, it can still make sense to place that person's inheritance in a special needs trust. This is particularly true for people who are unfamiliar with or incapable of prudently managing money. Even in the absence of an established disability, a special needs trust could be helpful for a person with mild developmental disabilities, mild autism, attention deficit disorder, or bipolar syndrome; or for someone who is easily influenced by financial predators.

In any of these circumstances, the special needs trust by its very nature would help, because the trust names a qualified person to help the beneficiary manage and spend trust assets. This helper is the trustee. The trust puts a host of rules in place to make sure that that the trustee manages the money in the best interests of the beneficiary. Such trusts are often called "spendthrift" trusts, when used to keep assets out of the hands of a beneficiary (and of his or her creditors) and in the firm control of a wise trustee. So, even for those persons who never need or use public benefits, a special needs trust can be used to optimally manage an inheritance.

Ultimately, only you can decide whether it makes sense to provide the long-term management of a loved one's inheritance that a special needs trust provides, instead of leaving the inheritance directly to that person. If you decide to use a special needs trust, the beneficiary is sure to receive much the same benefit from the inheritance as would be the case with an outright gift, even though a small portion of the trust assets may be spent on administrative fees over the years.

Alternatives to a Special Needs Trust

Special needs trusts may not be the right solution for every family. Trusts can cost time and money to administer, and the person serving as trustee may be called on to make difficult decisions about investing and spending trust assets.

Leaving Money to a Friend or Relative

Rather than rely on a special needs trust, you might be inclined to leave some money to a friend or relative who agrees to watch out for your loved one's needs after your death. With this plan, you would leave nothing to your loved one with disabilities.

Unfortunately, this informal approach has several serious downsides.

The main problem is that because the person to whom you leave the property will own it outright, you can't ensure that the money will end up benefiting your intended recipient, no matter how honorable everyone's intentions at the outset. In addition, the money would be subject to the friend's or relative's creditors in a lawsuit or bankruptcy. If your loved one is still alive at the friend's or relative's death, the property could pass to that person's heirs if the relative or friend fails to direct otherwise in a will or trust. Then again, it could go to a spouse in the event of a divorce. The biggest problem is that because the laws that govern how trustees must manage assets (described in Chapter 5) won't apply to the person who has control of the money, if that person spends the money on a new car instead of on your loved one's needs, there is nothing that anyone will be able to do about it.

This method is usually a big mistake because it leaves the person who needs the most protection reliant on the continued goodwill of others—with no recourse if your wishes are not honored.

Leaving Money Directly to Your Loved One

Leaving money directly to a person with a disability will almost certainly eliminate his or her eligibility for SSI and Medicaid. It also can have devastating results if that person lacks the capacity to manage money or is susceptible to financial predators. The only time it might be better to leave property directly to someone with a disability is if that person is unlikely to ever qualify for SSI and Medicaid and has the ability to manage the funds.

Using a Pooled Trust

If you don't want to set up your own special needs trust, you might wish to join an existing "pooled trust." Almost every state has at least one nonprofit organization that operates this type of trust. In a pooled trust, gifts to many disabled beneficiaries are combined so that they can be efficiently and professionally managed and have better investment options. The trustee invests and spends funds for the beneficiaries without affecting their eligibility for SSI and Medicaid. If you sign up for one of these pooled trusts, you can leave the trust details to them.

One of the benefits of pooled trusts is that the administrative fees, like trustee fees, are generally much lower than the costs of maintaining a special needs trust that has been drafted or customized for a specific individual. The downside of a pooled trust is that the beneficiary will receive less attention from his or her trustee. Because the pooled trust is managing hundreds, if not thousands, of beneficiary subaccounts, their approach to administration is less hands-on than that of a trustee managing a customized third-party special needs trust for one individual. The trustee of a pooled trust acts more like a specialized bill payer. However, as mentioned above, the investment options are sometimes better, and the management of the trust is still professional in nature.

Pooled trusts can prove convenient when you are concerned about whether there will be enough funds at the time of your death to absorb the administrative cost of a third-party special needs trust. If you are unsure about committing to a pooled trust at the outset due to the administrative cost of an individual special needs trust, you can take a more middle-ground approach: You can provide in your estate plan that your loved one's inheritance will go to a pooled trust if it is below a certain dollar amount, or to a third-party special needs trust if it is over that amount. Consult an attorney about the wisdom of this approach, and for help in adding this trigger to your estate plan. Chapter 6 discusses pooled trusts in detail.

Private Health Care and the Affordable Care Act (ACA)

Until recently, Americans' access to health care was typically tied to employment. This created a challenge for people with disabilities, because their disabilities often kept them from being able to work. Even if they could afford the cost of individual (nongroup) health care premiums, insurance companies would refuse to provide individual coverage because of their preexisting conditions.

Under the ACA (also known as Obamacare), many of the barriers to private health care for persons with disabilities have disappeared. The biggest change is that a preexisting condition no longer denies an individual access to private health care. The ACA also makes private health care more attractive because it removes the lifetime limits on health insurance that made private plans unattractive to many persons with profound disabilities. Another benefit of the ACA is that it requires private health care coverage for children (to age 26) on a parent's plan, even if that child has moved away from home, has a disability, is going to school, or is married. The ACA also caps the amount of money that a person will have to pay out of pocket each year on premiums and deductibles.

The Trump administration made some changes to the ACA. The most notable concerned the original mandate that all persons in the United States have health care insurance; failure to procure insurance could result in a tax penalty. The Trump administration reduced the tax penalty to $0, essentially removing the tax altogether. Without the negative consequence that would result from not obtaining insurance, the insurance mandate was effectively nullified.

The Trump administration also returned to the practice of linking healthcare to employment when it modified the ACA to give states the option, with approval by the federal government, to require Medicaid recipients to provide documentation that they either go to work or school. As of February 2021, 19 states have requested this link from the federal government. Some have been approved, though only two states have implemented it.

Despite the many challenges to it over the last administration, the ACA remains mostly in place. It provides people with limited incomes—like many people with disabilities—ways to pay premiums at a reduced cost.

The ACA makes these subsidies available to individuals who earn up to 400% of the Federal Poverty Limit (FPL). (For 2021, the income limit for a single person to qualify for a subsidy is about $51,040.)

In many states, you can search for and compare health care plans on the state's health care website (called an exchange). If your state doesn't have an exchange, use the federal government's website at www.healthcare.gov.

Medicare

Medicare is a government-run health care system. It pays for most medical services (but very limited long-term care and very limited in-home care) required by people with disabilities who are eligible for Social Security or Social Security Disability Insurance (SSDI) benefits. Medicare is like health insurance—it is designed to get you well, but not take care of you if you cannot take care of yourself. For example, it will not pay for somebody to assist you in activities of daily living, such as bathing, toileting, dressing, transferring from bed to chair, or feeding. A person need not be poor to get Medicare benefits, but because eligibility for Medicare is based on wage contributions, many people with disabilities fail to qualify for coverage.

Medicaid

Medicaid is a state-managed program that pays for virtually all health care delivered to people who don't have private insurance and who don't qualify for Medicare. Some programs, such as sheltered workshops, mental health supports, and independent living supports, are available only under the Medicaid program. (Some states give Medicaid a different name—for example, Medi-Cal in California and MassHealth in Massachusetts.)

Before the ACA, to get Medicaid you had to be classified as either "disabled" or older than age 64, and you had to have been poor enough to qualify for SSI, which provides income support for people with limited income and resources below $2,000.

The ACA expands Medicaid to cover persons with disabilities who have incomes up to 138% of the FPL ($17,609 in 2021). People with a disability can have more than $2,000 in resources and still qualify for Medicaid, if their income is below 138% of the FPL. This expanded program does not apply to persons currently receiving Medicaid, those over age 65, those applying for long-term nursing home care, and some others.

However, not every state has agreed to participate in the Medicaid expansion program. To learn whether your state has agreed to it, visit www.healthcare.gov/medicaid-chip/medicaid-expansion-and-you. This website also explains the options for your loved one with special needs who resides in a state that refuses to expand Medicaid eligibility.

Medicaid Eligibility Rules

Within limits set by federal law, each state can determine who is eligible for its Medicaid program. In most states, someone who is eligible for SSI is also automatically eligible for Medicaid.

Nine states, however, determine eligibility for Medicaid separately from eligibility for SSI. In these states, the income and resource limits for Medicaid are either roughly the same as for SSI or somewhat lower. So someone could be eligible for SSI but not for Medicaid. These states are listed below. They're called "209(b) states" after a section of the Social Security Act that allows states to determine Medicaid eligibility separately.

This book assumes that someone who is ineligible for SSI because of excess income or resources is also ineligible for Medicaid. However, in most states, a person with excess income or resources can become eligible for Medicaid by spending down the resources or excess income. And a person with disabilities who does not qualify for SSI could still qualify for Medicaid by being determined to be "medically needy."

For the many people with disabilities who don't qualify for Medicaid, health care costs cause serious financial complications. For example, if parents leave money directly to an adult child with a disability, the gift will disqualify the child from SSI and from Medicaid until the money is used up. This is where the special needs trust comes in. It allows people with special needs to enhance their quality of life with money and assets received from others without losing SSI and Medicaid.

Medicaid and SSI Eligibility: State Differences			
Eligibility for SSI and Medicaid determined separately ("209(b) states")		Medicaid for all SSI recipients, but must separately apply to Medicaid agency ("SSI Criteria states")	Eligibility for SSI same as eligibility for Medicaid ("1634 states")
Connecticut Hawaii Illinois Minnesota Missouri	New Hampshire North Dakota Oklahoma Virginia	Alaska Oregon Idaho Utah Kansas The Common- Nebraska wealth of the Nevada Northern Mariana Islands	All other states and the District of Columbia

For more information about Medicaid eligibility requirements in a 209(b) state, contact that state's Medicaid agency.

TIP

Using your work record to establish eligibility for your disabled child. If your child is disabled before age 22, he or she may qualify for SSDI *and eventually Medicare* based on your work record. Inform the Social Security Administration of the child's condition now, so that when the working parent becomes disabled, retires, or dies, the child with disabilities may qualify for SSDI and Medicare. This often is a better result for a child compared to relying solely on SSI and Medicaid because benefits are typically better and are easier to manage.

How Trustees Can (and Cannot) Use Trust Funds

This chapter explains how a special needs trust can provide your loved one with a disability with a large variety of goods and services, while at the same time preserving SSI and Medicaid benefits.

SSI Income and Resource Limits: An Overview

As you've learned by now, the purpose of a special needs trust is to enhance the quality of life of a person with a disability, without jeopardizing SSI and Medicaid benefits. This means that the people whom you've chosen to serve as trustee and successor trustee must know the rules about using trust money. Otherwise, your loved one's benefits could be cut or even lost altogether. To help your trustee and successor trustee, we have summarized much of the information in this chapter in a letter you can give to them (see Chapter 4 and Appendix A).

RESOURCE
Learn more about administering a special needs trust. For a detailed explanation about how to properly administer a special needs trust, read *Administering the California Special Needs Trust*, by Kevin Urbatsch and Michele Fuller (iUniverse), available on Amazon.com.

Here's a quick summary of the points covered in this chapter:
- Monthly SSI payments can be reduced or eliminated if the person serving as trustee gives the beneficiary cash or pays for the beneficiary's food or shelter.
- SSI benefits can be lost for any month in which the beneficiary receives too much cash or owns too many "countable" assets. In most states, a beneficiary who no longer qualifies for SSI won't qualify for Medicaid either.

! CAUTION

SSI and Medicaid rules can change at any time. The people whom you name to serve as successor trustees will be responsible for keeping up to date on SSI and Medicaid rules. See Chapter 11 for information about how to keep up to date.

Resource Limits

Anyone who owns more than $2,000 worth of countable resources is not eligible for SSI. (The limit for a couple eligible for SSI is $3,000.) Examples of countable resources include:

- cash
- checking and savings accounts
- stocks and bonds
- vacation home, rental property, or other real estate that is not the beneficiary's primary residence
- IRA, 401(k), and other retirement assets
- investment accounts, and
- Uniform Transfer to Minor Accounts.

Some assets are not counted toward the $2,000 limit. Examples of these exempt assets include:

- the beneficiary's primary residence (house and land, condo). This home may be of any value, if the beneficiary is on SSI. If the beneficiary receives only Medicaid—and not SSI— the state may limit the value of the home.
- one car or van of any value
- furnishings and personal effects
- life insurance with a face value of up to $1,500, and
- an irrevocable prepaid funeral plan.

If the person serving as trustee (you or a successor trustee) buys the beneficiary things that are counted as the beneficiary's resources, there is a danger that the $2,000 resource limit will be exceeded, making the beneficiary ineligible for SSI as well as Medicaid. So, the trustee must be careful.

The value of property is measured by how much it could be sold for, not what it originally cost.

EXAMPLE 1: Pete receives SSI and Medicaid and is the beneficiary of a special needs trust. He already owns a car that he uses for everyday transportation (not a countable resource). If the trustee spends $5,000 on a motorcycle, Pete will lose his SSI and Medicaid eligibility. The motorcycle is a countable resource, so its value puts Pete over the $2,000 resource limit. The solution to this situation is to have Pete's special needs trust own the motorcycle.

EXAMPLE 2: Sam also owns a car and a motorcycle. But his motorcycle would bring only $1,500 if he sold it, so, by itself, it wouldn't make him ineligible for benefits. However, if he owned $500 or more of other nonexempt assets—a savings account, for example—he would lose his SSI and Medicaid eligibility, at least temporarily, because the value of his assets would be more than $2,000.

How does the SSI program know what and how much a recipient owns? Generally, the bureaucracy relies on the recipient's own required reports and on information from the IRS, state motor vehicle departments, and banks. If, for some reason, the SSA begins an investigation, it will examine the recipient's financial affairs more closely.

Income Limits

Besides resource limits, the SSA imposes limits on a recipient's monthly income. An SSI recipient can receive only a certain amount of income in a given month. Federal regulations divide income into four categories: earned, unearned, in-kind, and deemed. The SSA treats each type differently.

Earned income comes from a job (including wages earned in a sheltered workshop, which is a supervised workplace for persons with disabilities) or a business. When beneficiaries earn more than $65 a month, their SSI payments will be reduced one dollar for every two dollars earned. If earnings are too high, the SSI grant (and, as a result, Medicaid benefits) can be lost altogether.

Unearned income is cash (or assets that can be easily converted into cash) from gifts, donations, prizes, rental income, interest from bank accounts, dividends, and similar sources. When a trustee gives a beneficiary money from the special needs trust, it is counted as unearned income. If you leave money directly to your loved one, that sum will be unearned income in the month it is received; whatever is left the next month will be treated as a resource and subject to the $2,000 resource limit.

For example, suppose John receives an outright inheritance of $25,000 in May and in the same month spends $20,000 on a car and puts the remaining $5,000 in his bank account. The SSA will count the entire $25,000 as income in May and disqualify John from his SSI for that month due to excess income. The $20,000 spent on the car is appropriate because John is allowed to spend his money without penalty and if the car is his only one, it is an exempt resource. On June 1, the SSA reviews John's resources to see if he is over the $2,000 limit. He will be because of the $5,000 he placed into his bank account. John will lose his SSI for June, and if by July 1, he still has not spent his countable resources below $2,000, he will continue to lose his SSI check each month.

The first $20 of unearned income each month has no effect on a beneficiary's SSI grant. After that, the SSA will reduce the grant, dollar-for-dollar, up to the amount of the unearned income.

EXAMPLE: Sadie receives SSI. In August, she was given $200 by her boyfriend as a birthday gift. The SSA treats the gift as "unearned income" that will reduce her SSI check for August by $180.

However, a special needs trust can avoid the unpleasant consequence of unearned income in two ways. One, if a gift is made directly to an SSI recipient's special needs trust, the SSA will not treat it as unearned income and it will have no effect on benefits. (However, people providing such gifts should speak to their own tax professionals regarding potential tax implications to themselves for providing the gift.) Two, if the trustee of the special needs trust makes a distribution on Sadie's behalf and the distribution is done correctly, it will not be treated as unearned income.

EXAMPLE 1: Sadie's boyfriend gives $200 to Sadie's special needs trust as her birthday gift. Because the gift was made directly to the special needs trust, there is no reduction of Sadie's SSI benefit. This way, Sadie continues to receive her full SSI check and has $200 available to her to enhance her quality of life.

EXAMPLE 2: The trustee of Sadie's special needs trust uses the $200 to buy Sadie a television set. Because the trustee paid for it directly from trust assets, the payment will not be counted as unearned income and Sadie will continue to receive her full SSI check.

In-kind income consists of food or shelter, including payments for shelter costs, such as rent, a mortgage, or utilities. When an adult SSI recipient lives rent free in the family home, the market value of such housing is considered in-kind income. Gifts of other items are not in-kind income, though they might count as unearned income (see above). They may also be considered a resource after the month in which they were received.

In-kind income reduces an SSI grant up to the lesser of:
- the value of the gift, or
- one-third of the maximum federal portion of the SSI grant plus $20. For 2021, the maximum reduction is $284.66.

Food stamps, low-income housing assistance, state-funded cash benefits, and noncash government benefits don't count as income in-kind for purposes of computing an SSI grant.

Deemed income is the income and resources of another person who has a "duty of support" to the person with special needs. One common example occurs when minor children live with their parents. In this situation, the parents' assets and income are counted as the minor's for the purposes of determining SSI eligibility.

Deeming applies whether or not the supporting person actually provides money to the minor. When the child turns age 18 (or age 22 if in school), the SSA will count only the minor's assets and income when determining SSI eligibility. Keep in mind that deeming applies only when a minor child is living with a parent. If the child lives in an institution or with a grandparent, the SSA does not deem the parents' income.

Similarly, deeming occurs when an SSI-eligible person lives with a spouse. The SSA counts the spouse's assets and income as the SSI-eligible person's, regardless of whether the spouse actually provides money to the SSI-eligible person. Like the parent–child case, if the SSI-eligible spouse moves out, the SSA will no longer deem the spouse's income.

The rest of this chapter discusses how these rules affect the management of the trust funds by you and the people you name as successor trustees.

RESOURCE

More information on SSI and related issues. For an in-depth discussion of the SSI system, see *Social Security, Medicare & Government Pensions*, by Joseph Matthews (Nolo).

Assets in the Special Needs Trust

Assets contributed by you or another third party to a properly drafted special needs trust are not considered resources of the beneficiary, because the beneficiary has never had control over them. Most importantly, they are not subject to the $2,000 resource limit. Theoretically, a special needs trust could hold millions of dollars in cash, houses, cars, jewelry, stocks, and commercial properties of enormous value, and yet the trust beneficiary would still financially qualify for SSI.

EXAMPLE: A vacation cabin that Estelle's family has owned for years has been left to a special needs trust naming Estelle as the beneficiary. Although the cabin is worth far more than $2,000, it is not considered a resource owned or controlled by Estelle, so it does not affect her eligibility for SSI.

How Trustees Use Special Needs Trust Funds

The person serving as trustee of the special needs trust can pay for anything for your loved one, as long as the purchase is not against public policy or illegal and does not violate the terms of the trust. Certain types of disbursements, most notably those for food or shelter, may reduce the amount of SSI, but are generally still allowed.

Trustees commonly pay for a broad variety of services provided to the beneficiary—for example, travel, education, caregiving, or medical services not provided by Medicaid. In fact, now that the Affordable Care Act has made private insurance available to most Americans, it may be in the beneficiary's best interest for the trustee to purchase private health insurance, as private insurance can usually offer many more health care options than Medicaid.

The person serving as trustee can also buy the beneficiary noncountable assets without worrying about how much they're worth. That means the beneficiary can own a substantial amount of property without losing eligibility for SSI and Medicaid.

> **EXAMPLE:** Pauline, the trustee of Meg's special needs trust, buys Meg a special van that Meg, who can't drive an ordinary car, can use. Because the van is a noncountable asset under SSI rules, Meg still qualifies for SSI even though the van is worth much more than $2,000.

Exempt Resources

Exempt resources are those goods and services that a trustee can purchase for a beneficiary that will not affect eligibility for government benefits. As noted above, they are not counted towards the limits. Here are details about some of the most common types of exempt resources.

One Home of Any Value

Owning one home as a primary residence won't disqualify your loved one from receiving SSI. However, it might be better to own the home in the special needs trust, so the person serving as trustee (you or a successor trustee) can make important decisions about the home. Important decisions include selling it someday if your loved one no longer needs it or cannot continue to live there, deciding who has the right to live in the home, having the authority to make improvements to the home, and fulfilling the obligation to pay property taxes and insurance. Ownership by the trust would also help to protect the resident from predators who might try and trick your loved one into signing a deed.

Having the trust own a residence will work only if the trust has enough cash to purchase the home without a mortgage. Most banks will not lend to trusts, so the trust must be able to cover the entire purchase.

When purchasing a home, the effect on the loved one's SSI check is minimal. In the month that the trustee buys the home, the beneficiary will lose $270 as an in-kind income penalty from his or her SSI check. After that, even if the beneficiary doesn't pay market rent to the trust, the SSA will not reduce the SSI amount, because the beneficiary is considered to have an "equitable" ownership interest in the house. The beneficiary can also move from the home at any time without affecting SSI. The trustee can then rent out the home and earn income for the trust or sell the home and keep the proceeds without any penalty against the beneficiary's SSI check.

The scenarios just described apply only when the special needs trust owns the home. If the beneficiary owns the home in his or her own name, the home is exempt only if it is the beneficiary's primary residence. So, if the beneficiary moves out of the home at any time and gets a new primary residence, the beneficiary-owned home will no longer be considered an exempt resource.

CAUTION

Additional restrictions apply to homes owned by some Medicaid recipients. Many Medicaid programs limit the value of a home owned by a person who receives Medicaid benefits to $500,000 or $750,000. However, this limit does not apply if a trust owns the home. So if a person with a disability does not qualify for SSI, but does receive Medicaid, it is important that either the value of the home be lower than the applicable amount or the home be owned by the special needs trust.

One Motor Vehicle

The beneficiary can own one motor vehicle, regardless of value, without affecting SSI eligibility.

EXAMPLE: Conor, the beneficiary of a special needs trust, urges the person serving as trustee to buy him a second car. If the trustee spent $10,000 on a second car, Conor's resources would go over the $2,000 resource limit, making him ineligible for SSI. Such a purchase is forbidden by the terms of the trust in this book, because the trustee is required to avoid disbursements that would make Conor ineligible for SSI and Medicaid. However, the trustee could purchase a second car and have the special needs trust own it, which would not affect Conor's SSI eligibility.

If the beneficiary is a minor and the family needs a car to take the beneficiary to and from therapy appointments, doctor appointments, or school, the trustee can also purchase the car and have title placed in the name of the parent or guardian who will be driving the car. The trustee can then have a lien placed on the car with the Department of Motor Vehicles, so that the car cannot be sold without the trustee's knowledge. Giving title to a parent or guardian, plus placing the lien, would preserve the trust's interest in the car as well as the beneficiary's eligibility for SSI.

Home Furnishings and Personal Effects

These categories are extremely broad. While there are technically no limits as to what a trustee can purchase for a beneficiary as home furnishings or personal effects, a trustee must use common sense.

> **EXAMPLE:** Bob, a trustee of a special needs trust for his niece Sandra, buys her a $1,200 computer. The computer is not counted as a resource because it's considered a household furnishing. Owning it doesn't affect Sandra's SSI eligibility.

Property and Services Essential to Self-Support

This category encompasses property that a beneficiary uses for work, either as an employee or running a trade or business. The SSA places limits on the value of these items, depending on the rate of return they provide (how much the beneficiary earns by using the item versus the cost of the item) and other variables.

More information about this category is available in the guidelines relied on by workers at the Social Security Administration and local district offices. For more about these guidelines, called the *Program Operations Manual System* or *POMS*, go to http://policy.ssa.gov. If you still are uncertain about whether a particular type of property will be treated as a resource, consider asking for a written opinion from the applicable SSA agency.

 SEE AN EXPERT

Get help from a professional if you're unsure about exempt property used for work. It can be tricky to figure out what is "essential to self-support." To avoid a disruption in benefits, get help from an attorney, a public benefits consultant, a CPA, or a professional fiduciary to figure out what goods and services fit into this category.

Items That Special Needs Trusts Can Pay for Without Worry

Here is a list of items that a special needs trust can pay for without jeopardizing eligibility for public benefits. This list is not exhaustive, but it shows how many common things and services can be paid for without worry.

Automobile (car, van)

Accounting services

Acupuncture/acupressure

Appliances (TV, VCR, DVD player, stereo, microwave, stove, refrigerator, washer/dryer)

Bottled water or water service

Bus pass/public transportation costs

Camera

Clothing

Cell phone and phone service

Clubs and club dues, book clubs, health clubs, service clubs, zoo passes, advocacy groups, museums

Computer hardware, software, programs, and Internet service

Conferences

Cosmetics

Courses or classes (academic or recreational), including books and supplies

Curtains, blinds, and drapes

Dental work not covered by Medicaid, including anesthesia

Dry cleaning and laundry services

Education expenses including tuition and related costs

Elective surgery

Eyeglasses

Fitness equipment

Funeral expenses

Furniture, home furnishings

Gasoline and maintenance for automobile

Haircuts and salon services

Hobby supplies

Holiday decorations, parties, dinner dances, holiday cards

Home alarm, monitoring, and response systems

Home improvements, repairs, and maintenance (not covered by Medicaid), including tools to perform home improvements, repairs, and maintenance by homeowner

Home purchase (to the extent not covered by benefits)

House cleaning and maid services

Insurance (for automobile, home, or possessions)

Legal fees

Linens and towels

Magazine and newspaper subscriptions

Massage

Musical instruments (including lessons and music)

Nonfood grocery items (laundry soap, bleach, fabric softener, deodorant, dish soap, hand and body soap, personal hygiene products, paper towels, napkins, Kleenex, toilet paper, and household cleaning products)

Items That Special Needs Trusts Can Pay for Without Worry (continued)

Over-the-counter medications (including vitamins and herbs)	Telephone service and equipment, including cell phone and pager
Personal assistance services not covered by Medicaid	Therapy (physical, occupational, or speech) not covered by Medicaid
Pets, pet supplies, and veterinary services	Tickets to concerts or sporting events (for beneficiary and an accompanying companion, if necessary)
Physician specialists if not covered by Medicaid	
Pornography (as long as legal)	Transportation (automobile, motorcycle, bicycle, moped, gas, bus passes, ride-hailing services such as Uber and Lyft, insurance, vehicle license fees, or car repairs)
Private counseling if not covered by Medicaid	
Repair services (for appliances, automobile, bicycle, household, or fitness equipment)	
	Tuition and other educational expenses
Snow removal, landscaping, and gardening (lawn) services	Utility bills (satellite TV, cable TV, telephone—but not gas, water, or electricity)
Sporting goods, equipment, uniforms, and team pictures	
Stationery, stamps, and cards	Vacation (including paying for a personal assistant to accompany the beneficiary if necessary)
Storage units	
Taxicabs	

Occupational Goals

Under SSI's Plan for Achieving Self-Support (PASS) program, the government allows SSI recipients to use specific assets toward an occupational goal, such as college, vocational training, or starting a business. The assets used can be earned income, unearned income, or even countable assets of over $2,000.

Normally, using these assets would result in ineligibility for benefits or would lower the SSI monthly payment amount. However, under PASS, a person with a disability can use assets toward an approved occupational goal without penalty. To have a PASS plan approved, an SSI recipient submits form SSA-545-BK to an SSI field office for review. In the form, the recipient describes how using the funds will help that person obtain employment. If the office's PASS expert approves the plan, the assets used to fulfill the PASS will not be counted as resources. To learn more about PASS, go to www.ssa.gov.

Burial and Life Insurance Policies

Life insurance policies with cash surrender values less than $1,500 are not counted toward the $2,000 SSI resource limit. Burial insurance policies of any value are not counted. However, funds set aside for burial expenses in an account or a trust are limited to $1,500 or less, and states may place limits on the value of a prepaid funeral plan. Most funeral homes are accustomed to helping people properly plan for and purchase a Medicaid-compliant irrevocable prepaid funeral plan.

Gifts of Cash

It's not a good idea for the trustee to give an SSI beneficiary cash from a special needs trust. When a beneficiary receives cash or its equivalent (countable resources that can be readily converted to cash, such as a bank CD or shares of stock), the SSI grant will be reduced, dollar for dollar, in the month the beneficiary receives the income. (A small exception to this rule is that the first $20 of a gift received in a given month is not counted.) You shouldn't count on flying under the radar here: SSI recipients must make regular reports to the Social Security Administration about income they receive or any change of circumstances. A recipient makes these reports under penalty of perjury, and failure to properly report gifts can have serious consequences.

> **EXAMPLE:** Peter is the trustee of Erica's special needs trust. For Erica's birthday every year, Peter writes her a check from the trust for $100. Erica then goes shopping with the money. Erica must report the receipt of this cash and, as a result, $80 will be deducted from her SSI grant.

The trustee can, however, give the beneficiary noncash items that aren't countable resources because such items are not income.

EXAMPLE: Peter stops writing Erica checks and instead starts taking her shopping for her birthday. He lets her pick out $100 worth of birthday gifts and pays for them with trust funds. The gifts—things for her apartment and personal items such as clothing and jewelry—qualify as "personal effects and household furnishings" (discussed above), and Erica's SSI grant stays intact. This result holds even if Erica picks out the very items she would have purchased on her own, had Peter given her the money directly.

If a gift of cash is large enough to reduce the SSI grant to zero, in many states, the recipient will also lose Medicaid eligibility for that month.

EXAMPLE: Peter writes Erica a trust check for $1,000 for her birthday. Because Erica's monthly SSI grant is only $680, Erica will lose her SSI eligibility for that month as well as her Medicaid benefits because the $1,000 check is counted as unearned income and will reduce the SSI check dollar-for-dollar on anything over $20. She regains her SSI and Medicaid benefits the month after that, provided that the balance of the $1,000 doesn't send her over the $2,000 resource limit, which can happen if she does not spend enough money so that all her other countable assets combined exceed the $2,000 limit.

The trust in this book prohibits the person serving as trustee from making disbursements like the one in this example, which would make the beneficiary ineligible for SSI and Medicaid. The trustee is also directed to conserve trust assets so they'll be available to the beneficiary for as long as possible. So, the trustee should avoid making disbursements that reduce the size of the SSI grant unless there is a very good reason to do so.

TIP

Avoid making distributions directly to the beneficiary. To avoid wasting trust funds or interfering with SSI eligibility, trustees almost always make disbursements for goods and services to a third party on the beneficiary's behalf, not directly to the beneficiary.

EXAMPLE: Jonas, age 35, receives SSI and Medicaid because the brain injury he suffered in a car accident as a teenager left him unable to work. Ten years ago, his mother left $50,000 in her will to a special needs trust set up for Jonas's benefit. The trust's value is now down to $30,000.

The person serving as trustee, Jonas's sister Peggy, would like to give Jonas $300 a month in spending money. But she knows that this would result in a dollar-for-dollar reduction of Jonas's SSI grant and so would be a waste of trust money. In addition, it would deplete the trust assets in about eight years. So Peggy decides to use trust funds to pay for goods and services he wants. That way, the trust disbursements don't affect his SSI grant.

Addressing the No-Cash Problem: True Link Cards

One way around no cash rule is for the trustee to use something called a True Link card. True Link is a financial services firm that offers a range of money management, investment, and insurance products. One such service is the True Link card, a reloadable Visa card that protects the user from financial vulnerability while promoting independence, improving quality of life, and protecting eligibility for government benefits.

The True Link card acts like a debit card on which the trustee puts money, and the beneficiary uses it when out and about, such as on errands. The card allows the beneficiary to use some trust funds independently, without the trustee having to attend a shopping trip, for instance. The trustee can limit where the beneficiary can use the card, for example eliminating grocery stores to avoid an SSI reduction for food payments. The True Link card is a valuable tool for smaller trust distributions, such as those for personal care and hygiene items. See True Link website for more information (www.truelinkfinancial.com/card). The SSA has expressly accepted True Link cards (see the *Program Operations Manual System* (*POMS*) at https://secure.ssa.gov/poms.nsf/home!readform; search for "True Link").

Payments for Food or Shelter

If the person serving as trustee pays for a recipient's food or shelter using trust funds (or even the trustee's own money), the SSA considers the amount paid to be income to the beneficiary. Specifically, it's called in-kind income or in-kind support and maintenance (ISM). The SSI program treats ISM differently from other types of income.

If the ISM can be assigned a specific value, that amount is deducted from the SSI grant—up to a limit. The amount of the deduction is currently capped at $284.66 (for 2021). That's one-third of the maximum federal portion of the SSI grant ($794 in 2021) plus $20.

> **EXAMPLE:** Leo, who receives an SSI grant because of his Down syndrome, loves to eat out. Each month Leo's restaurant tab averages $120. If the cost of the meals is picked up by a special needs trust or another outside source like his parents, Leo's SSI grant will be reduced dollar for dollar by $120.
>
> If Leo had fancier tastes and, courtesy of his special needs trust, spent $500 a month eating out, his grant would also be reduced, but only by a maximum of $284.66 (in 2021).

These rules mean that if necessary, a special needs trust can provide loved ones with food or shelter—and still leave them with the lion's share of their SSI grant, as well as continued eligibility for Medicaid benefits.

If your loved one qualifies for an ABLE account, a trustee can avoid the SSI reduction for food and shelter by funding the ABLE account with the trust and then paying the food and shelter expense from the ABLE account (see Chapter 7).

Items That Are Considered In-Kind Support and Maintenance

Here is a list of items that the SSA has explicitly said in their policies are applicable ISM expenses:

- Food
- Mortgage (including property insurance required by the mortgage holder)
- Real property taxes (less any tax rebate/credit)
- Rent
- Heating fuel
- Gas
- Electricity
- Water
- Sewer, and
- Garbage removal.

The question of ISM comes up most often with shelter for those living in private, not government-run housing, because the SSI grant is so inadequate when it comes to paying today's rents and mortgages on the open market. Trust payments for rent or mortgage payments on a house owned by the beneficiary are considered ISM, so they trigger a reduction of the SSI grant. Still, if a beneficiary's shelter needs can be met only through rental assistance from the special needs trust, a $284.67 reduction in the monthly SSI grant is usually in the best interests of the beneficiary.

> **EXAMPLE:** Sonya, the beneficiary of a special needs trust, receives SSI and Medicaid. When Sonya's group home closes, she is forced to seek shelter at private market rents. She finds a suitable apartment for $2,000 per month—considerably more than her total $794 SSI grant. The trustee of Sonya's special needs trust decides to pay for all of Sonya's rent and utilities, a total of $2,300 a month.
>
> Trust payments for rent and utilities are ISM, so Sonya's SSI grant will be reduced. The federal portion of the grant in 2021 is $794, so Sonya will lose $284.66 of her SSI check. She will also continue to receive Medicaid. In other words, Sonya's trust pays $2,300 for a nice, safe and clean apartment for Sonya and she continues to receive $509.34 in SSI without any further reduction in SSI.

As the above example shows, it's critical that a trustee know how much the beneficiary is receiving in benefits. If Sonya were receiving less than $270 in SSI because she was receiving income from another source, the rent payment in the example above would eliminate her eligibility for SSI. Thus, it is important to know how much SSI the person with a disability is receiving to make sure that an expenditure doesn't result in a total loss of SSI and an accompanying loss of Medicaid.

Once the ISM maximum reduction of $284.66 (in 2021) is reached, the trustee can pay for all the beneficiary's food, rent, and utilities without any further reduction in SSI.

> **EXAMPLE:** Tonya is the beneficiary of a special needs trust. The trustee has been paying $3,500 for all Tonya's rent and utilities. Tonya's SSI check was reduced by $284.66 as a result of these ISM payments. Tonya then asks the trustee to pay her monthly grocery bill of $500. The trustee can pay the additional amount without any further reduction of SSI.

As mentioned earlier, if a special needs trust owns a house or has enough assets to buy one outright, the beneficiary may be able to live in the house rent free without affecting his or her SSI grant. (See "Resource Limits," above.)

However, if the trust pays other expenses associated with shelter—such as electricity, heat, or water—the amounts are considered ISM, and the grant is reduced dollar for dollar up to the $284.66 per month (in 2021) maximum deduction. If the trust were to make mortgage payments on the house, those payments would also be considered ISM and would result in an SSI reduction, up to $284.66 per month.

> **EXAMPLE:** Kathy, who uses a wheelchair because of a childhood accident, receives a $750 monthly SSI grant and Medicaid. Kathy is also the beneficiary of a special needs trust created by her mother. Kathy lives rent free in the family home, which is now held in the special needs trust. Kathy's SSI grant is not affected by the market value of the shelter because her local SSA office does not count the value of the shelter as in-kind income.
>
> The trust pays for the utilities, which average about $180 a month. Because this amount is considered ISM, Kathy loses $180/month from her SSI grant.

Computing the Maximum Deduction for ISM

The maximum federal SSI grant increases every year, as the cost of living increases. In 2021, it is $794. One-third of this amount is $264.66; add $20 to get the maximum deduction of $284.66 per month.

For more information on federal and state SSI benefits, visit the Social Security Administration's website at www.ssa.gov.

When to Use Trust Funds—And When Not To

If payment for food or shelter is:	Then use money from:
less than $284.66 (maximum reduction in 2021)	the SSI grant
more than $284.66 (maximum reduction in 2021)	the special needs trust

Valuing Gifts of Food or Shelter From Other Sources

When someone gives food or shelter directly to an SSI recipient, the SSA considers the value of the gift when calculating the recipient's grant. Because it is burdensome to place a precise dollar value on the gift, the SSA presumes that its value is one-third of the maximum federal SSI grant, even if its actual value is lower or higher. The penalty assessed against SSI recipients will depend on where they live and who is providing the free food or shelter. If someone who does not live with the SSI recipient pays for food or shelter (oftentimes the SNT trustee), the penalty is called the "presumed maximum value," or PMV. If the person providing free room or shelter lives with the SSI recipient (oftentimes the parents), then the penalty is called the "value of the one-third reduction rule" or VTR.

PMV EXAMPLE: Mohammed, an SSI recipient, receives an SSI grant of $794, lives in an apartment by himself, and has his food and shelter paid for by the trustee of his special needs trust. Because calculating the fair market value of his free food and shelter can be unduly burdensome, the SSA presumes the value is one-third of the federal SSI grant plus $20, or $284.66 ($794/3 = $264.66 + $20 = $284.66). So each month Mohammed receives $509.34 ($794 − $284.66= $509.34) from SSI.

VTR EXAMPLE: Mohammed, an SSI recipient, is an adult and receives an SSI grant of $794. He lives with his parents who allow him to live with them for free. SSA penalizes this, but slightly differently than under the PMV rules. The penalty is a third of the federal SSI grant or $264.66 ($794/3 = $264.66). Each month, Mohammed still receives $529.34 ($794 − $264.66= $529.34). The other difference with VTR is that the penalty is assessed in full, even if the value of the free food and shelter is less than penalty, (e.g., his share of utilities that he receives for free from his parents is $100, but his penalty is still the full $264.66 a month).

Generally, these issues are not the trustee's concern. The person serving as trustee is responsible for reporting trust activity; the beneficiary (or his or her representative payee) should report other income or income in-kind separately in the month it is received. But there are two things the trustee will need to know:

- The maximum reduction to the grant is $284.67 (in 2021) regardless of the combined value of income in-kind received through the trust and from outside resources.
- If the person serving as trustee is responsible for making the reports to SSI (for example, the trust document may make the trustee responsible for reporting), then these outside gifts should be reported along with any income in-kind provided by the trust. ●

Getting Money Into a Special Needs Trust

This chapter takes a closer look at actually getting money into the special needs trust you have created. (We give you step-by-step directions for creating the trust in Chapter 8.) In legal language, putting assets in the trust is called "funding the trust." You also need to decide just what kinds of assets to leave in trust for your loved one; this chapter discusses that issue, too. We'll start out with a short explanation of who can set up a special needs trust.

Who Can Set Up a Special Needs Trust

Most discussions on special needs trusts involve a parent or grandparent who wants to leave property to a disabled child or grandchild. However, third-party special needs trusts can work for special needs individuals of any age and relationship to the grantor.

Older couples sometimes set up special needs trusts for the surviving spouse or partner, to take effect when the first one dies. However, if the couple is married, these types of special needs trusts must be established through a will and cannot be established during life or through a revocable living trust.

EXAMPLE 1: Gavin and Denise, both 70, have been married for the past 20 years. Denise has been diagnosed with Alzheimer's disease and will need Medicaid in the near future. Gavin creates a special needs trust in his will for Denise, naming a friend as trustee. In his will, Gavin leaves $75,000 to the trust, to be used for Denise's benefit. When Gavin dies, the trust will be set up to supplement Denise's SSI and Medicaid benefits with money from the trust, by paying for items not covered by those programs.

EXAMPLE 2: Rolf and Juanita are both in their 60s and live together but are not married. Rolf suffers from severe rheumatoid arthritis and has been receiving SSI and Medicaid for ten years. Juanita has a stock portfolio worth $50,000 in her name alone. She wants to leave the stock to Rolf but doesn't want him to lose his SSI or Medicaid. Juanita creates a third-party special needs trust naming herself as trustee and uses a transfer-on-death beneficiary designation to leave the stock to the trust. When Juanita dies, title to the stock passes to the trust and the person Juanita has named to succeed her as trustee can manage the stock to enhance Rolf's quality of life. Note, however, that if Rolf and Juanita get married, she must create a new special needs trust by will.

You can also set up a special needs trust for someone to whom you're not related at all.

EXAMPLE: Agnes, age 75, leads a simple life in the house she grew up in. She puts in volunteer time at the local Boys and Girls Club and The Arc (an organization dedicated to people with intellectual and developmental disabilities). Unbeknown to the community, Agnes is worth several million dollars because of property she inherited from her father and mother. She gives handsome annual donations to the groups she works with, but has never given much thought to how to leave her property.

When Agnes learns about special needs trusts, she decides to create a special needs trust for 12 disabled children she has grown close to in her volunteer work. In her will, she directs that at her death, the trust will receive all of her property to be used for the benefit of the 12 children. If she meets other children whom she wants to include, she can make arrangements to include them as well.

Tell Family and Friends About the Trust

Family members or close friends might want to leave money or other assets to the person with special needs. Make sure they know that you have created a special needs trust, and give them clear and precise instructions about naming the trust as a beneficiary. If they leave money directly to your loved one, they will disrupt the protections your trust has created.

If you use the special needs trust provided in this book, your family members and friends can add money or assets to the trust while you and they are still alive, as well as after they pass away. For instance, the trust can receive cash amounts that family members or friends wish to gift to the person with special needs as a birthday present or on other important holidays. Those gifts of cash can be used by the trustee to enhance the person's quality of life, without impacting eligibility for public benefits.

Assets You Can Put in a Special Needs Trust

A special needs trust can hold virtually any type of property. This includes real estate, collectibles, deposit accounts, stocks, bonds, heirlooms, furniture, jewelry, intellectual property (patents, copyrights, trademarks), businesses, cars, tools, hobby collections, wheelchairs, and just about anything else you can think of.

But a trustee usually has little use for assets that gather dust in an attic or a safe deposit box. The person serving as trustee needs cash to invest in assets that provide a return, which the trustee will spend on the beneficiary's special needs. The primary function of a special needs trust, after all, is to enhance the quality of life of the person with a disability. And trustees do that by paying for goods and services for the trust beneficiary.

To raise cash, most trustees sell tangible trust assets and keep the proceeds in liquid assets, such as deposit accounts, certificates of deposit, stocks, or other types of property that can easily be converted to cash.

> **EXAMPLE:** Fred was born with Fragile X syndrome. Among other symptoms, Fred has profound mental deficiencies, qualifying him for SSI and Medicaid. In her will, Fred's mother, Jolene, leaves all of her property to a special needs trust she previously established for Fred's benefit. Jolene had named her brother Carl as successor trustee. When she dies, Jolene leaves a broad array of items to the special needs trust (actually to Carl as trustee of the trust), including clothing, furniture, appliances, a boat, a vacation cabin, and the house where Fred grew up and still lives. She leaves almost no liquid assets.

Although Fred can use some of what Jolene left, most of it is not essential to his well-being and has no particular sentimental value to him. What Fred does need is supplemental services from various health and disability professionals, which he won't get unless the trust can pay for them. To fulfill his duties as trustee, Carl keeps the house and furniture that Fred can use, but sells everything else to raise cash for Fred's special needs.

Sometimes a beneficiary wants to use tangible property owned by the trust. In that case, there is no point in selling it. However, if the trust owns items that have no direct practical benefit to the beneficiary—jewelry, for example—it will probably make sense to sell it and invest the proceeds in a way that will produce income.

EXAMPLE: Violet is the person named as successor trustee of a special needs trust created for her nephew Sam by Sam's mother, Peg. Peg funded the trust with jewelry valued at $14,000, a coin collection worth $5,000, family heirlooms valued at $25,000, and a house in which Sam lives rent free. The trust document gives Violet the power to sell any property in the trust to further the purpose of the trust.

Violet sells the jewelry, coin collection, and heirlooms and invests the $44,000 in a series of mutual funds and some bonds. Sam continues living in the house.

How Much Money Will Your Loved One Need?

If your loved one is the only person you want to provide for after your death, then you'll probably want to put your entire estate into your special needs trust and hope it lasts as long as the beneficiary needs help. Many people, however, want to leave money not just to someone with a disability, but also to other family members or charities. Or, you might have more money than you think your loved one will need. In either case, you'll need to decide how much to leave to the special needs trust and how much to others.

Deciding on how much money to put in the trust depends on:

- **Your family.** Do you want to divvy your property up evenly or leave a larger share to the special needs trust, on the theory that your other beneficiaries can take care of themselves? There are no easy answers, but talking with family members may help you reach a conclusion you feel good about.

- **Your life insurance.** Many parents of children with disabilities obtain life insurance. This approach lets you leave a sizable sum to the special needs trust under the life insurance policy and still provide for your other family members out of your other property. Types of life insurance are discussed later in this chapter.

- **Your retirement accounts.** On January 1, 2020, a new law was released called the SECURE Act. This law creates certain tax advantages to leaving your retirement accounts to a special needs trust, rather than your other family members or charity. This new law and its repercussions are discussed later in this chapter.

- **Your loved one's life expectancy.** Grim as it is, you'll have to take your loved one's life expectancy into account when deciding how much property to leave to the special needs trust. To state the obvious, if the beneficiary's life expectancy is short, the trust will need less money than if it were long.

- **The beneficiary's needs.** Although it involves some guesswork, you need to think about the services you want the trust to supply, and how much money that will take.

So, how should you juggle all of these factors so that you come out with the right funding for your special needs trust? The short answer is, you shouldn't—unless you are a professional in the area of financial management. It's almost impossible to come up with meaningful numbers on your own, without the right calculators and expertise at your fingertips.

The right move for most people is to get help from a professional. At least two companies have created departments specially designed to assist in financial planning for persons with disabilities:

- MassMutual has a program called Special*Care*, dedicated to special needs financial planning. The program provides information, specialists, and financial solutions to families with dependents of any age who have a disability. To get started, visit the company's website, www.massmutual.com/specialneeds.
- Merrill Lynch & Co. has set up a program that focuses on financial planning for special needs families and has a training program for its brokers. Call 877-456-7526 or visit the company's website, www.ml.com.

You can also get help from certified financial planners. (See Chapter 11.)

How to Leave Money After You Die to a Special Needs Trust

Nearly always, you'll leave money to a special needs trust after your death. You might want to use more than one method to do that.

It is very, very important that you consult with a tax attorney or CPA if you wish to fund a special needs trust during your lifetime. Unless you have a very specific reason to leave assets to a special needs trust while you are living, you shouldn't do so because the high value of the assets might result in tax consequences (such as capital gains and gift taxes). Besides, during your lifetime you can use funds held in your name (your own money) to take care of your loved one with special needs. So, it is almost always unnecessary to fund a special needs trust before you die. If you believe that you need to add money to the trust while you are living, you should consult with a tax attorney or CPA to fully understand any capital gain and gift tax consequences.

Wills

The best-known estate planning document is the will or "last will and testament." It's relatively simple to create and you can use it to specify the property that you want placed in the special needs trust.

> **EXAMPLE:** In her will, Phyllis leaves her valuable art collection to her elder daughter, Katie, and her house to her other daughter, Ruth. She wants to leave her vacation cabin to her son, Mickey, who enjoys spending his summers there. However, Mickey qualifies for SSI because of a long-term disability and Phyllis knows that if he inherits property of more than $2,000 he will no longer be eligible for SSI and Medicaid. (See Chapter 3.)
>
> So instead of leaving the cabin directly to Mickey, Phyllis creates a special needs trust and uses her will to direct that the cabin be held in the trust at her death. This allows Mickey to use the cabin and preserves his eligibility for his public benefits.

Will Basics

You can leave almost any kind of property in your will—bank accounts, houses, businesses, personal property of any description, or intellectual property (patents, copyrights, and trademarks), to name a few examples.

Contrary to popular belief, you don't need to use magic words or legal jargon in a will. In fact, the more simple and straightforward the language, the better. (Take the will of the French philosopher Rabelais: "I have nothing, I owe a great deal, the rest I leave to the poor.")

A will must, however, be signed in front of at least two witnesses who also sign it, stating that the person making the will appears to be of sound mind. Witnessing is intended to provide protection against forgery or duress. It is important to check your state law to make sure you are meeting the legal requirements.

You can prepare a will at any time during your life and change it whenever you wish, provided any changes are signed and witnessed. After you die, the person handling your estate—called an executor, a personal representative, or an administrator, depending on the circumstances—distributes your property to persons and entities you named in the will to inherit it (for example, the trustee of a special needs trust). These recipients are your will beneficiaries.

![icon] CAUTION

Property left through a will might get held up in probate after your death. One downside to passing property to a special needs trust through a will is that all property that passes through a will must go through probate. With a few exceptions (for example, many states have simplified probate rules for small estates), probate is likely to take many months and cost many thousands of dollars. This will cause a delay in funding the special needs trust and, because the costs of probate are shouldered by the estate, might reduce the sum available to your loved one. In some states, probate proceedings are also open to the public, which means that your family estate would lose the privacy that other options (like a revocable living trust, discussed later in this chapter) might provide. To avoid these problems, consider using a revocable living trust instead; see below.

What You Can't Leave Through Your Will

You cannot leave property through your will if you have already arranged for that property to pass under another estate planning document— such as a beneficiary designation form, a revocable living trust, or a joint tenancy deed. In these instances, what you say in your will won't supersede those designations or decisions. (The one exception is in the state of Washington, which has a "superwill" statute allowing a will to override a previous beneficiary designation.) Here are some common ways that property can be distributed after death, outside of a will.

Jointly owned property. Certain forms of ownership give all co-owners the "right of survivorship." This means that when one owner dies, the surviving co-owners own the entire property. Forms of ownership that have the right of survivorship include joint tenancy, tenancy by the entirety, and community property with right of survivorship. If you're not sure how you own property with someone else, check the deed or other title document.

> **EXAMPLE:** Harvey makes a will leaving all his property in equal shares to his nine children. In addition to household furnishings and personal effects (worth a total of about $15,000), Harvey owns a house in joint tenancy with his second wife, Clara. At Harvey's death, Clara will own the house. Harvey's children will split the household furnishings and personal effects in equal shares.

Property held in a trust. If you've transferred title to assets to yourself (or someone else) as trustee of a trust, your will has no effect on the asset. For example, if you've transferred property to yourself as the trustee of the special needs trust you created for your loved one, your will won't determine who gets that property.

Property for which you've named a beneficiary in a binding document. If you've made an arrangement to give your money to a certain beneficiary at your death, then that agreement is legally binding. Your will has no effect on what happens to the property at your death. Beneficiary designations can be found on transfer-on-death deeds, some bank accounts, and most retirement accounts. (See "Beneficiary Designations," below, for more on leaving property this way.)

> **EXAMPLE:** On a beneficiary designation form provided by her bank, Flora names her son Angelo as the pay-on-death beneficiary of her savings account. Her will contradicts this and directs that the same account pass to her daughter Rosa. Angelo will get the money because Flora's will has no effect on property for which she has named a beneficiary.

Revocable Living Trusts

Because most wills must go through the probate process—which can be both costly and time-consuming—other estate planning devices have become very popular. One of these is the revocable living trust.

Like a will, a living trust can be used to fund a special needs trust that will become effective at your death. The trust document lists the trust property that should pass to the trust rather than directly to the beneficiary.

> **EXAMPLE:** Adam creates a special needs trust for the benefit of his son, Porter, who has spina bifida. Adam also creates a revocable living trust and transfers title to his main asset, his house, into the trust. As part of the living trust document, Adam directs that, upon his death, his house be transferred to the special needs trust. (Adam established the special needs trust independently of creating his own living trust.)

A simple revocable living trust works much like a will does to distribute property after your death. But a trust offers one big advantage over a will: Trust property does not need to go through probate court proceedings.

Here is how the most common kind of revocable living trust works. You, the "grantor," draft a trust instrument in which you name yourself as "trustee" of the trust and as its initial beneficiary. You transfer any property you want to pass after your death into the trust. Because you are both trustee and beneficiary while you are alive, you have absolute control over the property in the trust. You manage all of your assets, pay your bills, and pay your taxes the same way that you did before creating the trust. And because the trust is revocable, you can change your mind and take some or all of the property out of the trust at any point.

In the trust document, you direct what is to happen to the trust property upon your disability or after your death. When you become disabled or die, the person you named in the trust document as "successor trustee" takes over as trustee. The successor trustee will distribute the trust property as instructed by the trust.

No one will supervise your successor trustee except for the trust's beneficiaries. In contrast, with a will, the executor you name will probably be accountable to a probate court. But in both positions you want someone (perhaps the same someone) whom you trust completely.

A living trust controls only property that's legally held in the trust. As long as your property is formally held in trust, your will has no effect on it.

EXAMPLE 1: After creating a living trust and transferring title to his house to his name as trustee of the trust, Adam makes a will in which he leaves his house directly to Porter. The house will not pass to Porter under the will because it has already been disposed of in Adam's revocable living trust.

EXAMPLE 2: Joyce creates a living trust but forgets to transfer title to her house to her name as trustee of the trust. At her death, the house will pass under her will—not under her trust document, as she had intended.

Property that isn't held in your revocable living trust, or that hasn't been legally passed some other way, will pass under the terms of your will. It is precisely for this reason that most people with a living trust also make a will—to handle any property that hasn't been transferred to the living trust or left through some other means. This will is sometimes called a pour-over will, because any property that is accidentally left out of your trust can "pour over" into the trust via the will.

EXAMPLE: Julian creates a revocable living trust for his house, business, and investments. He then transfers title to these assets to the trust. He names two of his three children to each take one-third of the property. He leaves the remaining third to a special needs trust he has already set up for his other child, who has cerebral palsy. Julian also creates a will that leaves any property subject to the will (that is, not held in his trust or left some other way) to the successor trustee of the trust, to be distributed under the terms of the trust document (the trust has a catch-all provision that directs any stray assets to named beneficiaries).

After he makes his will and living trust, Julian inherits $200,000 from his sister. He never gets around to adding the money to his revocable living trust. So after his death, the money passes, under Julian's will, to the successor trustee of his trust. The trustee distributes it under the terms of the trust just like the rest of the trust property.

RESOURCE

Let Nolo help you make your will or revocable living trust. Nolo has put its best-selling and easy-to-make will online. Nolo's *Quicken WillMaker & Trust* can help you make your will and trust on your computer anytime, with a minimum of cost and effort. Nolo's product is updated regularly by Nolo's team of lawyers, and if you have questions while making your document, the product supplies practical help along the way. To get more information about wills and trusts, go to www.nolo.com.

Beneficiary Designations

These days, an increasing amount of property passes not by will or trust but under the terms of beneficiary designations that apply to specific accounts and items of property. For example, it's very common for people to name beneficiaries for bank and brokerage accounts, retirement plan money (IRAs, 401(k) plans), securities, and certificates of deposit. The owner of the funds simply uses a form provided by the fund or securities manager to designate who gets the property upon his or her death. Doing so ensures that the named beneficiary—a special needs trust, if you choose—will receive the property without probate. Also, in over half of the states, you can use a transfer on death deed to transfer real property to a named beneficiary when you die, without probate.

EXAMPLE: Justine wants to leave everything she owns to her only surviving relative, her younger brother Leonard. When she sets up her IRA, she names Leonard as the person to get the funds at her death. Similarly, Justine names Leonard as the pay-on-death beneficiary for her bank CD, using a form provided by the bank. And she can pass her stocks to Leonard by submitting a "transfer-on-death" beneficiary form to her broker.

Once she's taken these steps, Leonard will inherit the funds in the IRA, the CD, and the stocks—all without the need for probate court proceedings.

If you have established a special needs trust, you can name the trust as the designated beneficiary for any account or asset that offers this method of passing property. (Remember, leaving property directly to your loved one may jeopardize eligibility for Medicaid and SSI.)

> ⊘ **CAUTION**
>
> **Take care with the forms.** People often fail to complete their beneficiary forms, which can cause major problems for beneficiaries of a special needs trust. Many types of accounts will disburse assets through default disbursement provisions when an owner dies and leaves behind an incomplete beneficiary form. If these provisions leave the assets to your loved one with special needs, this could wreak havoc on that person's benefits. To avoid this outcome, review each of your beneficiary designations to ensure that you've completed them correctly.

> **EXAMPLE:** Leonard has severe brain damage from a childhood accident. Justine creates a third-party special needs trust for him and opens a bank account in the name of the trust. Justine then asks her broker to arrange for her to change the beneficiary on her IRA from Leonard to the trustee of Leonard's special needs trust. When Justine dies, the money in the IRA will be delivered to the trustee of the special needs trust, to be used for Leonard's special needs.

Retirement Plans (IRAs and 401(k) Plans) and the SECURE Act

You can leave a great benefit to your loved one with a special needs trust if you make the trust the "designated beneficiary" of a retirement plan, like an IRA or a 401(k) plan. Before 2020, beneficiaries of these plans could, for the most part, stretch out the amounts they received each year, until the money ran out. A beneficiary's ability to control the amount of money they took from their benefactor's plan enabled the beneficiary, for example, to defer distributions until the beneficiary was retired and earning less income (thereby reducing the tax hit on the distribution).

The SECURE Act changed the rules, requiring most beneficiaries to take the money within ten years. If the retirement plan is very large, the amount of tax the recipient will pay on these required distributions can be high, particularly if the beneficiary is working and already in a high income tax bracket. The not-so-hidden impact of this part of the SECURE Act was that it raised taxes.

Fortunately, Congress provided a way for a special needs trust to continue to stretch out the distributions and avoid the ten-year deadline, so that the taxes owed each year could be controlled. But as with most tax rules, it's complicated. The third-party special needs trust must include very special and specific language in order to avoid the ten-year rule and receive these retirement account tax advantages. *The trust in this book does not include this special language.* In addition, the IRS is expected to release regulations on the SECURE Act that might change these retirement account payout rules. If you plan to leave retirement accounts to your loved one via a special needs trust, you must consult an attorney to ensure the special language is included in the trust, allowing your loved one to avoid negative tax implications.

It is also important that you not name your loved one individually as a beneficiary of your retirement account. Doing so can jeopardize his or her public benefits. Fixing this error after your death is expensive and time consuming, requiring an attorney to file a petition with the court, during which time your loved one could be left without access to the public benefits he or she is relying on for daily needs.

Life Insurance

For many people, life insurance is the only feasible way to raise enough money to help a special needs trust beneficiary over many years or decades. While it is impossible for most people to save $100,000 or more during their life out of their paychecks, many people can afford a small monthly payment for a $100,000 life insurance policy.

> **EXAMPLE:** Frank and Jane, a married couple, buy a term life insurance policy that will pay out $100,000 when the surviving spouse dies, provided they keep the policy in force by paying the monthly premiums of roughly $25 a month. When it becomes clear to them that their daughter Emily will need SSI and Medicaid for life because of a childhood accident, Frank and Jane decide to direct the insurance proceeds to a special needs trust, by naming the trustee of the trust as beneficiary of the life insurance policy.

You can make sure that life insurance proceeds go to a special needs trust by creating the trust as detailed in Chapter 8 and naming the trust as the policy's beneficiary.

> **EXAMPLE:** Frank and Jane Jones create a special needs trust for their son Robert, naming themselves as cotrustees and Elmer, a close family friend, as successor trustee to take over after both Frank and Jane die. They also name the trustee of the special needs trust as the beneficiary of their life insurance policy, like this: Frank and Jane Jones, Trustees, or their successors in interest, of the Robert Jones Special Needs Trust, dated June 1, 2019.
>
> After the deaths of both Frank and Jane, the successor trustee receives the proceeds of the life insurance policy in his capacity as trustee and uses the money to provide for Robert's special needs under the terms of the trust.

There are many kinds of life insurance policies (or "products," as the companies call them) including term, universal life, whole life, and more. Term insurance is the simplest; if you die while the policy is in force, your beneficiary gets the proceeds. However, term insurance may not be the best product to ensure an inheritance, because if a person lets a term policy lapse and dies thereafter, there is no payout. Other kinds of policies are part insurance and part investment; they build up equity you can borrow against or cash in. Annuities can give you a steady income throughout retirement.

RESOURCE

More information on life insurance options. *Plan Your Estate*, by Denis Clifford (Nolo), discusses life insurance choices, including how to find the right kind of policy and a solid company. At least two financial companies have separate divisions specifically to deal with planning for loved ones with disabilities:

- MassMutual's special needs division. To get started, visit the company's website, www.massmutual.com/specialneeds.
- Merrill Lynch & Co.'s special needs division. Call 877-456-7526 or visit the company's website, www.ml.com.

Try to Head Off Mixing the Beneficiary's Property With Trust Property

Once the special needs trust you create is up and running, the trustee will be in charge of disbursing funds and doing as much as possible to protect the beneficiary's eligibility for Medicaid and SSI. But suppose the beneficiary comes into some property of his or her own—perhaps through a personal injury settlement or an inheritance from a relative that was not planned for?

At first thought, it might seem like a good idea to put that money straight into the existing special needs trust, to keep it from being counted as the beneficiary's resource and disqualifying him or her from getting SSI. In fact, this is a bad idea. Adding the beneficiary's own property to the special needs trust would make your loved one ineligible for SSI and Medicaid.

If the beneficiary's own property is mixed with the property you left in the special needs trust, it could all be considered the beneficiary's resource. The total amount would almost certainly exceed the resource limit (currently $2,000) that's imposed on SSI recipients. (Chapter 3 has more on resource and income limits.)

EXAMPLE: Bonnie, who receives SSI and Medicaid, is the beneficiary of a special needs trust created by her father and funded by him in his will. This has worked out well for ten years. However, Bonnie unexpectedly wins $10,000 in the state lottery.

She deposits the money in her existing special needs trust—and only later learns that as a result, all of the money in the trust is now considered her resource because her lottery winnings and the original funds from her father were mixed together.

How could Bonnie have averted this unfortunate consequence? A better alternative than adding property to a third-party trust is to create a separate, first-party special needs trust. That way, assets in the original trust will remain off-limits as a resource, and eligibility for SSI and Medicaid will not be affected.

Be sure to get help from a lawyer if you must decide what to do with funds owned by the beneficiary (do not use the trust in this book). A lawyer should know about the federal and state requirements for first-party trusts, and can explain to you how a first-party special needs trust must provide for reimbursement of Medicaid costs from trust assets (to the state's Medicaid agency) after the beneficiary's death. Chapter 11 can help you find and work with a lawyer. ●

The Trustee's Job

The trustee of your special needs trust will manage the trust for the benefit of your loved one. Whether the trustee is you, a relative, a friend, or a professional, the trustee has a critical job as the manager and guardian of the trust. Not only must the trustee spend trust funds in the best interest of the beneficiary (your loved one with a disability), the trustee must also keep up to date on SSI and Medicaid laws, invest trust funds, file taxes, maintain accurate records, and more.

This chapter describes the basic duties of the trustee. It will give you a sense of what your job will be as initial trustee, and it will also help you decide who should take your place when you (or the initial trustee you name, if not yourself) can no longer serve. Chapter 5 goes into more detail about how to choose the trustees.

Consider Signing Up for a Pooled Trust

If you don't know anyone whom you feel confident naming as trustee, you may want to consider joining a "pooled trust" instead of setting up your own special needs trust. If you use a pooled trust, you won't need to choose a trustee or successor trustee; the nonprofit organization that administers the trust will do so. Chapter 6 discusses pooled trusts.

The Trustee's Basic Duties

A trustee's most fundamental legal duty is to always act honestly and put the interests of the trust beneficiary first. This is commonly called the trustee's fiduciary duty.

EXAMPLE: Peter is the trustee of a special needs trust created for his younger brother Paul. Peter's older brother Simon needs money to fund a high-risk start-up company. Wanting to help Simon, Peter invests part of the trust money in Simon's company. By unnecessarily risking trust assets, Peter has violated his fiduciary duty to act in Paul's best interests.

The trustee may, however, take actions that indirectly benefit other parties, as long as the sole purpose of the action itself is to help the beneficiary. For example, it's all right to use trust money to buy a home for a beneficiary even if a relative may also live in the home and will also benefit.

Trustees who act in good faith generally won't be personally liable for losses caused by their actions. Trustees could be held personally liable for acts that are judged (after the fact) to be unreasonably careless or, to use the legal term, negligent. Negligence is generally defined as failing to take the proper care that a prudent person would take in similar circumstances.

For instance, if the beneficiary lost several months of SSI and Medicaid eligibility because the trustee forgot to prepare a report required by those programs, the trustee might be considered to have been negligent. The beneficiary, or the beneficiary's guardian, could sue the trustee.

Trustees must also:

- Avoid any activity that conflicts with the purpose of the trust —which is to enhance the quality of life of the beneficiary.
- Respond to the beneficiary's personal needs for goods and services that aren't covered by SSI or Medicaid.
- Keep up with SSI and Medicaid income and resource rules so that the trustee's spending doesn't affect your loved one's eligibility for SSI and Medicaid. (See Chapter 2.)
- Invest and manage trust property following the terms of the trust and state law, in the beneficiary's best interests.
- Keep your loved one with a disability and other interested persons up to date on trust activity.
- Keep accurate records, prepare reports that the SSI and Medicaid programs require, and file necessary federal and state tax returns.
- Go to court, if necessary and financially reasonable, to uphold the trust and require the SSI and Medicaid programs to comply with applicable law. (It's rare that trustees need to turn to the courts; see the discussion below, "Going to Court," for more information.)

All of these responsibilities are discussed in this chapter. And if you feel overwhelmed at the prospect of the time needed to attend to this list of duties, keep in mind that trustees are generally entitled to reasonable compensation from the trust assets for the time they spend administering the trust.

> **TIP**
>
> **Share the burden.** As you can see, there is a lot on a trustee's plate. You don't have to choose one person to handle everything; these tasks can be shared by two or more cotrustees, handled by experts hired by an individual trustee as needed, or carried out by a trustee working for a pooled trust. The pros and cons of each approach are discussed in Chapter 5.

Working With a Guardian or Conservator

People who have disabilities such as Down syndrome or a traumatic brain injury, which interfere with some aspect of their cognitive functioning, often need someone to help them make sound financial and personal decisions. Children under the age of 18 also require a parent or guardian to help make personal and financial decisions for them, unless they are emancipated or married.

For many people, this assistance comes from an informal advocate —a friend or relative who is always there to help the person with a disability cope with the world. But if the disability is severe, a court might need to appoint someone to make decisions on behalf of the beneficiary. This person is usually called a guardian or conservator.

Guardians or conservators can be in charge of a person's medical and personal decisions (called a guardian or conservator of the person), or in charge of a person's financial decisions (called a guardian or conservator of the estate). Sometimes, a guardianship or conservatorship of the estate is not necessary because all the funds available to a person are held in a special needs trust, rather than that person's own name.

If your loved one has a court-appointed guardian or conservator, the person serving as trustee of the special needs trust will have to work closely with that person. In essence, they must function as partners, each contributing to the business of meeting the needs of the person with a disability. Frequent communications—in person or by telephone or email—are necessary to make sure the guardian or conservator and the trustee are on the same page.

> **EXAMPLE:** Nicolas was diagnosed with severe autism when he was three years old. His father died when he was ten. His mother, Theresa, cared for Nicolas until he turned 18. At that time, she asked the probate court to appoint her as conservator, in charge of Nicolas's person and property. She also created a special needs trust and used her will to leave everything to this trust for Nicholas's sole benefit. The trust document named her brother Zeke as successor trustee to take over after Theresa dies.
>
> Shortly after Nicholas's 36th birthday, Theresa died. As part of the probate process, Theresa's executor (the person named in her will to wind up her affairs) asked the court to appoint Nicolas's aunt, Katie, as his successor conservator. As successor conservator, Katie made all necessary financial and personal decisions for Nicholas while Zeke, who became trustee when Theresa died, invested and spent trust assets for Nicholas's benefit. Katie couldn't require Zeke to make a disbursement, and Zeke couldn't second-guess any of Katie's decisions.
>
> Katie and Zeke made it a point to talk at least once a month to discuss any issues that had arisen. Zeke relied on Katie to tell him about Nicholas's day-to-day needs because Katie was more attuned to them than Zeke was.
>
> Similarly, Zeke, who was more comfortable with financial decisions than Katie was, frequently had good suggestions for Katie in that area.

Sometimes the person serving as trustee of the special needs trust is also the court-appointed guardian or conservator. In that case, the roles must be kept strictly separate. For instance, income received by a guardian for the benefit of your loved one must be kept in a separate account—it can't be placed in the trust. Similarly, records of trust activity must be kept separate from records kept as part of the guardianship or conservatorship.

Investing Trust Property

Trustees must safeguard and invest the trust property, following the instructions in the trust document. The trust provided by this book directs the trustee to act in accordance with the Prudent Investor Act, a law that has been adopted by most states. It makes significant demands on trustees, but also gives them flexibility in making investments.

> **SEE AN EXPERT**
>
> **The trustee can get help.** Investment decisions can become complex. For that reason, many trustees hire financial advisers to help them come up with sensible investment strategies that comply with the Prudent Investor Act. Chapter 11 explains how to find such people.

The Prudent Investor Act sets out four major rules for trustees:
- Balance risk against return.
- Diversify investments.
- Act in ways that will further the trust purposes.
- Evaluate the investment portfolio as a whole.

When you examine each of these principles, you'll see that they're nothing more than common sense. Basically, they tell the trustee to invest conservatively if the circumstances indicate caution, as may be the case with assets in a special needs trust. But if the purpose of the trust, the amount of funds available to invest, and the knowledge of the trustee combine to make a more aggressive strategy reasonable under the act's guiding rules, then it's allowed.

Trustees who act sensibly and follow the Prudent Investor Act rules will not be liable for losses to the trust caused by a particular investment that goes bad. Instead, in the event of a lawsuit challenging a trustee's actions, a court would look at the overall performance of the trust investments. Acting sensibly means having a reason for the investments you make, which fairly balances the four rules set out above.

The Old Rules for Investing

Many old state laws limited trustees to certain very low-risk, low-return investments. This gave trustees certainty, but didn't allow them to protect trust funds from being eroded by inflation or to diversify investments. In addition, every investment decision could be scrutinized separately if challenged in court. Under the Prudent Investor Act, the trustee's performance as an investor is looked at in its entirety.

A fairly detailed explanation of the Prudent Investor Act is in the Letter to Trustee provided in Appendix A. Take a look at the investment portion of that letter so you'll have an understanding of what the trustee and successor trustee must do, and what will happen to trust assets after your death. Assuming that the special needs trust will primarily be funded at your death, you won't be investing trust funds as the initial trustee, and you don't need to absorb all the details of investment rules yourself.

Leaving Investing Instructions

Should you leave specific instructions in your special needs trust about how to invest trust property? Probably not. It's not a good idea to be too specific about investing, because the trust may be around for decades. If the trustee does not have the flexibility to invest under changing conditions, trust investments may be either too aggressive or too conservative for the beneficiary's needs at that time.

If you want to give your trustee very specific instructions about how to invest the funds in the special needs trust you create, you'll need to consult an attorney to draft the appropriate provisions. You should also consult a financial adviser to assist with creating a plan. The trust in this book will not allow your trustee to deviate from the Prudent Investor rule.

Spending Trust Money for the Beneficiary

People who receive or expect to receive SSI or Medicaid are usually unable to work to support themselves. Their third-party special needs trust is probably one of the only large windfalls they will receive after their benefactor dies. This means that their third-party special needs trust should be treated by the trustee almost like a retirement plan. Accordingly, the person serving as trustee will have to keep an eye on two sometimes conflicting goals:

- meeting the trust beneficiary's current special needs (remember, basically that means things other than food and shelter—see Chapter 2 for more information), and
- keeping enough property in the trust to provide for the beneficiary's future needs for as long as possible. This approach involves taking into account any future needs before making payments for current needs. For example, can the trust afford to pay for a vehicle now and still afford an in-home caregiver later if one is needed?

Calculating an Annual Spending Plan

How much money can a trustee spend to meet the beneficiary's special needs? At the simplest level, to compute an annual spending plan, the trustee could divide the value of the trust property by the number of years the beneficiary is expected to live. For example, if the beneficiary's life expectancy is 30 more years, and there is $100,000 in the trust, the trustee could spend about $3,300 each year.

This calculation, of course, doesn't take into account any income that the trust assets might earn. If you assume an average return of 10% a year on the $100,000, then the annual spending plan would be increased to account for the trust income.

You or a successor trustee can get help in making these calculations simply by searching for the phrase "investment calculators" on the

Internet. But most trustees consult a financial planner or another adviser who's had experience with trust investing and with estimating how much a beneficiary's needs are likely to cost. For more about finding a financial planner, see Chapter 11.

TIP
Figuring life expectancy. Life expectancy tables are easily available on the Internet (search for "life expectancy tables"), but those figures might not apply to someone with a disability. If relevant figures aren't available, the trustee might ask the beneficiary's doctors for an estimated figure.

Use a Letter of Intent to Help Your Successor Trustee

Understanding the beneficiary's needs is an important part of a trustee's job. If you are the primary caregiver for your loved one, you might have concerns about whether a successor trustee will know your loved one well enough to make informed decisions concerning care.

To help with this problem, you can write a "letter of intent" to guide the successor trustees. In the letter, you describe the beneficiary's needs, including whatever information you think will be useful. For example, you can provide information about his or her disability, social life, medical concerns, interests and hobbies, employment, daily routine, and contact information for friends and family. For more about writing a letter of intent, see Chapter 10. For a sample letter of intent, see Appendix B.

Understanding the Remainder Beneficiary's Interests

The remainder beneficiary is the person you name to inherit any assets that are left in the special needs trust when your loved one with a disability (the trust beneficiary) dies.

Although the remainder beneficiaries will naturally be interested in how the trust is administered, the trust document you prepare with this book makes it clear that the interests of the person with a disability (the trust beneficiary) always come first. The person serving as trustee must provide for the trust beneficiary's special needs, even if nothing will be left when the trust ends and even if a remainder beneficiary complains about it.

> **EXAMPLE:** In their wills, Carlos and his wife, Maria, leave their property to each other and provide that when the second spouse dies, $25,000 will go to their son, Ricardo, and the rest to a special needs trust they created for their daughter, Rocio, who has a developmental disability. The trust provides that Ricardo will receive any property left in the special needs trust at Rocio's death. The leftover property (if any) is the remainder, and Ricardo is the remainder beneficiary.
>
> Carlos and Maria die together in a car accident, and their property (after the $25,000 gift to Ricardo) goes into the special needs trust for their daughter Rocio. The trust property is worth about $250,000. The successor trustee who became trustee when Carlos and Maria died can spend whatever is necessary to provide for Rocio's special needs, including a trip around the world or tuition at an expensive private college.
>
> Ricardo is resentful and thinks the trustee doesn't need to spend so much on Rocio. The trustee, obeying the terms of the trust, pays no attention to Ricardo's frustrations and concentrates on Rocio's needs.

Managing a Remainder Beneficiary's Property

If money is left in the trust when the special needs trust beneficiary dies, the trustee's job might not be over. If a remainder beneficiary is younger than 18, an adult must manage the property for the remainder beneficiary's benefit. Under the terms of the trust document in this book, the person serving as trustee for the original beneficiary has that job.

This book's trust document makes the trustee the "custodian" of the remaining property, under a law called the Uniform Transfers to Minors Act (UTMA). The UTMA, which has been adopted in all states except South Carolina, sets out the custodian's duties. Basically, the job is like that of a trustee—a custodian must prudently invest and spend the money on behalf of the minor beneficiary.

The custodianship ends when the beneficiary reaches an age between 18 and 25, depending on the state. This book's trust document directs that the custodianship end when the beneficiary turns 21, unless the state's law requires distribution at age 18. In some states, you can extend an UTMA custodianship to age 25 (see below). When the custodianship ends, the custodian simply gives any remaining property to the beneficiary.

> **EXAMPLE:** Greta creates a special needs trust for her daughter Frieda and funds the trust through her will. In the trust document, Greta names her grandchildren, Hans and Lena, as remainder beneficiaries to inherit any funds left in the trust when Frieda dies. About a year after Greta's death, Frieda dies. At that time, Hans is 23 and Lena is 18.
>
> The person succeeding Greta as trustee gives half of the remaining money to Hans and keeps the other half in a custodial bank account for the benefit of Lena. When Lena turns 21 (the age custodianships end in her state), the trustee gives her what's left in the account outright.

If you wish to leave assets to a remainder beneficiary by using something other than an UTMA account or with outright distribution, you should consult an estate planning attorney for help. Your options may include setting up a trust for the remainder beneficiary, staggering distributions (for example, leaving one-third at age 18, one-third at age 25, and the balance on age 30), or leaving assets only for education of grandchildren. You should discuss these decisions with an attorney. See Chapter 11 for more on finding and working with a lawyer.

Extending the UTMA Custodianship to Age 25

In a few states—Alaska, California, Florida, Nevada, Ohio, Oregon, Pennsylvania, Tennessee, Virginia, and Washington—you can choose to extend an UMTA custodianship until the beneficiary's 25th birthday. If you live in one of those states and want the UTMA to end at age 25 instead of age 21, modify Article 13 of your trust document to read: "The custodianship shall end when the remainder beneficiary turns 25 years old." You can learn more about UTMA custodianships, including the age at which the custodianships must end in your state, in Nolo's article, "The Uniform Transfers to Minors Act" (at Nolo.com, choose "Articles" and type the title in the search box).

Preserving Eligibility for SSI and Medicaid

Preserving the beneficiary's eligibility for SSI and Medicaid is a crucial part of a trustee's job. This is one of the main reasons for creating the trust.

Understanding SSI and Medicaid Rules

When spending trust money, the person serving as trustee must comply with either SSI or Medicaid income and resource rules so that the beneficiary's eligibility for SSI and Medicaid is not compromised. Trustees must have a sound understanding of these rules and must keep up to date on any changes. A summary of these rules appears just below and in the "Letter to Trustee," in Appendix A.

Making Reports to SSA

To remain eligible for SSI and Medicaid, your loved one (or someone authorized to act on his or her behalf, called a representative payee by the Social Security Administration) must submit an annual report to the state agency administering the SSI program, as well as report monthly on any changes in income, resources, or living arrangements.

The trustee's job is to make sure that the beneficiary or guardian has accurate information about the trust activity—such as a record of all disbursements on behalf of the beneficiary and all trust income received during the reporting period. If the trustee buys things that are countable assets under SSI rules and gives them to the beneficiary—that is, if they're not held in the trust—each month, the beneficiary or his or her representative must report them. Similarly, if the trustee pays for food or shelter, the beneficiary or his or her representative must report it to SSA so that the SSI reduction for in-kind support and maintenance (ISM) may be applied. For more information on ISM, see Chapter 2.

Disbursements made for property that is held in the trust don't, at least theoretically, need to be reported, because the beneficiary doesn't acquire income or resources as a result. But some SSI offices might take exception to this approach if the beneficiary actually has exclusive use and control over the property in question, even when the trust owns it.

EXAMPLE: Grace, the beneficiary of a special needs trust, wants a motorized wheelchair that has features that aren't available on the chairs that Medicaid will pay for. The person serving as trustee buys the chair in the name of the trust by making sure the receipt or bill of sale references the trust as the purchaser. The trustee also itemizes the chair as a trust asset in the trust records. Because the chair is held in trust in this manner, it probably doesn't need to be reported as an asset belonging to Grace. But the trustee decides that it's better to report the chair with an explanation that it's owned by the trust, so the trustee provides Grace with the receipt, bill of sale, and trust records in order for her to inform SSA.

Medicaid and SSI Eligibility Rules: A Summary

- With some exceptions, someone who is eligible for SSI is automatically eligible for Medicaid.

- An individual who owns resources worth more than $2,000 (not counting a primary residence, car, or furnishings) does not qualify for SSI.

- Assets in a special needs trust funded with assets other than the beneficiary's are not counted as a resource.

- If the beneficiary earns income, the first $65 is exempt and the earned income over that amount results in a one-dollar reduction from the SSI grant for every two dollars earned. Too much earned income causes loss of SSI benefits.

- After a $20 exemption, unearned income results in a dollar-for-dollar reduction of the SSI grant. Too much unearned income causes loss of SSI eligibility.

- If the trustee distributes countable resources to the beneficiary, in the first month it will be treated as unearned income and on the first day of each calendar month it will be treated as a countable resource.

- If this property is kept, in later months it is counted as a resource and if its value—along with the value of the person's other assets—is $2,000 or more, he or she will lose SSI and Medicaid eligibility.

- If trust funds are spent for food or shelter, the SSI grant is reduced, up to one-third of the federal portion of the grant plus $20. The beneficiary does not lose SSI eligibility (unless, because of other income, the SSI grant is less than the amount deducted).

- If the trustee makes payments to third parties on the beneficiary's behalf for anything other than food or shelter, the payments are not counted as income for purposes of SSI eligibility (unless the items purchased can easily be converted to cash).

Changing or Terminating the Trust

Due to advances in medical technologies, people with disabilities who might have survived only until 25 or 30 in the early 20th century can now count on a fairly long life—to age 60 or beyond. For example, the average life expectancy for a child born with Down syndrome is now more than 60. This, of course, means that a special needs trust can last for decades. And, needless to say, massive—and completely unpredictable—changes in agency rules and medical treatments can occur over this period. To take this uncertainty into account, the special needs trust you create with this book lets a "trust protector" change the terms in the trust to keep it current.

The need to change or modify the trust can arise when the trust's continued existence would jeopardize the beneficiary's eligibility for SSI and Medicaid. In that event, the trust protector would have the right to modify the trust to make sure it is updated to take into account any new requirements that may arise. The trustee could even terminate the trust before the death of the beneficiary ("early termination").

> **EXAMPLE:** Roberto is the beneficiary of a special needs trust created by his aunt, Mary. Years after Mary dies, changes in SSI and Medicaid eligibility rules make Roberto ineligible for those programs because of the trust assets. To get around these changes in the eligibility rules, the person serving as trust protector makes an amendment to the trust to make sure it conforms with any changes in the law.

Stand Your Ground If You Opt for Early Termination

Current government rules and regulations allow early termination provisions in *third-party* special needs trusts, like the one you can create with this book. However, the rules and regulations on early termination provisions for *first-party* special needs trusts—those created with the assets of the loved one with a disability—require Medicaid payback. If a government employee tells you that an early termination provision is not permitted in your third-party special needs trust without Medicaid payback, it might be because that person does not understand the difference between these types of trusts.

When the Beneficiary No Longer Needs the Trust

A condition that is disabling today might not be disabling in the future. It may be cured or ameliorated by advances in medical technology, or workplace demands may change, allowing someone who cannot now work to enter the job market. Or, the SSI and Medicaid programs might change in a way that makes a special needs trust unnecessary.

In light of these possibilities, the trust in this book lets the person serving as trustee terminate the trust if the trust isn't necessary to preserve the beneficiary's eligibility for government benefits.

> **EXAMPLE:** Vivian uses her revocable living trust to fund a special needs trust she created for her brother Charles, who has schizophrenia. Five years after Vivian's death, a cure for schizophrenia is found, and Charles no longer needs Medicaid or the protection of the trust. Using the authority granted by the trust document, the person serving as trustee ends the trust and distributes the trust assets directly to Charles.

Paying Taxes

The person serving as trustee must file a separate tax return for the trust every year, unless the income earned by the trust is below the reporting threshold ($600 in 2021). The special needs trust you create with this book is an irrevocable trust, meaning it can't be revoked after it takes effect. The trust must have its own tax ID number, which you can get from the IRS by submitting a simple form (IRS Form SS-4), or applying online at www.irs.gov (type "SS-4" in the search box on the home page).

Trust income (the money earned from investing trust assets) is taxed at a special trust rate (in 2020, 37% for income over $12,950). If you place only a minimal amount in the trust when you create it, you needn't worry about paying taxes. However, taxes will become a concern once significant funds land in the trust. Because the tax rate for trust income is so much higher than the rate that applies to most individuals, most types of trusts direct the trustee to distribute trust income to the beneficiary rather than keep it in the trust. But for special needs trusts, the person serving as trustee may keep all income in the trust rather than give it directly to the trust beneficiary, because requiring a disbursement of all trust income will make the beneficiary ineligible for SSI and Medicaid, defeating the purpose of the trust.

There is a way, however, to give the beneficiary the benefit of trust income but avoid the high trust tax rate. Under IRS rules, trust income that is spent on the beneficiary's behalf is taxed at his or her individual rate, not the trust rate. So, if the trustee spends the income on the beneficiary's behalf—and keeps careful records showing that trust income, not assets, was spent—the IRS will tax the income at the beneficiary's lower rate. The trust records must clearly show that the source of the disbursements was the income (interest), not the principal, and that the income was spent for the benefit of the beneficiary, not the trust itself.

> **EXAMPLE:** Joey is the trustee of a special needs trust for his sister Angela. The trust funds are invested in several funds managed by a big brokerage company, which sends Joey a monthly statement showing interest earned on the money. For the current year, the interest amounts to $5,000. In his trust accounting book, Joey records that disbursements for Angela's benefit were made out of this income, not the trust principal.
>
> When the trust taxes are computed, any money spent from the income for Angela's benefit is taxed at Angela's rate. Income that is added to the trust and not disbursed is taxed at the higher trust rate.

Going to Court

It's unlikely, but some person or government agency might attack the validity of your special needs trust or question the trustee's actions. For example, the SSI or Medicaid program might change its rules and try to force the person serving as trustee to contribute to the beneficiary's support even though that would deprive the beneficiary of SSI and Medicaid. If this happens, this book's trust authorizes the trustee to defend the trust in whatever forum is available, including court.

Going to court is expensive. It can easily cost $5,000—possibly more—in court costs and attorneys' fees. So, if a special needs trust has just $10,000 worth of assets, the trustee's decision may be to terminate the trust. On the other hand, if the trust were worth $500,000, it would be worth it to hire a lawyer and challenge the government decision.

If a lawsuit is ever necessary, the trustee will generally have to hire a lawyer to handle it. In many states, the trustee cannot represent the trust in court; only a lawyer can do that. (Chapter 11 discusses finding and working with lawyers.)

Letter to Trustee

Appendix A contains a long letter that you may want to adapt and give to the people you expect to serve as trustees of the special needs trust. The letter provides an overview of the trustee's job. You may find the letter a good source of information for you, too, if you're going to be the initial trustee of the special needs trust or if you want more detail about the responsibilities of the trustees who will succeed you.

The letter also explains how a successor trustee can prove his or her authority under the trust, resign as trustee, or appoint a successor trustee if all named successors are unavailable.

You can also download an electronic version of the letter, so you can tailor it to your situation. (See Appendix C.) Parts of it may not apply to you. For example, if you're appointing individual successor trustees, you'll want to delete the information about cotrustees. ●

Choosing Trustees

Who should you put in charge of the special needs trust? It's a hugely important question. You will probably name yourself as trustee to manage the trust while you are alive and healthy. But who will take over when you're unable to, or when you are no longer around to make sure that things go right?

Choosing reliable people to manage the trust is crucial, because trusts operate on the honor system. The law imposes a duty on trustees to honestly and faithfully carry out the trust's terms, but in most cases, a judge does not supervise the trustee. If a beneficiary (or someone acting on behalf of a beneficiary) sues the person serving as trustee, a court will examine the trustee's behavior and can remove a trustee who has failed to meet the standards set out by law. But because getting a trustee replaced usually involves at least one court filing—and possibly even a difficult lawsuit—it doesn't happen often. And by the time a trustee can be replaced, it may be too late to recover assets that have been misspent or misused.

After reading Chapter 4 and the letter in Appendix A outlining the trustee's duties, you should have a good idea of what trustees will be called on to do when serving as trustee. This chapter can help you make the best choice given your individual circumstances.

An Overview of Your Options

The trust in this book offers several options for naming the initial and successor trustees of your special needs trust. Here's an overview of the choices:

- Name yourself as initial trustee, or name yourself and a spouse or partner as initial cotrustees.
- Name someone else—perhaps the beneficiary's parent or parents.
- Name family members or friends.
- Name a professional trustee.
- Name an individual and a professional trustee to serve as cotrustees.
- Join a pooled special needs trust instead of setting up a trust yourself.
- Name a nonprofit trustee.

Picking the Ideal Trustee

If you decide to create your own special needs trust, then you must also decide who to name as initial trustee and successor trustees of that trust.

If the beneficiary of the trust is your child, you will probably name yourself to serve as the initial trustee. If you are married or partnered, you might name yourself and your spouse or partner to serve together as initial cotrustees. If the beneficiary is someone other than your child, the child's parent or parents might be the logical choice for initial trustees.

When you create your trust you will also name successor trustees—people to manage the trust when the initial trustee or cotrustees can no longer serve. The successor trustees will most likely be friends or family, but not just any friend or family member will do.

The job of trustee requires a unique balance of care for the beneficiary, fiscal responsibility, ability to understand SSI and Medicaid laws, and more. Ideally, you want your trustee to be:

- willing to serve
- able to manage the trust for your loved one's benefit
- personally acquainted with your loved one
- of roughly the same age as (or younger than) your loved one
- able to understand and apply government benefit eligibility rules able to maintain excellent records, and
- able to conduct financial affairs in a consistent, organized, and responsible manner.

The following subsections describe these qualities in detail. Keep them in mind when you choose your trustees.

Willingness to Serve

Every trustee and successor trustee you name must be willing to serve, so talk to all potential trustees in advance. Clearly explain under what conditions they would serve and what their duties would be. You might give them a copy of the Letter to Trustee, provided in Appendix A. The letter will help the potential trustee make an informed decision.

Before you name your trustees in the trust, make sure they know and accept the role you assign to them. Otherwise, when it comes time for them to serve, they might decline.

> **EXAMPLE:** Loretta, 60 years old and recently widowed, creates a special needs trust for the benefit of her blind daughter, Luanne. She names herself as trustee and names Luanne's cousin Peter as successor trustee. Because Peter and Loretta are very close, she assumes that Peter will agree to serve as trustee but doesn't get around to mentioning it to him.
>
> When Loretta dies ten years later, Peter learns that he has been named to succeed Loretta as trustee. Surprised and overwhelmed by the idea of taking on this responsibility, Peter refuses the appointment. Fortunately, Loretta had named a secondary successor trustee, her cousin Jim, who agreed to serve.

This example also highlights the importance of naming more than one level of successor trustee—so that there is always another named choice to take over if someone is unable or unwilling to serve. (See "Naming Successor Trustees," below.) But suppose, you might wonder, both successor trustees decline? If no named trustee is able or willing to serve, the special needs trust in this book authorizes the executor of your will (if you have one) or your successor trustee of your revocable living trust (if you have one) to choose someone to serve as trustee of the special needs trust.

You should speak to the executor of your will and successor trustee of your living trust about the possibility that your named trustees might decline to serve when the time comes, despite their initial agreement. You can make the job of finding someone to serve a lot easier for the executor of your will and successor trustee if you leave a list of potential successor trustees in your Letter of Intent. You can give your Letter of Intent to your named successor trustees, the executor of your will, and the successor trustee of your living trust, so they then can name your preferred successors if called on to appoint someone. See Chapter 10 on how to write and what to include in your Letter of Intent.

If any of the people whom you want to name as trustee or successor trustee don't want to do the job on their own, consider naming a cotrustee to serve with them. (See "Naming Cotrustees," below.) Also, you can reassure prospective trustees that as trustees they will have the authority to hire experts if and when they're needed.

TIP

Ask again later, too. Those whom you've chosen as successor trustees might not be called on to serve for years or even decades. For example, if you name yourself as trustee and are now 50 years old, the successor trustee might not be needed for 30 or more years. So even if your choice for successor trustee happily agrees to serve at the time you ask, circumstances could change. Check in with your choice every few years so that, if necessary, you can exercise your authority as trustee to name a replacement. Similarly, the person you name initially might not be the best choice as time goes on, so look at your trust every few years to review your choices.

No Conflicts of Interest

A special needs trust must be managed for the benefit of the beneficiary. This means that people serving as trustees must not act in their own interests—or the interests of others—when making investment or spending decisions. Put another way, the trustee must avoid conflicts of interests. Ideally, this means that the trustee should not have anything to gain from the trust, either while it is in operation or after it ends.

In real life, however, it is not uncommon to name the same person as both successor trustee and remainder beneficiary. (The remainder beneficiary is the person who gets any trust property that is left when the beneficiary dies or, in some cases, when the trust is dissolved.) This arrangement creates a direct conflict of interest when the successor trustee takes over as trustee, because every dollar of trust money spent on behalf of the beneficiary is one dollar less that the remainder beneficiary (the successor trustee) could receive at the beneficiary's death.

EXAMPLE: Jonas creates a special needs trust for his sister Clara. He names himself as trustee and names his brother Ralph as the successor trustee. The trust also provides that Ralph should receive any remaining trust property if Clara dies before Ralph. Jonas dies ten years after creating the trust. Ralph takes over as trustee and spends the money appropriately for Clara's benefit, even though every dollar he spends on her reduces the amount he will take when Clara dies. When Clara dies five years later, Ralph receives the $50,000 that remains in the trust.

There is no absolute rule against naming the same person as trustee and a remainder beneficiary. An honest and honorable trustee will make decisions based solely on the beneficiary's needs. If you don't expect the remainder beneficiary to inherit anything—for example, if the trust funds just won't last that long—it might not be a big issue for you.

Whenever possible, name different people to serve as successor trustee and remainder beneficiary. One path that works for some families is to name a favorite charity as the remainder beneficiary—perhaps a church, senior center, or disability organization, such as The Arc or Centers for Independent Living.

CAUTION

Consult an Attorney. If you are planning on putting your retirement assets, like an IRA or a 401(k), in the special needs trust, you might not want to name a charity as the remainder beneficiary. Doing so can prevent your loved one from receiving special tax benefits when they inherit your retirement asset. Planning with retirement assets is extremely complex and involves a new law called the SECURE Act. Consult an attorney if you are planning to leave your retirement account to a loved one with disabilities or their special needs trust. See Chapter 3 for more information on Retirement Accounts.

Familiarity and Empathy With the Beneficiary

A special needs trust is intended to give the beneficiary goods and services in addition to the food and shelter paid for by the SSI grant.

So a special needs trust functions most smoothly when the person serving as trustee has a good working knowledge of the beneficiary's needs. This relationship requires good communication, which is most likely to exist if the trustee has—or is able to develop—a close personal relationship with the beneficiary. A personal relationship is especially important if the beneficiary's ability to communicate is impaired.

> **EXAMPLE:** Douglas has schizophrenia and lives in a group home. He is the beneficiary of a special needs trust managed by his brother, Phil. Douglas has little awareness of the special needs trust or the benefits that it can provide.
>
> Fortunately, Phil is familiar with Douglas's likes and dislikes and makes sure that his special needs are provided for within the limits of the trust funds. For instance, Phil knows that Douglas likes to play video games and so makes sure that he receives a steady supply, courtesy of the trust.

Even when the beneficiary can communicate effectively, familiarity— and empathy—between the trustee and the beneficiary are still important. A good relationship makes it easier for them to negotiate requests that the trustee may be reluctant to grant because they threaten to deplete trust assets. Also, the more familiar a trustee is with a beneficiary, the less likely it is that the trustee's decisions will be based on bias or misconceptions about people with disabilities that are, unhappily, all too common.

> **EXAMPLE:** Angela, the beneficiary of a special needs trust, became quadriplegic after an automobile accident when she was a girl. She graduated from regular high school thanks to support she received from her family and accommodations offered by the school. Now, Angela wants to attend college and major in communications so she can pursue a career in television broadcasting.
>
> Tomas, the trustee of Angela's trust, is her distant cousin and has not spent much time around Angela or other people with disabilities. Tomas believes that given Angela's physical condition she is chasing a pipe dream and rejects her request for tuition and other expenses of college. Tomas thinks he is being reasonable. Angela believes he is making unwarranted assumptions about what she can accomplish. Because the trustee has full authority to make decisions, Angela will not be able to use trust funds for her education.

While serious disagreements between the beneficiary and the trustee are rare, they can be devastating to the purpose of the trust. For that reason, even if you choose a trustee who has an ideal relationship with the beneficiary, it's wise for the trust to name someone who can remove and replace the trustee, if necessary. See "Using a Trust Protector or Trust Advisory Committee," at the end of this chapter.

Close in Age to the Beneficiary

Special needs trusts can last for months, years, or decades. In many instances, their duration is very hard to predict. Today, many people with disabilities live much longer than their doctors or families originally expected. Such dramatic increases in life span are due both to medical advances and shifting attitudes toward people with disabilities. Institution-alization used to be the norm for people with many kinds of disabilities, but now they often live at home and are integrated into mainstream educational and social activities—and live a lot longer as a result.

When you're choosing a trustee, do your best to estimate your loved one's likely life span, despite the inherent uncertainty. The beneficiary's life span will give you some idea of how long you can expect the trustee will manage the trust.

It's best, of course, when the trustees will be around as long as the beneficiary is alive. So if you are creating a special needs trust for your child, who may outlive you by decades, your choice for successor trustee should be someone closer to your child's age than to yours. On the other hand, if your loved one's disability makes a long life very unlikely, it's reasonable to choose a successor trustee who is closer to your age.

Keep in mind that the special needs trust you create is likely to be fully funded at your death through a will, revocable living trust, or life insurance policy. If you're in your 40s or 50s, you likely have several decades to live, so it is wise to choose a successor trustee who is likely to live even longer.

You could also consider giving your named trustee the ability to appoint his or her own successor if you are no longer able to do it. Another option is to name a trust protector, as described at the end of this chapter.

> **TIP**
>
> **Keep your estate planning documents current.** You can amend your will or revocable living trust—and the money you are leaving to the special needs trust you created—right up until your death or until you lose legal capacity to handle your affairs. So, if it appears that a special needs trust is appropriate when you create it, but it later becomes unnecessary because of changes in your loved one's disability or in the laws governing SSI and Medicaid, you can make changes to your estate plan. Also, if you've named yourself initial trustee and your choices for successor trustees die before you, you can use your position as the trustee to name new successor trustees. See Chapter 8 for more specifics in keeping the special needs trust up to date.

Willingness to Get Help With Government Rules

Each trustee you name will need to become familiar with the rules that determine eligibility for SSI and Medicaid—and how the special needs trust can be used to supplement the beneficiary's needs without violating these rules. Some of the basic rules can be understood fairly easily. However, unless the trustee already has some experience with the rules of the public benefits programs, it may be best to get help from a professional—either a special needs planning lawyer or a nonlawyer with an expertise in public benefits counseling—at least until the trustee is comfortable that he or she understands the rules. See Chapter 11 for more information on how to get help from lawyers.

While it is important to name someone with basic common sense, common sense alone will not be enough to administer a special needs trust, because SSI and Medicaid eligibility rules and regulations rarely make sense. Trustees who do not get professional help might believe that they are doing the right thing, but may in fact be acting in a way that might destroy the beneficiary's public benefits eligibility. This is particularly worrisome because the SSA often catches mistakes, and if the problem isn't caught for many years, unwitting beneficiaries could be required to pay back benefits that they were not entitled to receive during that time.

Successor trustees who succeed a diligent and rules-abiding initial trustee can learn a lot by studying how the original trustee used trust funds. The initial trustee will write checks drawn on the trust's bank account, to cover goods or services that supplement your loved one's needs. Assuming the expenditures were within the SSI guidelines, the record of that spending will provide valuable guidance to the successor trustee about the types of expenditures the trust can confidently make. (But the successor trustee must not forget to keep track of SSI guideline changes.)

If the trust was established many years ago, under possibly different SSA rules, you'll want assurance that the trust will still qualify as a third-party special needs trust. You might want to give a copy of the trust to the local Social Security Administration (SSA) office, and ask them if it still qualifies. See Chapter 11 for more information on how to get help from SSA personnel. The appropriate time to do this would be when the trust gains significant assets (typically, when the grantor dies and the trust receives money from the estate or a life insurance policy). See Chapter 9 for more information on funding the trust.

Besides hiring a professional for help keeping up to date, trustees should consider the resources listed in this book's Letter to Trustee.

Financial Knowledge and Competence

Using trust money to provide for the special needs of a beneficiary is usually the rewarding part of being a trustee. In contrast is the business side of trust management: making reports, keeping records, filing tax returns, and making appropriate investment decisions. There are plenty of people who are quite comfortable with these tasks, but you might not know any among the group of people whom you would naturally choose to serve as trustee.

In this situation, you have several options. You could name cotrustees, one of whom has financial expertise; name a professional or corporate trustee or cotrustee; or join a pooled trust. Each of these options is discussed in this chapter.

Also keep in mind that a trustee who does not have the financial knowledge required to manage the trust can always get help. A trustee who isn't savvy in business matters is authorized, by the trust document, to hire experts for financial advice. For instance, an accountant or a tax service could help prepare the trust tax returns, while a financial planner could give advice on investment strategies. See Chapter 11 for more information on how to get help from financial planners.

Of course, the fact that the trustee gets help from experts doesn't mean that the trustee is not responsible for managing the trust. The trustee's ultimate responsibility for carrying out all the terms of the trust cannot be outsourced (delegated) to anyone else.

It might be hard to know now just how much of the trust property will be spent on these experts to support the trustee. It could end up costing the trust more for your trustee to rely on experts than it would cost to hire a professional trustee with whom you could negotiate the fee up front. (See "Naming a Professional or Corporate Trustee," below.) If you do stick with a relative or friend as your choice for trustee, you'll want that person to understand that he or she should do as much of the work as possible and use outside experts only when necessary.

Using Trust Protectors

Some special needs trusts name people to serve as "trust protectors" or "trust advisers" on various issues, such as investment strategies or compliance with SSI and Medicaid rules. These advisers have no legal authority over the trust, but the trust instructs the trustee to consult them in certain matters.

This might sound like an ideal solution if your choice for trustee lacks expertise in certain areas. However, having to consult advisers could add to the trustee's burden and be the last straw that drives a trustee to resign. If you prefer this option, you can include a trust protector provision in the trust you make with this book. Or you can have a lawyer help you to include a trust protector in your trust. Read more about using a trust protector or trust advisory committee near the end of this chapter.

Naming the Initial Trustee

When you create your special needs trust, you will name someone as the initial trustee (or more than one person, as cotrustees) to manage the trust. If you are married or otherwise partnered, you can name yourself and your partner as cotrustees. (See "Naming Cotrustees," below.) If you choose this option and one cotrustee becomes unavailable, the survivor will serve as an individual trustee.

If the trust starts out with just a small deposit in a bank account, there won't be much for the initial trustee to do until the trust is fully funded. However, if you (or friends or relatives) deposit a sizable sum in the trust account, the initial trustee's job will get more complex, as described in Chapter 4.

Most people who create a special needs trust will name themselves as initial trustee and then name others as successor trustees.

EXAMPLE 1: Lona Clark, age 43, creates a special needs trust for her autistic daughter, Julie Clark. She names herself as the initial trustee and her nephew David as the first successor trustee. She also names her niece Maya as second successor trustee, in case David is unable or unwilling to serve. She deposits $500 in a bank as trustee of the Julie Clark Special Needs Trust. From time to time Lona deposits her own money in the account and writes checks against the account to provide for Julie's special needs.

When Lona dies at the age of 63, there is $750 left in the trust. However, Lona had paid for a $50,000 term life insurance policy payable to the "trustee of the Julie Clark Special Needs Trust." David takes over as trustee and receives the life insurance payment. The account now has $50,750 for David to manage. Maya will take over if David becomes unavailable.

EXAMPLE 2: Now, assume instead that when Lona creates the trust, she has a domestic partner Ken who is also Julie's father. Lona names herself and Ken as initial cotrustees, David as first successor trustee, and Maya as second successor trustee. Ken survives Lona by 20 years and serves as sole trustee during that time. When he dies, David is unwilling to serve, so Maya becomes the trustee.

Under some conditions, you may want to name someone other than yourself as initial trustee. For example, if the beneficiary of the trust is not your child, it might make more sense to name the beneficiary's parent or parents as initial trustee or cotrustees. Also, even if the beneficiary is your child, if you don't expect to be able to manage the trust for very long—for example, if you are near the end of your own life—you may want to name someone other than yourself as initial trustee.

EXAMPLE: Deborah creates a special needs trust for her son, Billie. Deborah does not expect to live much longer because she has advanced lung cancer. Instead of naming herself as initial trustee, Deborah names her sister, Catherine, as initial trustee and her brother, Eugene, as successor trustee.

Naming Successor Trustees

In your trust you will name one or more people to take over when the initial trustee (probably you) can no longer serve. Unfortunately, the person you name to serve as successor trustee might not be available when the moment arrives. Things happen—people may become ill or die, move to another part of the country, or simply get too busy to serve because of their own responsibilities. Whatever the reason, it's important to name a short list of subsequent successor trustees who can take over, if necessary.

EXAMPLE: Edward creates a special needs trust for his domestic partner Sam, who has three siblings, Drew, Kai, and Chris. Any of them would do just fine as trustee. Edward names himself as trustee and Drew as first successor trustee. He also decides to name Kai as the second successor trustee, to serve if Drew can't or won't serve. He also names Chris as third successor trustee, to serve if neither Drew nor Kai is available.

The successor trustee who takes over for the initial trustee is called the "first successor" trustee. The successor trustee who takes over for the first successor trustee is called the "second successor" trustee, and so on. You can name as many levels of successor trustees as you wish. You should name as many people as you feel comfortable naming. As long as you name several people who are relatively close in age to the beneficiary, you should be fine.

Even if you name an agency or institution as trustee, rather than an individual, you'll still want to name successor trustees. Companies do go out of business and their policies change from time to time. Some corporate and professional trustees have minimum funding requirements for a trust, meaning they will serve as trustee only on a trust with a certain amount of money in it. Even though you expect to leave enough money in the trust to make it feasible to hire a corporate or professional trustee, there might not be enough when the trust goes into effect years from now. If a problem like this does come up, you'll want someone to step in to carry out the terms of the trust. If no person is able and willing to serve as trustee, a court will have to appoint a successor.

If the unlikely happens and none of the people you named as successor trustee are available, the terms of the trust allow the executor or administrator of your estate to name a trustee to manage the trust.

> ⚠ **CAUTION**
>
> **Name qualified successor trustees.** When naming successor trustees, keep in mind the critical qualities for *all* trustees discussed earlier in this chapter. Consider each potential successor trustee as if he or she will eventually manage the trust. Do not name someone just to be nice or out of a sense of obligation— naming an unqualified person will put the trust, and your loved one's benefits, in jeopardy.

Naming Cotrustees

You can name cotrustees for any level of trustee. For example, you can name two or more people to serve as initial cotrustees, first successor cotrustees, second successor cotrustees, and so on.

> **EXAMPLE:** Marla is ten and has Down syndrome. Her parents create a special needs trust, naming themselves as initial cotrustees. Marla's older sister Beth is willing to be named as successor trustee for Marla's special needs trust. However, Marla's parents are hesitant to put Beth in charge of all the record keeping, investments, trust disbursements, and tax obligations. So they name Marla's cousin Paul, who is a CPA, to serve as a cotrustee with Beth.

You might consider naming cotrustees if:

- You want a couple to serve together.
- You want to pair one trustee who knows the beneficiary well with another who has stronger financial skills.
- You want two or more people to share the burden of managing the trust.

But if you go this route, keep in mind that naming cotrustees creates additional questions and concerns. Will the cotrustees cooperate? Should each be able to act for the trust alone, or must all agree to every action? These issues are discussed next.

Picking People Who Work Well Together

As you can probably imagine, naming cotrustees who can't work together can cause difficulties. Record keeping, investment decisions, and tax reporting all become problematic unless there is excellent communication among the cotrustees.

Just finding people willing to work with each other and commit to trustee obligations over a period that might last decades can be difficult. Don't name more than one trustee to serve at a time unless you're confident that they can work together well over the long term, on both financial and emotional issues. When people must act together as cotrustees, it is like they are running a three-legged race. The cotrustees must act in perfect sync or things can fall apart, causing the trust administration to stall completely. When there is a disagreement among the cotrustees causing a delay in administration, the only person to truly suffer is your loved one.

Also, keep in mind that all cotrustees are legally responsible to the trust. So if one cotrustee acts negligently, all costrustees could be held legally responsible for those actions, even if they had nothing to do with it. This is another reason to name cotrustees who will work well together and who won't act without consulting the others.

Some Alternatives to Cotrustees

Pay a professional. If the trust contains enough money to pay the fees charged by professional and corporate trustees, this could be the preferable option. (See "Naming a Professional or Corporate Trustee," below.)

Let one trustee name cotrustees. Why not let your successor trustee name cotrustees if needed? This might seem sensible, but it can get messy. For example, it might be hard to get rid of a new trustee if the original one decides the arrangement isn't working. You'll need to see a lawyer if you want your trustee to have this authority.

Name more levels of successor trustees. If you are blessed with a number of good candidates for trustee, consider naming them as subsequent successor trustees rather than as cotrustees. Then, if one person becomes unable to shoulder the burden, the next person in line can take over. (See "Naming Successor Trustees," above.)

The law does not limit the number of cotrustees you can appoint to manage a special needs trust. For example, if your loved one has four siblings, all of whom want to be involved in managing the trust, you could legally name all of them to serve as cotrustees. However, it is in your loved one's best interest to keep the number of cotrustees to the absolute minimum. The more trustees serving at any one time, the harder it will be for them to make unified decisions. Disharmony among the cotrustees could seriously affect trust management and even risk legal problems, including the loss of SSI eligibility.

Can Cotrustees Act on Their Own?

Cotrustees—and the people, businesses, and institutions they deal with—need to know whether each of them can act independently, or whether they must sign off on everything jointly. For example, if you name cotrustees, and one of them wants to write a check from the trust account to pay for a plane ticket for your loved one, must the other one sign the check, too?

In your trust document, you must state whether cotrustees should act jointly or independently. Each way has its pros and cons. If you require that all cotrustees must agree before they can act on behalf of the trust, it could be tough to get any decisions made. There may be gridlock because the cotrustees disagree or simply because one or more of them is not available when decisions need to be made.

On the other hand, if you let each cotrustee act independently, you are increasing the chances that mistakes will be made that impair the beneficiary's eligibility for SSI and Medicaid. If that single but misguided trustee can act independently, the trust loses the value of the other trustees' oversight. But with a requirement of unanimous consent, one trustee's mistaken understanding of the rules can be caught by cotrustees who do understand them.

EXAMPLE: Melissa creates a special needs trust for her daughter Penelope and names Penelope's two siblings as successor trustees to take over at Melissa's death. Each trustee has authority to act independently. Penelope's brother, John, takes his duties seriously, learns the income and resource rules for SSI eligibility, and is judicious in the disbursements he makes from the trust.

Penelope's sister, Gwen, however, is very loving but has little sense of money or program rules. Gwen sees no harm in slipping Penelope cash as needed. When making her report to SSI, Penelope mentions the cash—which, because of its amount, makes her temporarily ineligible for SSI and Medicaid.

Assigning Specific Duties to Each Cotrustee

The trust document in this book does not spell out specific duties for each cotrustee. Instead, the trustees work out a division of labor on their own.

It's possible, however, to give each trustee specific responsibilities. For example, you could give one trustee financial responsibility (investment, spending, taxes, and so on), make another responsible for communicating the beneficiary's needs to the money person, and charge a third trustee with monitoring the other two and doing anything that falls between the cracks.

See a lawyer if you want your trust document to be structured in this way.

Naming a Professional or Corporate Trustee

If you don't want to put the special needs trust funds into the hands of a family member or friend, you have the option of naming an expert who will administer the trust for a professional fee. Known as a professional or corporate trustee, these individuals are often attorneys or CPAs. If you use a professional trustee, you'll get the benefit of that professional's knowledge about and experience with administering trusts. A professional trustee's job is to understand the trust rules, keep excellent records, make appropriate disbursements, pay all taxes, and prudently invest trust assets. But in order to enjoy that specialized knowledge, make sure that the trustees you choose have experience in running special needs trusts (for example, administering a living trust is a far cry from handling a special needs trust).

Another advantage of a professional trustee is the presence of insurance. Professional trustees generally carry liability insurance, which will cover the consequences of most mistakes that professionals might make. Even if the professional does not have insurance, a professional is more likely than a family member or friend to have sufficient assets to pay back the trust.

While hiring a professional may seem expensive, ultimately it could be cheaper than paying to fix problems created by a well-intentioned friend or family member who made a simple mistake. Nominating a professional might also provide comfort and reassurance that your loved one will be well cared for after you are gone.

Corporate trustees that will administer a trust for a fee include financial institutions such as banks, savings and loan institutions, and some brokerage houses. However, for many trusts, corporate trustees aren't really an option because most corporate fiduciaries will assume responsibility only for very large trusts—for example, trusts worth more than $250,000, or even $1,000,000.

If you do decide to hire a professional or corporate trustee, you might have to do a lot of shopping to find a trustee you are comfortable with. Talk to at least two or three people before you settle on someone. You can use our form, "Questions to Ask a Potential Private Professional Trustee," to guide your interview and as a place to record the professional's replies. When you're done speaking with a few prospects, consult your worksheets, compare the candidates, and pick the best one. You can download this form from this book's companion page, as explained in the Introduction.

Some uncertainty is always involved in naming a corporate or professional trustee as successor trustee. Most likely, the special needs trust will not be fully funded until your death—and by that time, the trustee's fees might have gone way up. The minimum dollar value of the trust that the trustee will accept could have risen as well. To avoid this problem, it's wise to name one or more successor trustees to take over if the professional trustee doesn't work out. Or you can add a trust protector, as described below.

Questions to Ask a Potential Private Professional Trustee

Trustee's Name _____

Phone Number _____

Address _____

Referred By/Source _____

Date of Conversation or Meeting _____

Background

1. How did you get involved in serving as a private professional trustee? _____
_____

2. What is your educational background? _____
_____

3. What work experience did you have prior to becoming a private professional trustee?
_____

4. How many years have you been serving as a private professional trustee? _____
_____

5. What kind of trusts do you serve as trustee (e.g. living trusts, special needs trusts, insurance trusts)? _____
_____

Current Administrative Practices

6. How is your trust company arranged (e.g. one person, a staff, part-time help)?
_____

7. If you have a staff, would I work with you or be assigned a case worker? _____
_____

8. How many trusts do you currently serve as trustee? _____
_____

9. Are any of these court-monitored trusts? _____
_____

10. Have you filed court accountings with the court before? _____
_____

11. What would the beneficiary have to do to review the records? _____
_____

Questions to Ask a Potential Private Professional Trustee (continued)

12. How many of these trusts are special needs trusts? _____

_____

13. Have you had any special training in serving as a trustee of a special needs trust?

_____

14. What services do you provide as trustee (e.g. record keeping, accounting, investments, making distributions)? _____

_____

Investment Decisions

15. How would you determine what to invest the assets of the trust in? _____

_____

16. Can the beneficiary (or a Trust Committee) assist in making the investment decisions? _____

_____

17. Do you provide the financial services or do you hire someone else to assist in making these decisions? _____

_____

18. What are the qualifications of the financial person that has been hired?_____

_____

19. How often are the investment decisions reviewed?_____

_____

20. If a beneficiary wants to review the records of his or her trust, can he or she do so?

_____

Start Up Procedure

21. If you were named trustee of this trust, how would we begin the process (e.g. a meeting, a letter, a welcome packet)?_____

_____

22. Do you set up a budget for distributions?_____

_____

23. How often is the budget reviewed? _____

_____

Questions to Ask a Potential Private Professional Trustee (continued)

Requesting Distributions

24. How would a beneficiary contact you to request a distribution? _____

_____

25. What kind of procedure do you go through in determining whether or not a distribution is warranted? _____

_____

26. If there is an emergency after normal business hours, is there a way I can contact you? _____

_____

27. If you are on vacation or otherwise unavailable, who would handle the management of your trust duties? _____

_____

28. What would happen to your business if you became incapacitated or died? Do you have a succession plan? _____

_____

Fees

29. How do you charge for your services? What is the fee? _____

_____

30. What is included for that fee? _____

_____

31. Is there an additional charge for investment services? How much? _____

_____

32. Is there an additional charge for tax preparation?_____

_____

33. Are there any additional charges?_____

_____

Next Steps

_____

_____

_____

_____

EXAMPLE: Bonnie creates a special needs trust for her grandchild Stacey. In addition to the small amounts of money that Bonnie puts in the trust during her life, the trust will be funded with the proceeds of a $300,000 life insurance policy. Bonnie names Stacey's mother, Francine, as successor trustee, but has great reservations about Francine's ability to manage the trust appropriately.

So she shops around and finds a corporate trustee that is willing to serve as a cotrustee with Francine as long as the trust has at least $300,000 in assets when the corporate trustee is called on to serve. Based on that information, Bonnie names that corporate trustee and Francine as successor cotrustees. Bonnie lives for another 20 years. When she dies, the corporate trustee accepts only trusts worth at least $600,000. The result? Francine will be sole trustee, in complete charge of the trust.

Keep in mind, it can be very difficult to find a professional or corporate trustee who is willing to serve as cotrustee with one of your family members or friends. The professional is concerned about the risk of cotrustee liability—the professional or corporate trustee can be held liable for a mistake by your family member or friend, and vice versa. If you want to name a professional and a family member or friend as cotrustees, make sure to speak with both of them beforehand to ensure they are willing to serve in the role together.

Using a Trust Protector or Trust Advisory Committee

When naming a trustee for a special needs trust, it's important to remember that the trustee will have absolute authority over the assets in the trust. The trustee must be given this authority to meet the legal definition of a special needs trust; however it gives the trustee broad power to make both good and bad decisions. For example, a trustee could refuse to make disbursements that are perfectly acceptable, or might make mistakes managing trust assets. If the trust contains no procedure for removing a poorly performing trustee and the trustee refuses to resign, there may be no way to get rid of the trustee unless he or she does something intentionally harmful to the trust, like stealing trust money or refusing to follow the trust's terms. And even then, only a judge can remove the trustee, after a court hearing (or full lawsuit).

> **EXAMPLE:** Ryan is the trustee of a special needs trust set up for the benefit of Amir by his parents. Amir has asked that Ryan make a distribution to pay for monthly Internet service. Normally, this is a great type of disbursement that will enhance the quality of life for Amir at a modest cost. However, Ryan believes that using the Internet is morally wrong and refuses to pay for it. Even though Amir's parents left a letter to Ryan saying they wished to encourage Amir to use the Internet, no one (not even Amir) can force Ryan to pay for Amir's Internet. Further, if Amir went to court to get Ryan removed as trustee, a judge might find that Ryan's refusal to pay for Internet access is an insufficient reason to remove him.

One way to provide a check and balance against a poorly performing trustee is to add a role in the trust called a "trust protector." (If you want to name more than one person to this role, the trust can name those people to serve as an "advisory committee.") If you include this role, the trust gives the trust protector or trust advisory committee the right to fire and replace the trustee at any time for any reason. Neither the beneficiary of the special needs trust nor the trust protector can serve as trustee.

> **EXAMPLE:** In the above example, if Amir's special needs trust named Sean as the trust protector with the right to remove the trustee at any time for any reason, then Sean could remove Ryan as trustee. The trust can also empower Sean to name a successor trustee. The trust protector has only the power of removal, so Sean cannot force Ryan to pay for the Internet. He can only remove Ryan as trustee.

The use of a trust protector can work particularly well when you want a friend or family member to oversee a professional or corporate trustee. That said, while most trust protectors are friends or family members, if there is no one close to the beneficiary who can serve this role, a financial advisor, CPA, or special needs planning attorney might be willing to serve.

Deciding whom to name trust protector can be easier than naming a trustee, because the trust protector does not generally have day-to-day responsibilities and is often needed only when something is not going well with the trust administration. Still, be cautious about whom you name as trust protector—bad trust protectors can cause big problems for trusts if they abuse their power to remove and replace trustees.

When choosing whom to name for this role, consider that a good trust protector will:

- stay in contact with the beneficiary
- be able to review and understand trust financial statements
- be willing to confront a poorly performing trustee
- listen reasonably when a trustee explains his or her decisions, and
- make thoughtful and reasoned decisions about removing a trustee.

You might have other good reasons to name a trust protector (or an advisory committee). You can provide the trust protector with additional rights—such as the right to amend the trust if changes to the law make it prudent to do so. Or you could give the trust protector the right to interpret "ambiguous provisions," (provisions that could be interpreted in more than one way). If you don't name a trust protector, the solution to these issues is to ask a court to fix the trust, which requires court costs and attorneys' fees.

Rules about including trust protectors in special needs trusts vary from state to state. This book's trust includes a simple trust provision that you can include in your trust. If you want a more robust trust provision, or one that is tailored to your specific circumstances, see an experienced special needs planning lawyer in your state for help. See Chapter 11 for tips on finding a good lawyer.

Signing Up for a Pooled Trust

If you sign up with a pooled trust, you won't choose a trustee—all pooled trusts offer their own trustee services. A pooled or community trust is a special needs trust, run by a nonprofit organization, that has many beneficiaries. You contribute money, which is held in a separate account but pooled with other families' funds for investing. The trustee distributes funds in the trust on behalf of the beneficiaries, according to the amount in each beneficiary's separate account. (Chapter 6 discusses pooled trusts in detail.)

Understand the Difference Between First-Party and Third-Party Pooled Trusts

Most pooled trusts are established to protect the beneficiary's own assets. These "first-party" pooled trusts are also called "(d)(4)(C)" trusts (after the federal code that permits them, 42 USC 1396 (p)(d)(4)(C)). Generally, any funds left in a first-party trust after the death of the beneficiary are kept by the nonprofit that manages the trust. In contrast, "third-party" pooled trusts use the assets of people other than the beneficiary—usually contributions from friends and family. After the death of the beneficiary, funds remaining in a third-party trust are generally returned to the family. If you use a pooled trust for your loved one, you'll be using a third-party pooled trust.

One way to use a pooled trust is to sign up while you are alive, if the pooled trust will allow it. This means you pay an initial fee, sign an agreement that creates an account for you with the pooled trust, and commit to paying an annual fee. You don't have to contribute money to the trust now. Rather, you can provide in your will or living trust that the trust be funded at your death. If you do it this way, your annual fees will be modest up until the trust becomes operational at your death. The administrative fees will be based on the amount of funds you contribute. Fees vary from one pooled trust to another.

Whether you fund the trust when you sign up or at your death, you'll have the security of knowing that your loved one's inheritance will be managed by experienced people affiliated with a nonprofit organization intended to benefit people with disabilities. You will also get the added benefit of being able to take the pooled trust for a test drive, and if you don't like what you see, you can choose another one. Keep in mind, if you funded the trust when you signed up, you might need to spend down any amount already funded in the trust, as it can be difficult to move funds from one pooled trust to another.

Pooled trusts are not for everybody and they come with some risks, including these:

- They are generally much more expensive to administer than naming your own trustee to serve in your own third-party special needs trust, because family members often do not charge a fee. Fees charged by pooled trusts vary widely, so be a good consumer and do some comparative shopping. This said, fees for pooled trusts are generally low compared to other professional trustees.

- If for any reason the charity loses its funding or status as a nonprofit, the pooled trust could be shut down and the beneficiary would not have access to trust funds until the situation is resolved.

- If the pooled trust administrators and the beneficiary do not get along, it is very difficult to get out of the pooled trust or join a different one.

- Some pooled trusts are more trustworthy than others. You'll need to do some research to find a pooled trust with a mission and structure that works for your family.

Almost all states have pooled trust programs. Most prefer to accept members only from their state. The reason for this restriction is that the trustee of the pooled trust doesn't want to take on the extra burden of keeping up to date on the laws in different states.

Instead of signing up while you are alive, you can direct the executor of your will or the successor trustee of your revocable living trust to determine which pooled trust is the best choice at that time. If the executor or trustee can't find a suitable pooled trust, the inheritance can be routed through your will or revocable living trust to the special needs trust you create, as a backup. Read Chapter 6 for all of the details about pooled trusts. ●

Joining a Pooled Trust

Instead of naming a trustee to handle the special needs trust you create, you might be able to have your loved one's inheritance managed as part of a group trust. These pooled trusts, also known as community or master trusts, are managed by nonprofit organizations.

Pooled trusts are a good alternative to creating your own special needs trust when you have no appropriate people to nominate to serve as trustee. Similarly, if the trustees you have nominated are unavailable or unable to serve, you could always switch gears and use a pooled trust. The trust in this book does not allow for a transition to a pooled trust, however, so if you want to make the switch, you should consult an attorney. The attorney would need to amend your estate plan (your living trust or your will), directing funds in your estate to the pooled trust rather than the third-party special needs trust.

> **EXAMPLE:** Mildred's daughter Cassie will need SSI and Medicaid for the rest of her life. Mildred wants to leave Cassie $50,000 cash, without jeopardizing Cassie's benefits. A special needs trust is perfect for this purpose, but Mildred can't think of anyone she can count on to assume the role of successor trustee. Mildred decides to join a pooled trust and have it act as successor trustee.
>
> Because many pooled trusts are run by people dedicated to serving an entire community of disabled persons, Mildred has faith that Cassie will be well taken care of and that her special needs will be met by the pooled trust as she continues to receive SSI and Medicaid benefits.

Pooled trusts can also be helpful when a professionally managed third-party special needs trust starts running low on funds. If you create your own special needs trust for your loved one, at some point, that trust will run low on funds, especially if it is being managed by professionals who are charging for their services. To slow down depletion and stretch out the trust's longevity, the professional trustee could turn over the funds to a pooled trust that, as a nonprofit organization, will likely charge a much lower fee.

TIP

Pooled trusts can also be used for funds owned by the beneficiary. This book focuses on third-party special needs trusts—trusts in which the trust funds originate from anyone except the beneficiary. However, if your loved one does have money of his or her own, you can use a pooled trust to shelter those funds from consideration as a resource when qualifying for SSI and Medicaid. These trusts are commonly referred to as (d)(4)(c) trusts.

Finding a Pooled Trust

This chapter gives you a general description of pooled trusts and how they work. If you think a pooled trust might work for you, search for a pooled trust in your state on the website of the Academy of Special Needs Planners at specialneedsanswers.com (choose "Pooled Trusts" on the home page).

An Overview of Pooled Trusts

Pooled trusts are run by nonprofit organizations set up to expertly and efficiently administer special needs trusts on behalf of individual beneficiaries with disabilities. But instead of handling multiple stand-alone trusts, each created for one person, the nonprofit administers one "master trust" agreement that covers everyone. With a pooled trust, your loved one becomes a member of the trust when you sign a contract with the nonprofit trustee. This contract is often called a "joinder agreement." The nonprofit combines and invests the assets that each member brings to the table, an arrangement that tends to increase investment power and reduce costs when compared to investing and administering single trust funds. The nonprofit spends funds for beneficiaries in proportion to their share of the total amount on deposit for them.

No two pooled trusts are exactly alike. Each has its own fees, menu of available services, and contracts under which it operates. Some offer many options, complicated contracts, and complex fee schedules. Others offer a single agreement and an easy-to-understand fee schedule. Some are organized to provide complete care of beneficiaries, while others just manage the money in an appropriate manner. Some pooled trusts are run by people who are technologically savvy, which could be a plus for beneficiaries (or their advocates) who are comfortable with smart phones, apps, spreadsheets, and so on.

But whatever their differences, all pooled trusts share some basic features that make them worth considering:

- The people managing a trust and its assets will be knowledgeable about agency rules regarding income and resources. They will be able to deal with questions from the SSI or Medicaid programs.
- The trust directors usually are relatives of people with disabilities and are attuned to that community.
- If you don't have a lot of money to leave to your loved one, a pooled trust can give your loved one the benefits of a special needs trust and expert trust administration for a lower cost than other professional trustees.

If you find a pooled trust that looks like it might work for you, call it or visit its website. The information in this chapter should help you understand what you learn from the program itself.

Anticipating Your Use of a Pooled Trust

As a general rule, if you plan on using a pooled trust, it is good to set up an account for your loved one during your life, even if you don't put much money into it. It gives you an opportunity to see how the program works and get to know the people who will be caring for your loved one after your death. In fact, some pooled trusts insist on this approach so that they can become fully conversant with your loved one's background and needs and can benefit from your experiences as a caregiver.

Some pooled trusts let you establish an account without funding it immediately. The trust will usually require that you pay a small annual renewal fee to keep the account active (some trusts will waive these fees if you keep a minimum amount in the trust). Then, you can use your will, a living trust, or another estate planning tool, such as life insurance, to leave property to the account at your death.

EXAMPLE: Craig creates an account for his daughter Ashley with the ABC Pooled Trust. Although he doesn't have to, Craig transfers a $10,000 CD into Ashley's account to avoid paying renewal fees. He also plans to leave $25,000 to the account through his living trust and another $25,000 through a term life insurance policy payable at his death.

If you don't set up an account with a pooled trust during your life, you can direct your executor or successor trustee of your revocable living trust to join a pooled trust after your death, if one is available. However, this approach deprives you of control over which pooled trust to use and makes it more difficult for the pooled trust to smoothly arrange the switch from your care of the beneficiary to theirs.

EXAMPLE: Billie, a Tennessee resident, creates a special needs trust for her developmentally disabled granddaughter Kai. Billie names Kai's brother Thom to serve as trustee when Billie dies, but she's uneasy about whether Thom can do the job.

A few years later Billie learns that Tennessee has a pooled trust that would give Kai the same benefits as the special needs trust she created. Billie visits the pooled trust's website and learns that the trust program offers all the services that, in Billie's opinion, Thom might be unable to handle. Billie can sign up for the trust and introduce the program's staff to Kai right away.

Billie decides to use the pooled trust instead. She creates an account with the pooled trust and changes her will to leave Kai's inheritance directly to the pooled trust account. Then, to end the special needs trust that she had previously created, she uses her power as trustee to spend the trust funds and terminate the trust.

How Pooled Trusts Came About

Many pooled trusts were created in response to a 1993 change in the Social Security Act. The change authorized persons with disabilities to shelter their own money (from consideration as a resource by SSI and Medicaid) by placing it with a nonprofit organization for management. The new law also allowed the nonprofits to keep a portion of any funds remaining in the trust after the beneficiary's death—creating a lucrative fundraising opportunity. (Not all pooled trusts impose this requirement.) Some nonprofit pooled trusts then expanded this concept and developed third-party pooled trusts to allow friends and family to utilize the benefits of a pooled trust for their loved ones.

Can You Use a Pooled Trust?

A pooled trust might not be an option for you. It all depends on where your loved one lives, what kind of disability he or she has, and the amount of funds you have available to place in the trust.

The Beneficiary's Residence

Pooled trusts currently exist in almost every state. Some of them accept only beneficiaries who live in the state where the trust is established.

EXAMPLE: Ralph's mother Charlene wants to join a pooled trust on Ralph's behalf. Ralph lives in Vermont; his mother lives in California. Even though there are several pooled trusts in California, Charlene can't use them; it is the beneficiary's (Ralph's) state of residence that counts. If no pooled trust has been established in Vermont, the only option for Charlene is to try to make arrangements with a pooled trust that is willing to operate across state lines.

If you don't find a pooled trust in your loved one's state, consider one of the national pooled trusts, or call one in an adjoining state. The other state's pooled trust program might be able to steer you in the right direction.

Why Most Pooled Trusts Stick Close to Home

Some pooled trust organizations operate a variety of trusts: third-party pooled special needs trusts (trusts funded with assets belonging to anyone other than the beneficiary), first-party pooled special needs trusts (trusts funded with the beneficiary's own property), and even pooled minor's settlement trusts (trusts funded with a minor's litigation settlement). The state laws and agency policies on administering first-party pooled special needs trusts are very complex and vary from state to state, making it very difficult to keep up with all the rules in all states.

Most pooled trust organizations are experts on the rules of their own state, and prefer not to venture into uncharted territory. And, pooled trust administrators who are familiar with the local scene are likely to know about resources available in their own states. This practical knowledge helps them ensure that beneficiaries receive the help they need to be as independent as possible.

Kind of Disability

Virtually all pooled trusts require their beneficiaries to meet Social Security disability standards set for SSI and SSDI. They may also require that a beneficiary have the type of disability for which the pooled trust was created in the first place. For instance, a pooled trust intended primarily to help people with developmental disabilities might not accept a person with quadriplegia as a beneficiary.

The reason for this "discrimination" is not sinister. Most pooled trusts are dedicated to providing a broad range of services to people with a certain disability. Staff members trained to deal with autism, for example, might not be familiar with the needs of persons with certain types of physical or mental disabilities.

On the other hand, most pooled trusts are willing to at least consider each applicant on a case-by-case basis—which means there is no harm in asking a particular program what its disability requirements are, if any.

The potential that a particular pooled trust might not accept your loved one is another good reason to sign up while you are alive, so that you can advocate for your loved one yourself, or make another choice if you need to. Otherwise, you risk leaving this important step to your executor or successor trustee.

Property Accepted by Pooled Trusts

Most pooled trust programs accept only cash, which can be invested to earn more money for the beneficiary. They don't want to be in charge of tangible items that incur the expense of storage, insurance, and maintenance. So you probably don't want to use a pooled trust if you are leaving tangible property—for example, jewelry, heirlooms, vehicles, or collections—that you would want preserved in its tangible form. If you leave that type of property to a pooled trust, it will be sold for cash.

Some pooled trusts, however, accept a beneficiary's home as a trust asset. But because a home is not counted as a resource by SSI or Medicaid, regardless of its value, you could leave it directly to your loved one and leave the cash part of your loved one's inheritance to the pooled trust.

Advantages and Disadvantages of Pooled Trusts

Advantages	Disadvantages
• If you don't know someone who is willing and competent to be trustee, a pooled trust program can provide one. • Pooled trust staff or volunteers often have expertise and experience with people who have disabilities. • You can get professional management for trusts that are too small (less than about $250,000) for most banks and trust companies. • Pooled trusts usually work closely with banks and trust companies and can tap their investment expertise. • Experts manage the trust assets and make the required reports after the fund starts disbursing money. • You don't have to worry about what might happen if an individual trustee dies or can't serve. With a pooled trust, there will likely be someone on staff who can serve as a trustee. • Management fees are generally much lower than those of banks and trust companies.	• Pooled trusts can be very expensive. Generally, they charge a one-time setup fee that can run from a few hundred dollars to several thousand dollars. Plus, there is an annual fee—based on a percentage of the assets that are put into the trust—that can be several thousand dollars a year. If you're putting only a modest amount of assets into the trust, the fees of the pooled trust can seriously deplete these assets. In contrast, a friend or family member may not charge anything to serve as the trustee of an individual trust. • Pooled trusts are inflexible. If you change your mind after joining a pooled trust and withdraw, you may forfeit some or all of the enrollment fees you've already paid. Once the assets are in the pooled trust, it is difficult if not impossible to move the assets to another trust. Your beneficiary is then stuck with this pooled trust even if the beneficiary doesn't like the program or the trustee does not do a good job. • Your agreement with the pooled trust program might give it the right to keep part of any assets that remain in a trust after the beneficiary dies—a result you might not want.

Advantages and Disadvantages of Pooled Trusts (continued)

Advantages	Disadvantages
• You don't have to draft and maintain your own special needs trust document; the program will provide one. It might have been reviewed by Medicaid and SSI to make sure it complies with their rules. • The program will probably be overseen by volunteers who likely include legal and financial experts, family members of people with disabilities, and disability advocates.	• If the pooled trust requires that it be allowed to keep a portion of any remainder, an unethical program could refuse to disburse funds to your loved one in an attempt to keep more money for itself. • A pooled trust is only as good as the nonprofit that is managing it. Some may do a good job for a while, but in the face of financial problems or management changes, may end up doing a terrible job or even going out of business altogether. (Many program contracts address this possibility.) • Many pooled trusts will not agree to own real estate or authorize other nontraditional investments. If your inheritance will include these types of investments, an individual special needs trust would serve you better. • Investment decisions are beyond your control and might not be as conservative as you would provide in your own special needs trust. • Pooled trusts might not be as responsive as personal or professional trustees and disbursements might be delayed. • Some pooled trusts distribute assets only at certain times of the month. This can be a problem for a beneficiary who may need distributions more frequently.

Amount of Property Required by a Pooled Trust

Most pooled trusts require a minimum level of funding. The "buy-in" amount for a pooled trust is surprisingly affordable, usually between $5,000 and $25,000. That's about 1% to 5% of the minimum amount many banks and trust companies require. A few pooled trusts require more—much more—than these amounts, but they, in turn, offer a higher level of service. (See "Extra Services," below.) Keep in mind, however, that in many states another option is to hire an individual professional trustee who may require no minimum at all.

Funding requirements change over time. If you fund the pooled trust while you are alive, you will be sure to meet the minimum funding requirement. However, if you plan to leave money to the pooled trust at your death, you risk having less in your estate than is necessary.

> **EXAMPLE:** Trudy joins the ABC Pooled Trust for her daughter Emily. At that time, the buy-in is $15,000. Instead of depositing money in Emily's account then, Trudy decides to wait and fund the account with the proceeds of a $25,000 life insurance policy payable at her death.
>
> When Trudy dies 15 years later, however, the buy-in amount has gone up to $50,000. Because Emily will not qualify for that pooled trust, the $25,000 will need to be placed in a first-party special needs trust. From the time the inheritance is made available to her through to the time it is placed in a first-party special needs trust, her eligibility for SSI and Medicaid is jeopardized.

How Pooled Trusts Work

Most pooled trust programs have similar structures and work in similar ways.

Organization

The typical pooled trust is a federally recognized nonprofit corporation, overseen by a board of directors. Directors are commonly volunteer nonprofit organization leaders, members of the charity, parents and relatives of the disabled, and professional and business leaders. The board sets the direction for the organization.

A trustee who is knowledgeable about the resource and income rules of the SSI and Medicaid programs is responsible for managing the trust. The trustee usually works with an independent bank trust department or financial adviser responsible for managing trust funds. The bank or adviser might have professional staff making the actual distributions for the benefit of the trust beneficiaries. A professional money manager will be responsible for managing the money. Most pooled trusts also hire expert legal counsel to make sure they stay compliant with state trust law as well as changing SSA and Medicaid policies.

Finally, often a pooled trust has a social services component dedicated to providing individualized services for each beneficiary of the trust.

Your Contract With the Trust

When you want to put assets into a pooled trust on behalf of a loved one, you sign an agreement—called a joinder agreement—authorizing the program or trustee to manage the account as part of the pooled trust.

Typically, the contract also:

- authorizes the program to provide typical special needs services—such as making disbursements appropriate to the beneficiary's needs on a timely basis
- authorizes specific life services
- names remainder beneficiaries (those who will inherit what is left in the trust after the trust is terminated), and
- sets the fees, if any, for those services.

The joinder agreement is discussed in more detail in "Joining a Pooled Trust," below.

Basic Trustee Services Under a Pooled Trust

A pooled trust program usually takes on all the responsibilities of a regular trustee (discussed in Chapter 4). The trustee and program staff hired by the program will:
- invest trust property
- handle requests for disbursements
- keep up to date on government rules regarding eligibility for SSI, Medicaid, and other benefits
- keep records for each beneficiary's account, including your loved one's account
- prepare necessary reports for the beneficiary and other interested parties, and
- prepare tax returns.

Extra Services

For many people, it's enough that the pooled trust manages the trust fund and makes disbursements to meet the beneficiary's special needs. But some pooled trusts do much more.

Some beneficiaries, for example, can't make appropriate decisions for themselves and need somebody to act as a substitute parent. If a court has appointed a guardian or conservator, that person will make care and custody decisions, or a beneficiary might be able to use a power of attorney to name an "agent" to make these decisions. If not, however, the pooled trust may furnish, for an additional fee, someone who will provide a wide range of services. This person might frequently visit the beneficiary, attend meetings with SSI and Medicaid officials about the beneficiary, and be the beneficiary's advocate in dealings with benefit agencies. This advocate might also:
- periodically evaluate the beneficiary's health and health care
- evaluate the suitability of living arrangements
- promote and improve social contacts and recreational opportunities

- monitor daytime activities by making random visits and obtaining feedback from the beneficiary
- assist the beneficiary with daily money management
- provide help and support in emergencies, and
- identify and find solutions for problems that affect the beneficiary's quality of life (for example, obtaining psychological help if the beneficiary seems depressed).

If you want these personal one-on-one services, which are often called "life services" or "care coordination," you'll need to meet with the appropriate program personnel to complete a plan and arrange for payment. But be careful. As with any social service program, the services delivered might be less than what you were promised. If these services are a major reason you are choosing a pooled trust, ask for the names of people currently receiving the services and get their opinions. Also, use your common sense. The longer and more detailed a plan, the less likely it is to be read or followed.

As you would expect, highly personalized services cost more, depending on the beneficiary's needs. Each pooled trust offering these services sets its own fees. If several pooled trusts are available to you, do some comparison shopping; the cost of the services you need will help you determine which trust is the best fit for you and your family. If only one pooled trust is available, you'll have to decide whether the services are worth the price.

How Pooled Trusts Manage Your Funds

In a pooled trust, the funds you contribute stay in a separate "subaccount" for accounting purposes, but are combined with other trust funds for investment purposes. This, naturally, saves on investment fees.

The nonprofit administrator keeps records of the amount of each beneficiary's subaccount and the amount spent for that person. These figures are reported to the beneficiaries, to interested members of the beneficiary's family, and to the remainder beneficiaries.

How the Trustee Spends Trust Funds

Like the trustee of an individual special needs trust, the trustee of a typical pooled trust has complete discretion over spending—provided, of course, that disbursements don't make the beneficiary ineligible for SSI, Medicaid, or similar government benefits.

Some trusts require beneficiaries or their representatives to ask for disbursements in writing with supporting invoices or receipts; other trusts are more informal. Family members have no control over how trust assets are spent, but are encouraged to give the trustee information that will help the trustee make good decisions.

When you enroll your loved one in a pooled trust program, you'll probably be asked for lots of information about him or her and how you would like to see the trust funds used. Some programs gather this information in an interview. Others will give you a questionnaire to fill out.

If the pooled trust you choose is oriented toward a type of disability that is different from that of your loved one, it will be up to you to provide the necessary information in an interview or in your own letter. (Chapter 10 discusses writing a "letter of intent," and a sample is in Appendix B.)

The trust will also want to know with whom they can consult when questions come up about the beneficiary's needs and personal situation. This person is sometimes called a "beneficiary advocate." Some pooled trust programs will let this person make disbursement requests on behalf of the beneficiary. In addition, some pooled trust programs will insist on speaking only to the person named as beneficiary advocate about the subaccount particulars, like balances and accountings. In most cases, you will be able to name a successor beneficiary advocate if the person named becomes unable or unwilling to serve. Of course, the more completely you document your wishes and desires regarding care of your loved one, the less likely such consultations will be necessary. But because it's impossible to predict what may happen, the more people you can line up to be available for the trust to confer with, the better.

EXAMPLE: Phil's father joins a pooled trust to handle the inheritance he plans to leave Phil, who needs a wheelchair. Phil himself gives the trust program personnel lots of information about his needs as a wheelchair user.

After his father dies, Phil develops a severe mental illness and is unable to direct his own needs. The trust is uncertain about what type of treatment to obtain for Phil. Fortunately, Phil's father gave the trust a list of relatives he trusted to act in Phil's best interest. The trust finds a relative who is eager to help and becomes an important liaison between Phil and the pooled trust.

Fees

Fees charged by pooled trusts vary greatly, and are generally higher than those charged by corporate and bank trust departments. As discussed above however, corporate and bank trust departments generally deal just with the money and don't know much about public benefits or local resources and services, while many pooled trusts offer additional life services, which arguably justify their higher fees. Obviously, these charges are much more than a family member would typically charge for doing these services.

Fee amounts, and when and how they are charged, vary from organization to organization. Some fees are due when you join the trust program. Others are paid out of the funds you leave the trust at your death. Most programs include a one-time nonrefundable enrollment or setup fee and an annual renewal fee for unfunded accounts. You might also be charged for:
- a management (or "consulting") fee for funded accounts based on the amount of funds, and
- fees for specific life services.

Typical Questions Asked of a Family

A pooled trust that is geared toward beneficiaries with mental illnesses should ask for some of the information below. A different set of questions would be appropriate for a person with cerebral palsy or paraplegia.

- Contact information for you and the beneficiary
- SSI and Medicaid eligibility status
- SSDI, SSA, or Medicare eligibility status
- History of hospitalization over last five years
- Status of current medications, if any
- Cooperativeness in taking meds
- Mental health services received currently
- Contact information for psychiatrist and case manager
- History of conservatorship or guardianship
- Type of crisis beneficiary is most likely to experience
- History of suicide or violence ideation, if any
- History of substance abuse, if any
- History of unannounced departures, if any
- Whether a relative manages the beneficiary's money
- Expenses that the family currently pays for on relative's behalf
- Whether the family is considering making a condo or house available for the beneficiary
- Beneficiary's private insurance, if any
- Whether the family desires that the beneficiary receive living skills training, recreation, vacations, travel, and/or quality of life enhancement out of trust resources; if so, prioritize
- What are the beneficiary's interests and pastimes, and which does the family wish to support and promote via the trust, and
- Anything else you think the social services staff or trustee should know.

An enrollment or setup fee can run as little as $500 and as much as $3,000, but most are between $500 and $1,500. If you join the trust and leave it without any money, annual renewal fees for unfunded trusts are typically $75 to $500. The management or consulting fees tend to be based on the amount you have deposited in the account; they are often between 1% and 3% of the funds in the account. Most pooled trusts also have a minimum annual charge that applies when the percentage fee doesn't provide sufficient funds.

Some pooled trusts charge an hourly or flat fee for specific services. Costs for services vary among programs; there is really no typical amount.

Program fees are likely to increase from year to year, so you'll want to get a written statement of fees and payment schedules when you're investigating different pooled trust programs.

Pooled Trust Fees	
Type of Fee	**Typical Amount**
Enrollment	$500 to $1,500
Renewal fees for unfunded trusts	$75 to $100 per year
Management	1% to 3% of the funds in the account, annually
Specific services	Hourly rate or flat fee

EXAMPLE: Katie sets up in her will that her daughter Val's inheritance will be sent to the DEF Pooled Trust. Katie dies and leaves Val $100,000. The trust charges a $1,000 enrollment fee plus an annual 2% management fee or a minimum fee of $1,800 a year, whichever is greater. To join the trust, Val must pay $3,000 of the assets for the enrollment fee plus the first year's management fee. In addition, there are specific services that incur an additional charge like $25 for each check after the first five checks a month; a $50 fee for rush service on checks; and an hourly rate of $100 per hour for care management consulting. Val needs to use ten checks a month to pay for her budgeted items, costing her an additional $1,500 each year. So, Val will pay at least $4,500 in fees the first year. Each year thereafter, the fees will be based on the amount of assets being held in trust and how many additional services Val requires.

Joining a Pooled Trust

If you find a pooled trust that you're really interested in, take the time to ask some detailed questions about how the trust will provide for your loved one.

Investigating Your Options

No government agency oversees pooled trusts to make sure they are managing assets wisely and honestly. In other words, they are unregulated. There is no certification or accreditation process for pooled trust programs.

As discussed above, pooled trusts vary considerably in terms of the services they offer. All offer trust management, investment services, and expertise in federal benefit resource and eligibility rules. The programs tend to differ in:

- the nature of the supplementary services offered (see "Extra Services," above)
- the relationship between a beneficiary and the trust manager
- fees, and
- what happens to money in the account when the beneficiary dies.

For this reason, it's very important to read the materials from any program you are considering, and to meet with a program representative to discuss the details of the program. Before you sign any papers, the program representative should carefully explain the process, including fees and the scope of services

In the course of this process, pay close attention to your feelings about the place you're dealing with and the people you encounter. For instance, if you get a polished presentation, you might be put off if you are more comfortable with "just plain folks"—or you might be impressed by the professionalism. If you are more confused than enlightened, it could be a sign to shop for a different program.

Here are some questions to ask before entrusting your loved one's inheritance to the program:

- Does the trust program have the financial or volunteer support of one or more well-known disability organizations?
- Does the board of directors include people with expertise or experience in disability, legal, and financial matters?
- Does the program use the services of a reputable bank, a trust company, or another financial institution as a trustee or for account management?
- Does the trustee's investment strategy make sense to you?
- Does the program give you clear and comprehensive information about how the trust operates, including its fees and services, or do you feel confused?
- What is the process for making distribution requests, and approximately how long does it take for the program to process the request?
- Are you satisfied that the program will always know about your loved one's special needs?
- Do program staffers answer your questions in easy-to-understand language?
- Are staff members knowledgeable about federal and state benefits, laws that affect planning, and the reporting requirements imposed by SSI and Medicaid after the trust is active?
- How happy are other families who use the pooled trust? Ask the program for evaluations it's received, and talk to other families directly if possible.
- Does the program's annual report make it clear that the program is operated in a businesslike manner? (If you're not comfortable deciphering the report, ask someone who is.)
- Is the trust financially self-sufficient, or does it depend on third-party funding (like private or corporate benefactors that provide donations during fundraising) that might decrease or, in the case of government funding, be withdrawn altogether? You want to be sure that the program could continue in the absence of those funds.

Signing the Agreement

Every pooled trust operates under a master trust document, which creates the special needs trust to which you'll be contributing. Master trusts contain provisions very similar to those of the special needs trust in this book, plus provisions unique to pooled trusts.

When you join the pooled trust, you sign a joinder agreement and pay the one-time nonrefundable enrollment fee described above. The joinder agreement links your loved one to the master trust provisions, describes your duties as the person supplying the money (the grantor), explains what happens if you wish to withdraw the funds later, and specifies what will be done with any funds left in your loved one's account when it terminates. Some joinder agreements also let you describe your preferences for disbursements once the trust is funded and goes into effect.

After you die, the joinder agreement becomes irrevocable, which means any funds that have been put in the account will stay there. The trustee will manage and disburse them for your loved one's benefit under the terms of the trust.

Making an Appropriate Estate Plan to Fund the Trust

You might want to sign an agreement with a pooled trust during your lifetime, but intend to wait until your death to have money go into the trust. To make that happen, all you have to do is use your will or living trust to route the property you are leaving your loved one to that pooled trust. Chapter 9 tells you how to do this.

Funding the trust with money that you leave behind will work when, obviously, your estate is solvent. If it's not, or if debts eat up most of the estate's assets, there's a risk that the trust won't in fact get funded. There might be a fee for terminating or cancelling the pooled trust. You should ask the pooled trust organization prior to setup whether they have a termination or cancellation fee and, if so, in what amount.

EXAMPLE: Paula joins the Greater Springfield Community Trust on behalf of her sister Annabelle. She does this by signing a joinder agreement, paying a $500 setup fee, and agreeing to pay an annual renewal fee of $75 until the trust is funded with at least $25,000. Paula's plan is to fund the trust through her will when she dies.

Paula makes the renewal payments while she is alive but dies broke. When the renewal payments stop and the trust is not funded, the account is closed.

If you don't want to sign up with a pooled trust now but would like the executor of your will or the successor trustee of your living trust to explore the possibility of using a pooled trust, you can provide for this in your will or living trust. As a backup measure, as part of your estate plan you should also establish your own special needs trust to take the property if a suitable pooled trust isn't available when the time comes.

EXAMPLE: Joe creates a special needs trust for his niece Sophie. In his will, Joe directs his executor (Sophie's sister Catherine) to try to join the ABC Pooled Trust and to place Sophie's inheritance in it. If the ABC Pooled Trust doesn't work out, he directs Catherine to place Sophie's inheritance in the special needs trust he created as a backup.

If the Pooled Trust Changes for the Worse

When selecting a pooled trust, keep in mind that the quality of the trust can change over time. For example, suppose at the time you investigated a pooled trust, it provided all the services you wanted, had an active and diverse volunteer board, and its fees met your expectations. However, years later after you have died, the pooled trust has withdrawn most services, the volunteer board has lost most of its members and meets only twice a year, and the fees have increased.

In this situation, beneficiaries or their legal representatives do not have a lot of options. It will be difficult, if not impossible, to change pooled trusts or to move out of a trust that is no longer performing adequately. The beneficiary can end up stuck in a pooled trust that at one time did great work, but by the time of funding has become a terrible institution.

After naming a pooled trust for the person with a disability in your will or living trust, you should periodically check to make sure it still meets your requirements. If not, you can change the pooled trust recipient in your will or living trust documents. However, if assets have already been transferred to the trust, you might have no way of changing the pooled trust. Whether you can get out will depend on the terms of the pooled trust document.

What Happens When the Trust Ends

Eventually, the pooled trust account for your loved one will no longer be necessary. The most likely scenario is that the account will end when your loved one dies. But it could also happen if Congress changes benefit laws, the pooled trust itself quits operating, or the trust runs out of money.

When the Beneficiary Dies

You might fully expect that all trust property will have been spent on your loved one by the time he or she dies. But your loved one might die sooner than expected. And if the trust account is quite large, some money might remain at the time of death.

If there is money left, some or all of it will go to beneficiaries you name in the joinder agreement. Some of it might stay in the trust, usually to help it provide services that other trust beneficiaries might not be able to afford. This arrangement is required by many pooled trusts, and policies vary greatly.

EXAMPLE: Joyce signs a joinder agreement with the XYZ Pooled Trust. The agreement provides that at her loved one's death, $300 of any money left in the trust account will be kept by the pooled trust. The rest will be paid to the beneficiaries Joyce names.

Be sure you understand exactly how remaining assets will be treated after the beneficiary's death, ask about options, and make sure that the policies are consistent with your wishes.

Pooled Trusts vs Individual Special Needs Trusts

The chart below shows some of the important differences between a pooled trust and an individual special needs trust. As you can see, in most circumstances, an individual trust will be a better fit for you and your loved one than joining a pooled trust. Pooled trusts really only make sense when there is no one in your life that you trust enough to manage money set aside for the person with a disability.

Issue	Pooled Trust	Individual Trust
Setup	You must sign a joinder agreement and the trust is provided by the organization.	You draft a trust yourself or with the help of a lawyer.
Trustee	The trustee is provided by the pooled trust.	You name a trustee to serve. This may be a trusted friend or family member, or a private professional or corporate trustee.
Costs and fees	Costs and fees include enrollment fees, ongoing management fees, and sometimes fees for specific services.	There are no fees if you name a trusted family member or friend. You will pay professional fees if you hire a private professional or corporate trustee.
Trust remainder	The pooled trust may keep some or all of the trust remainder.	The assets go to whomever you name.
Flexibility	The beneficiary most likely will have to stay with the trust, even if the trustee is doing a bad job.	You can set up terms in trust to have trustee removed or replaced if he or she is not doing a good job.
Administration	The beneficiary is stuck with the trust's management team, who are often paid professionals or volunteers.	A family member, friend, or paid professional will manage the trust. A family member or friend may have to hire professional help.
Administrator dies or charity goes out of business	The agreement may cover this—if not, the state's attorney general may decide where assets go to be managed.	If the trustee dies, then the successor named in the trust takes over. If no successor is named or if the successor is not available, a court will appoint one.

If the Pooled Trust Stops Operating

All corporations—profit and nonprofit—have the potential for eternal life, and most nonprofits have boards of directors who feel strongly about their organizations and want to keep them going if at all possible. But it's certainly possible that a particular pooled trust program will someday cease operations. Many possible causes can result in going out of business—financial difficulties, a failure of management, or lack of adequate membership, to name a few.

What happens to your money if the pooled trust goes out of business? Most if not all states require defunct nonprofits to distribute any remaining assets to another suitable nonprofit organization. The contract you sign with the pooled trust will probably address this question. ●

ABLE Accounts

As described in this book, special needs trusts are an excellent way to preserve eligibility for public benefits for persons with disabilities. However, these trusts do not allow persons with disabilities to manage their own funds. Fortunately, there is another tool that allows persons with disabilities to control their own funds, invest them, grow tax-free income, and still protect their eligibility for public benefits. As of 2014, federal law created the "Achieving a Better Life Experience Act of 2014" (the "ABLE Act"), which gives individuals with disabilities a tax-friendly way to save and have control over money in their ABLE bank accounts.

Along with the flexibility and power ABLE accounts give beneficiaries, they come with some limitations, and they aren't right for everybody. This chapter outlines the requirements for ABLE accounts and provides information that will help you figure out if an ABLE account is right for your loved one with a disability.

ABLE accounts have several eligibility and management limitations. The main limitations are:

- A person must have been disabled prior to age 26 to utilize the account.
- A person can have only one account.
- The account can only be funded annually with a single annual gift exemption amount (currently $15,000).
- Accounts can grow up to $100,000 and not disqualify a person from SSI; or up to a state's 529 plan limit (in California, that limit is $529,000) without disqualifying someone from Medicaid.
- Disbursements must be for "Qualified Disability Expenses" (or risk triggering a penalty).
- On the death of the person with a disability, any remaining funds in the account must be paid back to the state Medicaid program for any services paid since the opening of the account.

ABLE accounts have been opened all over the country and most states allow a nonresident to open an ABLE account in their state. So, if you live in a state that has not yet implemented the ABLE Act, or if you don't like your state's ABLE program, you can open an ABLE account managed in another state. If your state later opens its own program, you can transfer your ABLE account to your home state.

ABLE Law Updates

The rules and regulations governing ABLE accounts have been evolving since their inception in 2014. As of the writing of this edition, the following changes have been implemented:

- **529 funds.** A person can now roll over funds held in a 529 higher education account to an ABLE account for the same individual. This change benefits families who funded a 529 plan, expecting to use it for a child's future educational expenses, only to later learn that their child cannot use it because of a disability. Those funds can now be transferred to an ABLE account and used for disability expenses. The rollover counts against the annual funding limit of $15,000 a year.

- **Adding income to the ABLE account.** A person with a disability who works (but is not part of an employer-sponsored retirement program) now has the right to contribute the lesser of (1) their work income for the tax year, or (2) $12,760 ($14,680 in Hawaii or $15,950 in Alaska) per year of his or her earnings in an ABLE account, on top of the $15,000 annual limit.

- **Reducing tax liability.** People with a disability can use the Savers Tax Credit for Retirement as part of their ABLE accounts. This benefits persons with disabilities who need to reduce their tax liability.

You can read more about current and upcoming ABLE laws on the website of the ABLE National Resource Center, www.ablenrc.org.

Qualifying for and Opening an ABLE Account

Not all people with disabilities will qualify for an ABLE account, and each state's ABLE account provider will have its own process for qualifying for and opening an account. However, the basic rules are set by the federal ABLE laws and regulations. As you look into the workings of ABLE accounts, understand that ABLE laws and regulations use the term "designated beneficiary" to refer to the person who owns and benefits from an ABLE account.

The sections below explain the requirements for opening an ABLE account.

The Account Owner Must Meet Age and Disability Requirements

ABLE accounts are available only to those who became disabled early in life. Currently, this means that to open an ABLE account, a person must have a disabling "condition that began prior to reaching age 26." As of this writing, there is legislation before Congress (the ABLE Age Adjustment Act) that would increase the qualifying age from 26 to 46. First introduced in 2016 and then again on March 5, 2019, the bill unfortunately has not made any movement through Congress. To stay current with the age requirement, check for updates on the ABLE National Resource Center website, www.ablenrc.org.

The person opening an ABLE account must swear under penalty of perjury that the account holder is "disabled" and—if requested—the person must provide a signed physician's statement confirming the disability diagnosis and the age of onset of the disabling condition. This procedure is called "self-certification." If a physician's statement is not obtainable, account holders can satisfy the disability requirement by showing that they were receiving Supplemental Security Income (SSI) or Social Security Disability Insurance (SSDI) based on a disability that began prior to age 26.

For the purposes of opening an ABLE account, "disabled" means that the account holder must either already be receiving Social Security benefits based on his or her disability, or otherwise qualify as disabled by the Social Security Administration. Although the factors that qualify someone for disabled status are usually different for adults and children, the ABLE regulations use the child definition, regardless of age. The Code of Federal Regulations §416.906 defines "disability" for an individual under the age of 18 as:

[A] medically determinable physical or mental impairment or combination of impairments that causes marked and severe functional limitations, and that can be expected to cause death or that has lasted or can be expected to last for a continuous period of not less than 12 months.

One Account Per Owner

A person with a disability can have only one ABLE account. If a person with an ABLE account opens another ABLE account, the second account will be closed. Otherwise, benefit programs will treat it as an available resource. If you want to open an account in another state, make sure that out-of-state residents can join.

Most states currently offer ABLE accounts. Visit www.ablernc.org to review which states have programs, and to learn important facts about each program. Below is a sample of four programs.

ABLE Accounts by State					
State ABLE	**Website**	**Limitation on Non-residents**	**Funding Minimum**	**Basic Fees**	**Number of Investment Options**
Iowa	IAble.gov	None	$25	$45 annual fee or $60 if want paper statements	6 options
Michigan	miable.org	None	$25 (or $15 if enrolled in automatic investment plan)	$45 annual fee	5 options
Oregon	oregonable savings.com	None	None	$35 annual fee	3 options
South Carolina	SCable.org	Only state residents	$50	$42 annual fee	4 options

Opening an ABLE Account

An ABLE account can be *opened* by the designated beneficiary, or his or her agent, guardian, or parent (if a minor), by joining one of the active state programs. However, the ABLE account is always *owned* by the designated beneficiary. You can join an ABLE account in any state, as long as that state allows out-of-state residents to join. The original federal ABLE law required individuals to open ABLE accounts in their home state. However, Congress amended ABLE to eliminate this state residency requirement.

You can visit www.ablernc.org to learn which states have established their ABLE programs and which ones allow nonresidents to join.

Funding an ABLE Account

Any person is allowed to contribute to an ABLE account. This means that persons with a disability can fund their own ABLE accounts. Plus, "person" is defined by the IRS to include "an individual, trust, estate, partnership, association, company, or corporation." (26 U.S.C §7701(a)(1).) Unless the special needs trust terms expressly prohibit contributions to the ABLE account from the trust, a trustee of a special needs trust can fund an ABLE account with funds from the special needs trust.

Deposits Are Limited to $15,000 Per Year, Cash

The law limits the amount of money that can be deposited into an ABLE account each year. The limit is equal to the annual federal gift tax exclusion amount, as set forth in I.R.C. §2504(b). This number rises with inflation, usually by $1,000 increments. In 2021, the gift tax exclusion amount remains at $15,000. Keep in mind that this is a limit per account, not per depositor. In other words, multiple people cannot each fund it with $15,000 each year. The limit is $15,000 total per account, per year, regardless of the number of contributors.

Cash Contributions Only

Contributors must make contributions in cash. If they want to deposit funds from stocks, bonds, insurance policies, or other investments, they must turn them into cash before transferring the funds into an ABLE account. Deposits can be made in installments, and this can help control the beneficiary's spending. For example, instead of depositing $15,000 all at once, contributors could make twelve monthly contributions of $1,250.

The Consequences of Excess Contributions

As of 2021, if an ABLE account receives contributions of more than $15,000 in one calendar year, the plan administrator must return the excess to the contributor or contributors, including any income associated with the excess contribution. The excess funds must be returned by the due date of the designated beneficiary's tax return (including extensions) for the year in which the contributions were made. If the excess funds are not returned, the overage is subject to a 6% excise tax. (26 U.S.C. §4973(a)(6).)

Account Balance Limits

The ABLE Act limits the amount of money you can keep in an ABLE account. The limit varies, depending on the designated beneficiary's eligibility for government benefits. If the person with a disability qualifies for SSI, the account can grow to a maximum of $100,000. The SSA will count any overage as a resource for SSI eligibility, and they will suspend SSI benefits. When the account falls below $100,000 again, the SSA will automatically restore SSI, without the need to reapply. During the SSI suspension, the designated beneficiary continues to be eligible for Medicaid (at least until the account reaches the limit for the state's 529 plan contribution, see below). Here's an example drawn from the Social Security Administration.

EXAMPLE: Paul is the designated beneficiary of an ABLE account with a balance as of the first of the month of $101,000. Paul's only other countable resource is a checking account with a balance of $1,500. Paul's countable resources are $2,500 and therefore exceed the SSI resource limit. However, because Paul's ABLE account balance is causing him to exceed the resource limit (that is, his countable resources other than the ABLE account are less than $2,000), the SSA suspends Paul's SSI eligibility and his cash benefits stop, but he retains eligibility for Medicaid. When Paul spends at least $1,000 from his ABLE account, the SSA restores his SSI.

If the person qualifies for traditional Medicaid *but not SSI*, the limit is equal to the state's maximum contributions to the Qualified State Tuition Program, sometimes called 529 plans. The limit for these plans is usually much higher than the SSI limit—between $300,000 and $500,000 in most states. So designated beneficiaries who do not qualify for SSI can keep much larger account balances than those who do.

Spending ABLE Account Funds

The undistributed income held in an ABLE account is not subject to federal income tax, and distributions made to the qualified beneficiary are tax free as long as the money is used to pay for the beneficiary's qualified disability expenses (QDEs). The sections below explain QDEs.

Qualified Disability Expenses (QDEs)

"Qualified disability expenses" is a term used by the Internal Revenue Service to describe permitted expenditures from ABLE accounts. Such expenses must be "related to the blindness or disability of the beneficiary and for the benefit of the designated beneficiary." ABLE regulations indicate that this definition should have a broad interpretation that includes basic living expenses, as well as expenses that might also benefit others. The chart below gives you a nonexhaustive list of items that the IRS considers to be QDEs.

Here's an example from the IRS illustrating how QDEs can work:

EXAMPLE: B, an individual, has a medically determined mental impairment that markedly and severely limits her ability to navigate and communicate. A smart phone would enable B to navigate and communicate more safely and effectively, thereby helping her to maintain her independence and to improve her quality of life. Therefore, the SSA would consider the expense of buying, using, and maintaining a smart phone used by B as a qualified disability expense.

If designated beneficiaries use funds in an ABLE account for something other than QDEs, the amount of those unqualified expenditures must be included in the beneficiary's taxable income. Further, the IRS will assess a 10% penalty on that amount, unless the unqualified expenditures were made after the death of the qualified beneficiary.

SSA has clarified how non-QDE distributions will be treated for SSI. If money comes out of an ABLE account for a nonhousing QDE and that money is not spent on the intended purpose during that calendar month, the amount will remain exempt as long as the QDE purchase is made later. If the beneficiary changes the intended purpose, there is a risk that the disbursement will become a countable resource, jeopardizing the account owner's eligibility for SSI.

Here's an example from SSA illustrating how QDEs can work for SSI:

EXAMPLE: In June, Jennifer takes a $7,000 distribution from her ABLE account to pay an educational expense that is a QDE. Her educational expense is due in September. In August, Jennifer gets a job offer and decides not to return to school. The $7,000 becomes a countable resource in September, because she no longer intends to use it for an educational expense that is a QDE. Jennifer can avoid this consequence if she redesignates it for another QDE or returns the funds to her ABLE account before September.

The IRS has the right to ask beneficiaries to verify that they spent their ABLE money for QDEs. For this reason, beneficiaries should keep excellent records on how they use the money in their ABLE accounts.

Examples of Qualified Disability Expenses (QDEs)

Ohio was the first state to implement its ABLE program and has an informative website www.stableaccount.com. Ohio's STABLE Account lists the following nonexhaustive list of permissible expenditures on their website.

Basic Living Expenses
- Food
- Clothing
- Personal care items

Education
- Tuition for preschool through postsecondary education
- Books
- Supplies and educational materials

Housing
- Expenses for a primary residence
- Rent
- Purchase of a primary residence
- Mortgage payments
- Home improvement, modifications, maintenance, and repairs
- Real property taxes
- Utility charges

Transportation
- Expenses for transportation
- Use of mass transit
- Purchase or modification of vehicles
- Moving expenses

Employment Support
- Moving expenses
- Expenses related to obtaining and maintaining employment
- Job-related training

Health and Wellness
- Expenses for health and wellness
- Premiums for health insurance
- Mental health, medical, vision, and dental expenses
- Habilitation and rehabilitation services
- Durable medical equipment
- Therapy
- Respite care
- Long-term services and supports
- Nutritional management
- Communication services and devices
- Adaptive equipment
- Personal assistance

Assistive Technology and Personal Support
- Expenses for assistive technology and personal support (such as a smart phone for a child with autism)
- Remote monitoring equipment and services
- Communication devices
- Screen reader software

Miscellaneous Expenses
- Financial management and administrative services
- Legal fees
- Expenses for oversight
- Monitoring
- Funeral and burial expenses.

ABLE Funds Can Pay for Housing Without Penalty

An interesting benefit provided by the definition of QDEs is that paying for housing from an ABLE account does not trigger an SSA penalty for payment of in-kind support and maintenance (in-kind support and maintenance is known as ISM, explained in Chapter 2). The value of avoiding the ISM deduction is equivalent to an additional $3,416.04 in tax-free payments from the SSA annually.

If a *trustee* of a special needs trusts uses trust funds to pay for the housing expenses, the SSA will reduce the amount of the SSI check. As of this writing, that reduction is capped at $284.67 per month (for 2021). But there will be no reduction for the same expenses if they are paid with funds from an ABLE account.

A special needs trust and an ABLE account work best as companion tools, used together. When trustees of a special needs trust put money from the trust into an ABLE account, and the beneficiaries use the ABLE account to pay for the beneficiaries' housing expenses, the beneficiaries can avoid the ISM deduction to their SSI checks. SSA and attorneys have referred to this tactic as "legal money laundering." According to the SSA, here are some typical housing expenses that can be paid for with ABLE funds, without penalty:

- mortgage payments (including property insurance required by the mortgage holder)
- real property taxes
- rent
- heating fuel
- gas
- electricity
- water
- sewer, and
- garbage removal.

Debit or Prepaid Cards

Now that you have an idea of what the ABLE account can be used for, the next question becomes *how* do beneficiaries spend ABLE account money? All ABLE programs will allow beneficiaries to make wire transfers to and from their ABLE accounts, usually for no fee.

Additionally, all ABLE programs allow them to request a check, usually for a fee varying depending on which state program they are using.

Wire transfers can be difficult to initiate, and paying a fee for each check can be unsustainable. In addition, the mailing time for checks can lead to late fee penalties if beneficiaries plan on using their ABLE accounts to pay for bills. In response to this issue, several state ABLE programs have launched debit or prepaid cards. For example, the California ABLE program (CalABLE) offers a reloadable, prepaid card as an optional service to program participants. These cards are attached to the account and are much more practical for account access.

The states that do offer a debit or prepaid card usually do not automatically give them to account owners. The account owner must apply for it and request it. For example, the CalABLE program requires participants to request a card when opening the account or thereafter by clicking a link on their online profile. Once activated, participants can load money onto the card by requesting an ACH withdrawal from their CalABLE account and selecting the prepaid card option.

The availability of a debit or prepaid card can affect which state ABLE program you select. Relying on wire transfers and checks alone can be very inconvenient and make the ABLE account difficult to access. If your state ABLE program does not provide a debit or prepaid card option, you can explore other state programs that do on the ABLE National Resource Center website, www.ablenrc.org.

Medicaid Payback

When designated beneficiaries die with money remaining in their ABLE accounts, federal law requires that those funds first be used to reimburse state Medicaid for Medicaid-funded services that the beneficiaries received since they opened their ABLE accounts. All outstanding QDEs (mainly burial costs) will be given priority over Medicaid. After Medicaid is reimbursed, any remaining funds in the ABLE account will go to the beneficiary's estate. Despite this law, certain states have stated they will not seek payback from ABLE accounts. Because ABLE accounts are still new, we don't yet know whether the federal government will allow states to ignore the payback requirement.

EXAMPLE 1: When Jane dies, she is the designated beneficiary of an ABLE account that contains $85,000. From the time that she opened her ABLE account, Jane used $100,000 of Medicaid services. After her death, her estate has $11,000 of outstanding obligations for QDEs, including bills for transportation, caregiving, and legal fees. These bills can be paid from her ABLE account. The $74,000 remaining in her ABLE account is paid to the state Medicaid agencies. Nothing is left for her survivors.

EXAMPLE 2: Same facts as above, except that Jane used only $50,000 in Medicaid services. In this scenario, $11,000 would be used to pay the QDE bills, $50,000 would be paid to the state Medicaid agencies, and the remaining $24,000 would pass to her survivors through her estate.

Is an ABLE Account Right for You or Your Loved One?

An ABLE account is not a substitute for a special needs trust, but it can be used to provide persons with special needs:

- additional funds to be used for some expenses
- more control over their own money, and
- the ability to save for their future.

Because the account holder can manage his or her ABLE account, ABLE accounts are ideal for those who have the capacity to manage their own financial affairs. Managing an account of up to $100,000, provides a meaningful and practical experience. That said, ABLE accounts aren't a good fit for everyone. Here are some issues to consider:

- **Can the beneficiary manage money?** If yes, an ABLE account may be a good way for the beneficiary to exercise control over his or her own spending. If not, but the beneficiary has the capacity to learn to manage money, then an ABLE account might work if you provide the beneficiary with some financial management training. However, if the beneficiary does not have the capacity to manage money, an ABLE account is probably not a good fit, unless a legal guardian manages the account instead.

• **Could the beneficiary be a target for exploitation or fraud?**
ABLE accounts can give designated beneficiaries some welcome control over funds, but they also provide an opportunity for the beneficiary to be targeted for fraud, undue influence, or exploitation. The beneficiary of an ABLE account must have the capacity to identify and ward off potential abusers.

• **Can the beneficiary maintain account records?** Because account funds must be used only for QDEs, designated beneficiaries must maintain perfect records of how they have used account funds. Failure to do so could subject the account to tax penalties or cause the loss of SSI or Medicaid.

• **Would the account be funded with money from a third-party special needs trust?** When a beneficiary dies, funds in an ABLE account are subject to Medicaid payback, but funds in a third-party special needs trust (like the one in this book) are not. So, if you were to fund the ABLE account with money from a third-party special needs trust, you would be risking payback for funds that might otherwise be distributed to family, friends, or favorite organizations.

If you are unsure about whether an ABLE account is right for your loved one, consider discussing your questions and concerns with an experienced special needs planning attorney. (See Chapter 11.)

The chart below compares ABLE accounts and special needs trusts to provide a better understanding of how the two tools work together.

Comparison of Special Needs Trusts and ABLE Accounts

Issue	ABLE Account	Third-Party SNT
What is the purpose?	Allows an individual with a disability to have a cash account to pay for certain expenses without loss of SSI or Medicaid or any other federal benefit program	Enhances quality of life of person with a disability by paying for goods and services without the loss of SSI or Medicaid
Who is the beneficiary?	Person with a disability who was disabled before age 26	Person with a disability, but can be others; no age limit
Who creates or opens it?	Person with a disability or anyone	Any person or entity except the person with a disability
Who manages the trust or account?	State ABLE program runs account, but person with disability owns it	Any individual or professional, but not the person with a disability
How many trusts or accounts are allowed?	One	Unlimited
Whose assets fund the trust or account?	Assets of anyone	Assets of anyone but the person with a disability
How much can go into the trust or account annually?	Limited to annual gift tax exemption from all sources (currently $15,000 per year)	Unlimited
How much can the account hold?	$100,000 for SSI recipients, otherwise up to the state's 529 plan limit	Unlimited
How can the funds be used?	"Qualified disability expenses" as defined by the IRS code and regulations, otherwise a tax penalty will be incurred	No limitation, except for certain disbursements that may reduce or eliminate SSI or Medicaid eligibility
What is the effect of paying for food or shelter?	No penalty for paying for food or shelter as long as paid in same calendar month of disbursement from ABLE account	Implementation of SSI ISM penalty
How will the trust or account be taxed?	Taxed on gross income (not growth) plus a 10% penalty for nonqualified distributions	Taxed as a nongrantor trust except to the extent funds are used on behalf of the beneficiary
Who gets remaining funds when beneficiary dies?	Typically, Medicaid first, then heirs although some states have stated will not seek funds	Heirs or whomever is named in document

Creating Your Special Needs Trust

This chapter shows you how to create a valid special needs trust. During your life, you can hold property in the trust and you can use your will, living trust, or other estate planning device—such as a life insurance policy or a transfer-on-death designation—to route property to the trust at your death.

If you want a peek at what your finished document might look like, take a look at the sample trust at the end of this chapter. Of course, your trust will look a little different because of the choices you make to fit your own circumstances.

> **SEE AN EXPERT**
>
> **Get help if you want to create a trust that will be funded with the beneficiary's own money.** For example, if the intended beneficiary has money from a personal injury recovery or a direct inheritance, you'll need a "self-settled" or "first-party" special needs trust. Hire a lawyer to set up one of these trusts. See Chapter 11 for tips on finding and working with a lawyer.

Drafting the Trust Document

Now you're ready to start. We'll go through the clauses (called "articles") in order, explaining what each one means and letting you know whether you need to make any choices or fill in any information.

Every special needs trust must include certain language, or clauses, to ensure that the SSI or Medicaid programs won't count property held in the trust as a resource of the beneficiary. The trust document in this book includes these clauses, which lawyers call "boilerplate."

> **CAUTION**
>
> **Do not use this trust in Louisiana.** While Louisiana residents will find this book useful for its discussion about how special needs trusts work, the trust provided by this book was not designed to be used in Louisiana. If you are a Louisiana resident and want to make a special needs trust, see an experienced attorney.

For some articles, however, you must fill in a blank. We provide instructions and also refer you to the chapter that discusses the particular issue. If you need some help making the decision, just flip back and read more about your options.

The easiest way to assemble your special needs trust is to use the downloadable e-forms that come with this book (see Appendix C). Just modify the clauses to fit your situation. You will sign the finished product in front of a notary public. (Instructions for doing that are in Chapter 9.)

> ⓘ CAUTION
> **Don't change trust language.** We designed the trust in this chapter to comply with the minimum legal requirements that keep the trust from interfering with the beneficiary's public benefits. To keep the trust drafting process manageable, we don't offer all potential options. If you want something more than a bare-bones trust, you should consult an attorney. If you embark on editing the trust language on your own, your changes might inadvertently:
> - interfere with the purpose of the trust
> - create an inconsistency within the trust document, or
> - change the numbering of the trust clauses (that's a problem because of the extensive cross-referencing within the trust document).
>
> Chapter 11 has some advice on how to go about finding a lawyer.

Naming Your Trust

The name of your special needs trust should include the name of the beneficiary.

What you need to do: Replace "[*Name of Beneficiary*]" with the name of your loved one.

Name of the Trust
The [*Name of Beneficiary*] Special Needs Trust

Article 1. Creation of the Trust

The first clause of your trust document makes it irrevocable (that is, it can't be changed). Because the trust is irrevocable, you will not be able to make changes to it after it is signed, so make sure that information you enter into the blanks expresses exactly what you want. The first clause also identifies both you (the "Grantor") and your loved one (the "Beneficiary").

This trust is designed to have just one grantor, but if you are creating the trust with another person—for example, your child's other parent—you can alter the trust to name more than one grantor. Doing so names both of you as the creators of the trust, but it doesn't give either of you any power to manage the trust; only the trustees have that power. So, while you should feel free to name more than one grantor here in Article 1, your more critical decision will be whether to name yourselves as cotrustees in Article 4.

To name more than one grantor, put the grantors' names here in Article 1. Then go through the rest of the trust, add an "s" to every instance of "grantor" (Warning: There are a lot of them!), and make the following verb (and any pronouns) agree. For example, you would change Section 1 of Article 3 from "Grantor intends this trust…" to "Grantors intend this trust…."

What you need to do: Fill in your name(s) and the name of the beneficiary.

ARTICLE 1. Creation of Trust

[*Your name(s)*], Grantor, is creating this special needs trust for the benefit of [*name of beneficiary*], Beneficiary. This trust shall become irrevocable upon execution.

Article 2. Purpose of the Trust

Next, you state the central purpose of the trust: to provide for your loved one's special needs over and above the support and medical assistance provided by government programs. Should an agency or court be called on to interpret any part of this trust document, the purpose stated here will serve as the overarching guideline. It makes clear beyond any doubt that the trust property may never be considered available as a resource for the purpose of determining eligibility for SSI and Medicaid.

What you need to do: Decide whether to include a description of your loved one's disability (do so if you think it will help your successor trustee better understand your loved one). If you want to, use the first alternate article (shown below in Option 1), fill in the description and then delete the second alternate article. If you don't want to include a description, use the second alternate article (shown below in Option 2) and delete the first one.

Option 1: If you wish, include here a brief description of the beneficiary's disability. This will inform anyone who reads the trust document about the nature of the beneficiary's disability and clarify why the trust is being created. However, describing a disability is not legally required. Here are some examples:

- The nature of the disability is: major mental illness diagnosed as schizophrenia.
- The nature of the disability is: Down syndrome.
- The nature of the disability is: cystic fibrosis.

If you expect that your loved one's disability might change in the future, indicate that as well. (For example, if the beneficiary is a young child recently diagnosed with autism, you might not know how severe the condition will become.) Remember, the trust in this book is irrevocable, so you will not be able to make changes to it later. To the best of your ability, fill in the blank with as much flexibility for the future as possible. For example, using the autism example above, you might say that your son has been diagnosed with autism, though at the time this trust is created, it is unclear how severely he will be affected in adulthood.

OPTION 1

ARTICLE 2. Purpose of Trust

Beneficiary has a disability and will likely require government assistance during Grantor's life and after Grantor's death. The nature of the disability is: _____.

Grantor creates this special needs trust to enhance Beneficiary's quality of life while at the same time preserving Beneficiary's eligibility for government support and medical assistance programs, including SSI, Medicaid, or other similar programs. Grantor intends this Declaration of Trust to be interpreted in light of this purpose.

Option 2: If you don't want to describe the disability, simply omit the second sentence of the paragraph, as shown below.

OPTION 2

ARTICLE 2. Purpose of Trust

Beneficiary has a disability and will likely require government assistance during Grantor's life and after Grantor's death. Grantor creates this special needs trust to enhance Beneficiary's quality of life while at the same time preserving Beneficiary's eligibility for government support and medical assistance programs, including SSI, Medicaid, or other similar programs. Grantor intends this Declaration of Trust to be interpreted in light of this purpose.

Article 3. Defining Special Needs

This clause explains the types of goods and services you want the trustee to be able to provide for your loved one.

The fact that something isn't mentioned in this list doesn't preclude your trustee from providing it, as long as the good or service doesn't interfere with your loved one's eligibility for government assistance. And the fact that something is on the list does not mean that your trustee has to buy it for the beneficiary; it just means that the trustee has explicit authority to do so if it becomes necessary.

What you may want to do: Add items not included and delete ones that you're sure are not necessary in the circumstances. Or, you can just leave the clause as is.

ARTICLE 3. Examples of Special Needs

1. Grantor intends this trust to provide Beneficiary with goods and services to meet Beneficiary's special needs, which are needs that are not provided for by any government programs.

2. Special needs include but are not limited to: out-of-pocket medical and dental expenses; medical equipment not provided by Medicaid or similar programs; eyeglasses; exercise equipment; annual independent checkups; transportation; vehicle maintenance; vehicle insurance premiums; life insurance premiums; physical rehabilitation services not covered by Medicaid or similar programs; essential dietary needs; materials for hobbies; tickets for recreational or cultural events; musical instruments; cosmetics; home furnishings; home improvements; computer or electronic equipment; cable television; internet access, telephones; televisions; radios; cameras; trips; vacations; visits to friends; entertainment; membership in book, health, record, video, or other clubs; newspaper and magazine subscriptions; athletic training or competitions; personal care attendant or escort; vocational rehabilitation or habilitation; professional services; costs of attending or participating in meetings, conferences, seminars, or training sessions; and tuition and expenses connected with all types of technical degree programs and higher education.

Article 4. Identification of Trustees

Here you state whom you want to serve as trustee of the trust. Choosing your trustee is one of the biggest decisions you will make with regards to the trust. (See Chapter 5 for a full discussion on how to choose your trustee.) You can name one or more persons in each role as trustee or successor trustee. If you do name cotrustees, you will also need to decide whether you want them to act jointly or independently as they administer the trust. If you decide that they must work jointly, the cotrustees will have to agree on all decisions. If you decide that they can work independently, each may make decisions without the approval of the other cotrustee or cotrustees. (See Chapter 5 for a full discussion of the pros and cons of allowing cotrustees to act jointly or independently.)

EXAMPLE 1: When creating a special needs trust for her daughter Susan, Nora names herself and her partner, Mick, as cotrustees. Nora believes that she and Mick are both very responsible and good at communicating with each other, so in the trust document, she indicates that they can act independently to administer the trust for Susan's benefit.

EXAMPLE 2: Nora names Susan's two brothers David and Mark to serve as first successor cotrustees. They will serve as cotrustees when she and Mick can no longer serve. Even though Nora thinks that she and Mick can administer the trust independently, she has her doubts about David and Mark, so she requires that all cotrustees act jointly. This means that Mark and David must make every decision about the trust together.

SEE AN EXPERT

If you want some trustees to act jointly and others to act independently, you will need to hire a lawyer to draft a trust with more flexibility.

Article 4 gives the executor of your will (or the successor trustee of your living trust) the power to name a trustee for this special needs trust if none of the people you named to serve are available when you die. This article also gives the trustee the power to resign at any time and states that if you (the grantor) have named the same person to be both a trustee or successor trustee and a remainder beneficiary, that you are aware of the potential conflict of interest. (See Chapter 5.)

What you need to do: Decide whom you want to name as initial trustees and successor trustees, then fill in the blank lines of Article 4. If you're not naming any cotrustees, delete the unnecessary sections and renumber the remaining sections. To do all of this, read and follow the instructions below.

Naming the initial trustee. After the word "Trustee(s)," insert the name or names of the initial trustee or cotrustees for the trust. Most grantors serve as the initial trustee, but there are circumstances in which you might want to name someone else. (See Chapter 5.)

Naming successor trustees. After you've named your initial trustee or cotrustees, name the people who will take over if the initial trustee or cotrustees cannot serve. The successor trustees that you name to take over for the initial trustees are called "first successor" trustees. You can name one or more persons to serve as first successor trustee. In the clause, fill in the name or names after "First Successor Trustee(s)."

If possible, you should also name one or two additional successor trustees who will step in if your first choices for successor trustee cannot serve. The "second successor" trustee will take over, if necessary, for the first successor trustee and the "third successor" trustee will take over for the second successor trustee. Insert the names of your additional successor trustees on the corresponding lines of Section 1.

Specifying how cotrustees will act. If you decide to name more than one cotrustee to serve together, you must also decide how you want those cotrustees to work together to make decisions. They'll either need to act jointly or independently. (See Chapter 5.) Mark your choice in Section 3.

If you do not name cotrustees. If you decide not to name any cotrustees to serve together, remove the sections that refer to cotrustees —Sections 2, 3, 4, and 6. Then renumber the remaining sections.

ARTICLE 4. Trustees

1. The following persons or entities shall serve, in the order listed, as trustee(s) of this special needs trust:

   Trustee(s): _____

   First Successor Trustee(s): _____

   Second Successor Trustee(s): _____

   Third Successor Trustee(s): _____

2. If any person or entity named as a cotrustee or successor cotrustee is unable to serve, the trust shall be managed by the remaining cotrustees or successor cotrustees.

3. All cotrustees shall act: ☐ jointly ☐ independently.

4. Cotrustees shall cooperate with each other to carry out the trust purpose set out in Article 2, to prevent harmful and costly duplication of activities and to avoid unnecessary delay in making disbursements to Beneficiary.

5. If no successor trustee named here is available to serve, the trust protector named in this trust may name a trustee to manage the special needs trust. If there is no trust protector, the personal representative of Grantor's estate may name a trustee to manage this special needs trust. If there is no personal representative, the successor trustee of Grantor's revocable living trust, if any, may name a trustee to manage this trust. In the event there is no successor trustee of Grantor's revocable living trust, then, on petition of any interested person, a court of competent jurisdiction shall designate the successor trustee. In no event shall a court obtain jurisdiction over this trust by exercise of this provision.

6. All references to trustee in this trust document include each cotrustee named in this Article.

7. Any trustee may resign at any time. The resigning trustee shall give written notarized notice of the resignation to Beneficiary, Beneficiary's legal guardian or conservator, and all persons and entities named in the trust as successor trustees or remainder beneficiaries.

ARTICLE 4. Trustees (continued)

8. If a remainder beneficiary is also named as a trustee or successor trustee, Grantor is aware of the potential conflict of interest and intends for the trustee or successor trustee to serve as provided for in this Declaration of Trust.

Article 5. Powers of Successor Trustees

This article puts any successor trustee in the same position as the original trustee, once a successor trustee takes over. It lets the successor trustee show third parties—banks, for example—that he or she has power to act on behalf of the trust.

What you need to do: Nothing. This is boilerplate and you must include all of this language.

ARTICLE 5. Powers of Successor Trustees

All authority and powers, including discretionary powers, conferred upon a trustee or cotrustee shall pass to all successor trustees.

Article 6. Trust Protector

This provision allows you to name an individual or a group of individuals to oversee the trustee's actions and make changes to the trust, if necessary. (If you name successor protectors, the second takes over when the first can no longer serve or resigns, and so on.) Whether to include this provision is up to you.

A trust protector provides flexibility when you are no longer there to manage the trust. For example, you may want to give someone the right to remove and replace a trustee who does not work out. Other common provisions allow the trust protector to modify the terms of the trust or to interpret ambiguous language in the trust document. Chapter 5 details the benefits of naming someone to look after the trust.

When choosing a trust protector (one or more), name people whom you trust completely, but who might not be right to serve as trustee—perhaps because they are too busy or live too far away, or for another reason.

What you need to do. Decide whether you want to name a trust protector. If you decide not to, remove this clause and renumber the clauses that follow.

If you do want to name a trust protector, you will need to tailor your trust document to reflect your wishes. In Section 2, insert the name or names of the people you want to serve as a trust protector or as a trust advisory committee. Include your backup choices as "successors."

Next, decide which of the optional powers you want to include. Here are your choices:

- Section 3, the power to remove and replace a trustee
- Section 4, the power to amend the trust, or
- Section 5, the power to review the trustee's records.

Delete any section that you don't want to include, then renumber the remaining sections, if necessary.

If you decide to give the trust protector the power to remove and replace a trustee in Section 3, you must decide whether the trust protector needs to have a good reason to do so. In the first sentence, include "only for cause" if you want the trust protector to be able to remove a trustee only for a legal reason. Keep in mind, this gives the trustee broad power to make both good and bad decisions. For example, if the trustee refuses to make a disbursement that is perfectly acceptable, it could still be difficult to remove the trustee if the trust has a provision allowing removal "only for cause." If you include "with or without cause," the trust protector may remove the trustee for any reason, regardless of the trustee's performance.

ARTICLE 6. Trust Protector

1. The function of the trust protector is to assist, if needed, in protecting the interests of Beneficiary and in achieving the objectives and intent of this trust agreement.

2. The following persons or entities shall serve, in the order listed, as trust protector of this special needs trust:

   Trust Protector: _____

   First Successor: _____

   Second Successor: _____

   Third Successor: _____

3. The trust protector shall have the authority to remove any trustee [*choose one:* only for cause/with or without cause] and appoint a trustee under this agreement. Whenever the office of trustee is vacant and no successor trustee is effectively named, the trust protector shall appoint an individual or a corporate fiduciary to serve as trustee familiar with the administration of special needs trusts.

   A trust protector may not appoint himself or herself as a trustee and a trust protector may not simultaneously serve as both trust protector and trustee. This is in keeping with the intent and purpose that the trust protector's only interest will be to protect the financial resources governed by this agreement and the intent that the assets of this trust agreement not be considered income or resources for all needs-based and entitlement benefits from any government agency.

4. The trust protector may amend any provision of this agreement to:

   (a) Add or modify terms of the trust so that the trust will protect the financial resources governed by this agreement and to comply with the intent of this trust that trust assets shall not be considered income or resources for all needs-based and entitlement public benefits from any government agency for which the trust beneficiary is eligible;

   (b) Alter the administrative and investment powers of trustee to comply with any changes in the law;

ARTICLE 6. Trust Protector (continued)

(c) Reflect tax or other legal changes that affect trust administration; and

(d) Correct ambiguities, including scrivener errors that might otherwise require court construction or reformation.

Notwithstanding the foregoing, our trust protector shall not amend this agreement in any manner that would limit or alter the rights of Beneficiary in any trust assets held by the trust before the amendment, unless the purpose of the amendment is to modify an existing provision in the trust that defeats the trust's intent of preserving public benefits.

An amendment made by the trust protector in good faith shall be conclusive on all persons interested in the trust and the trust protector shall not be liable for the consequences of any amendment or for not having amended the trust. An amendment to this agreement shall be made in a written instrument signed by the trust protector. The trust protector shall deliver a copy of the amendment to the trust beneficiary, the trust beneficiary's legal representative, and the currently serving trustee.

5. The books and records of this trust agreement, including all documentation, inventories, and accountings, shall be open and available for inspection by the trust protector at all reasonable times.

6. Any trust protector (including successors) shall have the right to appoint a successor trust protector in writing. Such appointment shall take effect on the death, resignation, or incapacity of the appointing trust protector. If there are successor trust protectors named in this agreement, the appointment of a successor trust protector under this subsection shall take effect only if and when all trust protectors named fail to qualify or cease to act.

7. A trust protector may resign by giving notice to Beneficiary and to the trustee then serving. Such resignation shall take effect on the date set forth in the notice, which shall not be earlier than 30 days after the date of delivery of the notice of resignation, unless an earlier effective date shall be agreed to by the trustee.

Article 7. Contributions to the Trust

This provision requires the person serving as trustee to keep the trust as a third-party trust—that is, one funded exclusively with property from someone other than the beneficiary. It is important not to put any of the beneficiary's own money (such as a personal injury settlement, an unplanned inheritance, or work income) into this trust. Doing so could affect the beneficiary's eligibility for public benefits.

It's fine, though, to accept property from other third-party sources. For example, after the trust is operational, suppose that a relative or friend wishes to give some money to the beneficiary. Because a gift made directly to the beneficiary might interfere with the beneficiary's eligibility for SSI and Medicaid, the friend or relative could instead put the money in the special needs trust by giving it to the trustee.

CAUTION

This is crucial: If the beneficiary comes into some money— for instance, wins the lottery or a lawsuit, or receives a gift or inheritance —those funds may not be put into this trust. If any of the beneficiary's property were added to the trust, all the trust assets might be considered the beneficiary's property—and the trust would no longer serve its purpose. Instead, a separate trust should be established for the beneficiary's own funds, with the help of a lawyer. (See Chapter 11 for tips on finding a lawyer.)

What you need to do: Nothing. This is just boilerplate.

ARTICLE 7. Contributions to the Trust

Trustee shall accept contributions to the trust from any person or entity. However, Trustee shall not accept any assets that are owned by Beneficiary, including public assistance, Social Security benefits, or any other earned or unearned income.

Article 8. Use of Principal and Income

This article requires that income earned by trust assets be kept in the trust and not be distributed to the beneficiary. The reason is that income distributed to the beneficiary would be deducted from the beneficiary's SSI grant and would interfere with the beneficiary's eligibility for SSI and Medicaid.

For bookkeeping purposes, the retained income must be used first when the trustee spends trust money for the beneficiary's benefit. This way, the income spent for the beneficiary can be taxed as the beneficiary's income (even though he or she doesn't actually get it). That's desirable because typically the beneficiary's income tax rate is much lower than the trust income tax rate. (See Chapter 4 for more on the rules governing income earned by a special needs trust.)

What you need to do: Nothing.

ARTICLE 8. Use of Principal and Income

Income earned from trust property shall be retained in the trust to be used for trust purposes. When making disbursements for Beneficiary's benefit, Trustee shall keep adequate records to show that current and accumulated trust income is used first, and then trust principal.

Article 9. Trustee's Duty to Cooperate in Seeking Government Benefits

This part of the trust document requires that the person serving as trustee to cooperate with the beneficiary (or the beneficiary's legal representative) to secure all possible government benefits for the beneficiary. The greater the benefits, the longer the trust funds will last. This provision does not require your trustee to apply for the beneficiary's public benefits or maintain them, which could place a great burden on your trustee. The trustee might not have standing (the legal right) to seek public benefits for the beneficiary, or might be unable to obtain required confidential financial and medical records. Instead, this trust provision is limited to a duty to report information relative to the trust, a much more sustainable duty for the trustee to perform.

What you need to do: Nothing.

ARTICLE 9. Trustee's Duty to Cooperate in Seeking Government Benefits

Trustee shall cooperate with Beneficiary by providing information that is necessary for Beneficiary to obtain or maintain eligibility for needs-based public benefits and entitlement programs, including, but not limited to, Social Security payments, Supplemental Security Income, Social Security Disability Insurance, Veterans Administration benefits, HUD housing benefits, Medicare, and Medicaid. However, Trustee shall not be responsible to Beneficiary to obtain or maintain Beneficiary's eligibility for these programs.

Article 10. Trustee's Discretion Over Disbursements

This provision is the heart and soul of your special needs trust. It gives the person serving as trustee unlimited discretion to make disbursements, as long as the distributions:

- are consistent with the trust purpose described in Article 2
- are made for the benefit of the beneficiary (though it's okay for others to benefit indirectly), and
- won't deprive the beneficiary of eligibility for SSI, Medicaid, or similar programs.

What you need to do: Nothing.

ARTICLE 10. Trustee's Discretion Over Disbursements

Trustee shall have complete discretion in how the trust property is used, provided that the property is used only for the purpose of helping Beneficiary by providing Beneficiary with goods and services that supplement those provided by SSI, Medicaid, or similar programs, and never for a purpose that will eliminate Beneficiary's eligibility for those programs unless it is in the best interests of Beneficiary to do so. All actions of Trustee shall be directed toward carrying out the primary purpose of this trust to supplement Beneficiary's public benefits. Trustee's discretion to carry out this purpose is absolute. Hence, while Trustee is to be guided by the needs of Beneficiary, as determined by Trustee, in Trustee's sole and absolute discretion, Trustee is not obliged to make any specific distributions under the terms of this trust. Because Trustee shall be solely responsible for determining what discretionary distributions may be made from this trust, Beneficiary does not have access to principal or income of the trust or authority to direct distributions from the trust for any purpose.

Article 11. Trustee's Duty to File Tax Returns and Make Reports

This article requires the person serving as trustee to:

- prepare and file all required trust tax returns
- assemble all information necessary to prepare reports required by government agencies as a condition of eligibility for SSI and Medicaid
- submit all information required by government agencies as a condition of eligibility for SSI and Medicaid or, alternatively, turn over the information to the beneficiary if the beneficiary wants to submit it, and

- share basic information about trust activity with the beneficiary, a guardian or conservator if any, and other interested parties such as a person or an entity who has been designated by a government agency to receive funds on the beneficiary's behalf (a representative payee).

The required information about trust activity includes:

- income and contributions (for example, money contributed by a relative) received by the trust
- what trust income and assets were spent on, and
- the current amount of money in the trust.

This work must be done anyway to compute annual taxes and make reports required by SSI and Medicaid. This article requires that the people most interested in the trust be included in the information loop.

What you need to do: Nothing.

ARTICLE 11. Trustee's Duty to File Tax Returns and Make Reports

1. Trustee shall prepare and file all required trust tax returns.

2. Trustee shall provide to Beneficiary, or Beneficiary's legal guardian, conservator, representative payee, or agent, if any, all information necessary for the reports required by a government agency as a condition of Beneficiary's continued eligibility for SSI, Medicaid, and other similar benefits.

3. Trustee shall annually provide Beneficiary, Beneficiary's legal guardian, conservator, representative payee, or agent, if any, and the remainder beneficiaries named in Article 13, with written information about trust activity, including an accounting of current trust assets, income earned by the trust, contributions from outside sources made to the trust, disbursements made to meet Beneficiary's special needs, and an accounting of all purchases by Trustee.

4. Upon request, Trustee shall provide the persons named in Section 3 of this article with copies of the trust's annual income tax returns.

Article 12. Termination of the Trust

At some point, the person serving as trustee will have to end the trust. This part of the trust document describes the circumstances that justify ending the trust, and what the trustee should do with any money left in the trust. (Wrapping up the trust is discussed in Chapter 1.)

What you need to do: Nothing.

ARTICLE 12. Termination of the Trust

1. Trustee shall terminate this trust if:
    - in his or her sole discretion, the Trustee determines that the value of the trust property makes it impractical to administer the trust, or
    - in his or her sole discretion, the Trustee determines that changes in Beneficiary's disability make a special needs trust unnecessary, or
    - Beneficiary dies.

2. If Trustee terminates the trust for any reason other than Beneficiary's death, upon termination of the trust, and after all debts and taxes legally owed by the trust have been paid, Trustee shall distribute the trust property and accumulated income to Beneficiary or Beneficiary's legal guardian, conservator, representative payee, or agent, if any, unless such distribution would deprive Beneficiary of needed government benefits. In that event, Trustee shall distribute as much of the property as possible to Beneficiary consistent with maintaining the benefits and distribute the rest of the property to the remainder beneficiaries named in Article 13.

3. If Trustee terminates the trust because of Beneficiary's death, the trust property and accumulated income shall be distributed to the remainder beneficiaries as set out in Article 13 after all debts and taxes legally owed by the trust have been paid.

4. Any termination of the trust shall be in writing and notarized. Trustee shall provide copies of the termination to Beneficiary, Beneficiary's legal guardian or conservator, and all persons and entities named in the trust as successor trustees or remainder beneficiaries.

Article 13. Remainder Beneficiaries

Here, you name someone to inherit any property left in the trust after it's terminated. This "remainder" beneficiary can be one or more people or organizations. You can also name alternate remainder beneficiaries.

If you plan on using retirement accounts to fund this trust, be careful naming organizations or charities as remainder beneficiaries. Naming organizations or charities as remainder beneficiaries on a trust funded with retirement accounts can result in negative tax implications to the trust. Remember, planning with retirement accounts is very complex and nuanced, and an attorney must be consulted. (See Chapter 3 for a more thorough description on the impact of funding with retirement accounts.)

Usually, the trust ends when the beneficiary dies. But the remainder beneficiary could also inherit if the trust ends for another reason and giving all of the trust property to the beneficiary would interfere with his or her eligibility for SSI or Medicaid.

If the remainder beneficiary is under 18 when he or she inherits trust property, an adult must manage the property. It's the trustee's job to act as "custodian" under the Uniform Transfers to Minors Act or pick someone else to do it. A custodian, like a trustee, must manage, invest, and spend the money on behalf of the young beneficiary. Generally, the custodianship ends when the remainder beneficiary reaches age 18, 21, or 25, depending on the state. (See Chapter 4 for more on this.)

Finally, this article restates that the person serving as trustee must act in the beneficiary's best interest and always put that interest ahead of the remainder beneficiary's interest. Because every disbursement from the trust for the beneficiary's benefit means there is less money left over for the remainder beneficiaries, a natural conflict of interest exists. This conflict is most evident if the trustee is also the remainder beneficiary, which is common but best avoided. (See Chapter 5.) Regardless of any such conflict, the trustee is duty bound to always put the interests of the primary beneficiary first.

What you need to do: Fill in the names of the remainder beneficiaries (Section 1) and alternates (Section 2). If there's a chance that any of these people could inherit trust property before they're adults, in Section 5 fill in the state in which you (or the beneficiary) lives. If not, you can delete all of Section 5.

ARTICLE 13. Remainder Beneficiaries

1. If Trustee terminates this special needs trust, and there are trust assets that Trustee does not distribute to Beneficiary under the terms of Article 12, Trustee shall distribute the remaining trust principal and accumulated income, after all debts and taxes legally owed by the trust have been paid, to [*names of remainder beneficiary(ies)*].

2. If the remainder beneficiary or beneficiaries named in Section 1 of this article fails or fail to survive Beneficiary by 30 days, Trustee shall distribute the property to [*names of alternate remainder beneficiary(ies)*].

3. If the remainder beneficiary or beneficiaries named in Section 2 of this article fails or fail to survive Beneficiary by 30 days, Trustee shall distribute property to Beneficiary's heirs at law, per stirpes.

4. While administering this special needs trust, Trustee shall in all cases exercise discretion in accordance with Article 10 and without regard to the interests of any remainder beneficiary named in this article.

5. If, when a remainder beneficiary inherits property under this article, he or she is not yet 18 years old, or, in the opinion of Trustee, is unable to prudently manage the property to be distributed and is under the age of 21, Trustee shall either (a) retain that beneficiary's share as a custodian under the Uniform Transfers to Minors Act of [*state*] , or (b) name another person to serve as custodian for the property under that act and distribute the property to that custodian. The custodianship shall end when the remainder beneficiary turns 21 unless the law requires it to end at age 18. When the custodianship ends, the custodian shall distribute any remaining custodial property to the beneficiary.

⊘ CAUTION

Special rules for South Carolina residents. South Carolina has not adopted the Uniform Transfers to Minors Act, so you cannot direct your trustee to serve as a custodian for a young remainder beneficiary. You'll need to omit Section 5 of Article 13. If you want to name a minor as remainder beneficiary, see a lawyer for help.

Article 14. Trustee Powers

This long clause spells out the powers that the person serving as trustee will have while administering the trust. The idea here is to give the trustee maximum authority to deal with the trust and trust property in a way that will provide the most benefit for the beneficiary, consistent with Article 2 (which states the purpose of the trust, to benefit your loved one and preserve eligibility for SSI and Medicaid) and Article 10 (which gives the trustee unfettered discretion over how trust funds are spent). You will also notice that Section 2 allows your trustee to use this trust to fund the beneficiary's ABLE account if the beneficiary has one. (See Chapter 7 for more information on ABLE accounts.)

What you need to do: Nothing.

ARTICLE 14. Trustee Powers

Trustee shall, in addition to the powers given by law, have the following powers applicable to all property held in trust, whether principal or income, and exercisable without order of any court that has jurisdiction over Beneficiary:

1. To retain any property transferred to this trust, and to make such investments and reinvestments and in such proportions as Trustee considers beneficial and prudent in light of the trust purposes set out in Article 2, provided that the trustee's investment decisions shall be guided by the Prudent Investor Act as enacted by the state where this trust is administered, or if it has not been so enacted, by the Uniform Prudent Investor Act as originally published by the National Conference of Commissioners on Uniform State Laws.

ARTICLE 14. Trustee Powers (continued)

2. To contribute to a qualified ABLE account under Section 529A of the Internal Revenue Code on Beneficiary's behalf. All such contributions must be made in cash and may not cause the annual aggregate contribution limit (from all contributors) imposed by Section 529A(b)(2)(B) to be exceeded, and shall not cause the aggregate excess contribution limit imposed by Section 529A(b)(6) to be exceeded.

3. To (1) participate in any merger or reorganization affecting securities held hereunder at any time; (2) deposit stock under voting agreements; (3) exercise any option to subscribe for stocks, bonds, or debentures; and (4) grant proxies, discretionary or otherwise, to vote shares of stock.

4. To manage, operate, or repair real estate or other property and to lease real estate and other property upon such terms and for such period as Trustee deems advisable.

5. To buy or sell (and to grant options for the sale of) any real or personal property at public or private sale for such prices and upon such terms as Trustee thinks proper.

6. To purchase, maintain, improve, or replace a residence, or any interest in it, where Beneficiary may reside, including any portion of the residence that may be owned by a family member.

7. To permit any person to reside at any real property held in this trust at which Beneficiary is residing, on such terms as Trustee deems proper, for the purpose of providing care, supervision, or simple companionship to Beneficiary.

8. To seek court permission to amend the trust only if necessary to fulfill the trust purposes set out in Article 2.

9. To make loans, but not gifts, for Beneficiary's benefit, provided the loans do not interfere with the trust purposes set out in Article 2.

10. To pay premiums to provide supplementary health insurance for Beneficiary or life insurance policies that may be owned or acquired by the trust. If Trustee is also the insured of any life insurance policy owned by the trust, then Trustee may exercise all rights and incidents

ARTICLE 14. Trustee Powers (continued)

of ownership with respect to such policy only in a fiduciary capacity, including the power to change the beneficiary, to surrender or cancel the policy, to assign the policy, to revoke any assignment, to pledge a policy for a loan, or to obtain a loan against the surrender value of the policy from the insurer.

11. To start or defend such litigation with respect to the trust or any property of the trust as Trustee deems advisable, at the expense of the trust.

12. To carry, at the expense of the trust, insurance of such kinds and in such amounts as Trustee deems advisable both to protect the trust property against any damage or loss and to protect Trustee against liability with respect to third persons.

13. To prepare and file returns and arrange for payment with respect to all local, state, federal, and foreign taxes incident to this trust, to prepare all necessary fiduciary income tax returns, and to make all necessary and appropriate elections.

14. To prepare and, if necessary, file all reports required of providers of government benefits received by Beneficiary, and to prepare and distribute annual reports of trust activity to Beneficiary and any named remainder beneficiaries.

15. Upon termination of the trust, to pay all debts and taxes determined by the trustee to be legally owed by the trust.

16. To hire attorneys, accountants, investment advisers, financial advisers, tax preparation services, and any other experts should Trustee, in Trustee's unfettered discretion, determine such expertise to be necessary for proper management of the trust.

17. To appoint one or more persons or agencies to serve as successor trustee in case no other trustees or successor trustees named in this trust are available to serve. Such appointment shall be made in writing and notarized. Trustee shall provide copies of the appointment to Beneficiary, Beneficiary's legal guardian or conservator, and all persons and entities named in the trust as successor trustees or remainder beneficiaries.

Article 15. Trustee Compensation

The issue of compensation is most problematic when you choose a friend or relative to handle the trustee chores.

Although your choice for successor trustee may initially turn down your offer of compensation, this may change down the road; serving as a trustee can be a time-consuming job. So this trust document entitles the person serving as trustee to reimbursement for out-of-pocket costs and reasonable payment for services rendered. The trustee determines what is "reasonable."

There is no easy way to define reasonable fees. You just need to trust your trustee—and given that you are asking him or her to take on such an important job, you surely do.

> **SEE AN EXPERT**
>
> **If you are concerned about whether or how to compensate the trustee (particularly if you want to specify the compensation in your trust),** consult an attorney about customizing your trust document to address the issue of the trustee's compensation.

If you choose a corporate or professional successor trustee, you will be told about the trustee's fee. Most charge a flat rate—usually a percent of the property in the trust. (See Chapter 5.) Some add extra fees for particular actions, such as $50 per disbursement or $25 per phone conversation with the beneficiary. If you're paying a professional trustee, you can add this to the end of the last sentence of the clause: "unless the compensation has been set out in a written agreement between Grantor and Trustee."

What you need to do: Nothing. Unless you're using a professional trustee, in which case, add the clause described in the paragraph above.

> ### ARTICLE 15. Trustee Compensation
>
> Trustee shall be entitled to reasonable compensation, from trust assets, commensurate with the services actually performed, and to reimbursement for expenses properly incurred. Trustee shall determine what compensation is reasonable by referring to the fees charged for similar services in the community where Trustee is serving.

Article 16. Spendthrift Provisions

This clause puts the trust property off-limits to everyone but the person serving as trustee, including the beneficiary. It prevents beneficiaries from transferring their interest in the trust to a third party, and protects trust assets from being grabbed by a creditor if the beneficiary is on the losing end of a lawsuit or files for bankruptcy. It also makes clear to SSI, Medicaid, and similar benefit programs that the trust property and income are unavailable to the beneficiary, and that the trustee may use them only for the purposes stated in the trust document.

What you need to do: Nothing.

> ### ARTICLE 16. Spendthrift Provisions
>
> 1. Beneficiary has no right or power, whether alone or in conjunction with others in whatever capacity, to amend, revoke, or terminate this special needs trust. No interest in the income or principal of this trust may be anticipated, assigned, encumbered, or subject to any creditor's claim or legal process.
> 2. Because trust funds will be conserved and maintained for Beneficiary's special needs, no part of the income or principal shall be construed as part of Beneficiary's "estate" or be subject to the claims of voluntary or involuntary creditors for the provision of care and services (including residential care) to or for Beneficiary by any city, county, or state government; the federal government; or any public or private agency except as otherwise provided in this trust instrument.

Article 17. Bond

This article states that the person serving as trustee does not need to obtain a bond. In the world of trusts, a bond is a kind of insurance policy that would cover losses to the trust if the trustee embezzled trust funds or otherwise violated the duty of trust owed to the beneficiary.

With a special needs trust, there is rarely need for a bond. Here's why:

- You should have full faith in the persons you've chosen as trustee and successor trustee.
- Bond premiums will be paid with trust money.
- Something in the successor trustee's background—a bankruptcy, poor credit rating, or an old criminal conviction—might make it difficult or even impossible to obtain a bond except at an exorbitant cost. This could prevent your choice from serving, a result you might not want. However, if someone has a history of poor financial management, you may want to carefully consider his or her ability to properly manage your loved one's finances.

SEE AN EXPERT

If you want to require a bond, get help from an attorney. If you would gain peace of mind by requiring a bond and you're not concerned about the cost, see a lawyer.

What you need to do: Nothing.

ARTICLE 17. Bond

Unless required by a court of competent jurisdiction or a trust protector, Trustee and successor trustees are not required to post a bond.

Article 18. Photocopies

This provision makes it clear that a copy of the trust carries the same legal weight as the original. Because there is only one original, it's possible that somewhere down the line a successor trustee will have only a copy and will need to use it to do business in the name of the trust.

What you need to do: Nothing.

ARTICLE 18. Photocopies

All photocopies of this Declaration of Trust shall carry the same legal weight as the original.

Article 19. Trustee Not Liable for Good-Faith Actions

This clause states that a trustee who acts in good faith won't be personally liable to the beneficiary for losses caused by his or her actions. (See Chapter 5 for more on the trustee's fiduciary duty.) This adds a little protection for the person you have carefully selected to serve as trustee. If that person makes a mistake, as long as that mistake was made with good intentions, the trustee will be protected in the event a lawsuit is filed against them.

What you need to do: Nothing.

ARTICLE 19. Trustee Not Liable for Good-Faith Actions

A trustee of any kind nominated by this document shall not be liable to any beneficiary for the trustee's acts or omissions, except in cases of willful misconduct, bad faith, or gross negligence.

Certification by Grantor

A few legal formalities remain. You and any trustees other than yourself will sign the trust in front of a notary public. Your signature certifies that you are the maker of the trust. The signatures of any trustees other than yourself certify their willingness to serve in the role of trustee. When you sign the certification in front of a notary and the notary attaches a certificate of acknowledgment, your trust becomes legal.

What you need to do: First, in the section labeled "Certification by Grantor," insert your name under the signature line. Then, if you named yourself as trustee, remove the italics and brackets so that after your name are a comma and the words "Grantor and Trustee." If you named someone other than yourself as initial trustee, after your name, remove the brackets and the word "Trustee" so that only a comma and the word "Grantor" appear after your name. If there is another grantor, repeat this line for the second grantor. Do not sign the trust yet.

Certification by Grantor

I certify that I have read this Declaration of Trust and that it correctly states the terms and conditions under which the trust property is to be held, managed, and disposed of by Trustee, and I approve the Declaration of Trust.

Dated: _____

[*Your Name*], Grantor [and Trustee]: _____

Certification of Trustee

This section documents that the person you name as initial trustee (if other than yourself) agrees to serve in that role. Legally, this section isn't required, but it's a good way to show that the trustee has agreed to serve.

What you need to do: If you named only yourself as initial trustee, delete this entire section. Otherwise, insert the name of the initial trustee or cotrustee under the signature line. If you named only one initial trustee (other than yourself), change every instance of "I/we" to "I." If you named more than one person (other than yourself) to serve as cotrustees, change all instances of "I/we" to "we" and insert a signature line for each cotrustee.

Certification of Trustees

[I/We] certify that [I/we] have read The [*Name of Beneficiary*] Special Needs Trust, and, having been appointed as Trustee(s) by Grantor, [I/we] agree to serve as Trustee(s) and to manage the trust property under the trust's terms and conditions.

Dated: _____

_____
[*Name of Trustee*], Trustee

_____
[*Name of Trustee*], Trustee

CAUTION

Special rules for Florida trusts. If you're finalizing your trust in Florida, you must have two witnesses sign it. See Chapter 9 for details.

Making the Trust Legal and Effective

Congratulations! If you've worked your way through all of those clauses, you should now have the special needs trust language you want. To make your trust legal, you (and any other initial trustees) now need to take your trust (along with your photo ID) to a notary public (or another qualified official), sign it in the presence of the notary, and have the notary attach a certificate of acknowledgment. After that, you will obtain a taxpayer ID number and open a bank account for the trust. Read Chapter 9 for details about each of these tasks.

Keeping the Special Needs Trust Up to Date

Make it a point to review the special needs trust every few years. Changes in the law or in your loved one's condition may require you to make a change. For example, if a new SSI rule makes the special needs trust obsolete or if your loved one no longer needs government aid, you, as trustee, would need to terminate the trust under its termination clause (Article 12) or seek an amendment from the trust protector (Article 6). Or, if you can no longer serve as trustee and none of your named successor trustees are available, you can choose new successor trustees.

The good news is that SSI and Medicaid rules regarding third-party special needs trusts (the kind covered in this book) have not changed significantly over the past 25 years. SSI and Medicaid rules regarding the treatment of income and resources have changed somewhat more frequently, but these changes have had little effect on third-party special needs trusts.

Of course, the fact that this area of the law has been stable in the past doesn't mean that a cash-strapped federal or state government won't change the rules in the future. Chapter 11 tells you how to stay current on the rules affecting third-party special needs trusts.

Hiring a Lawyer to Keep You Up to Speed

Most lawyers who specialize in drafting special needs trusts offer updating services as part of their overall package. The lawyers periodically notify their clients to come in for a checkup—often for a fee. Clients are also notified if important changes in SSI and Medicaid rules occur. These update services are intended to give the clients peace of mind that comes with having a knowledgeable professional looking out for their interests. You'll have to decide whether this service is worth the price to you. See Chapter 11 for more information on finding lawyers who specialize in this area.

Sample Special Needs Trust

Here is a sample of a special needs trust. It was made for someone else, so it won't match your trust exactly, but it should give you a good idea of what your final document will look like.

The Bessie Escobar Special Needs Trust

ARTICLE 1. CREATION OF TRUST

Gloria C. Escobar, Grantor, is creating this special needs trust for the benefit of Bessie Escobar, Beneficiary. This trust shall become irrevocable upon execution.

ARTICLE 2. PURPOSE OF TRUST

Beneficiary has a disability and will likely require government assistance during Grantor's life and after Grantor's death. Grantor creates this special needs trust to enhance Beneficiary's quality of life while at the same time preserving Beneficiary's eligibility for government support and medical assistance programs, including SSI, Medicaid, or other similar programs. Grantor intends this Declaration of Trust to be interpreted in light of this purpose.

ARTICLE 3. EXAMPLES OF SPECIAL NEEDS

1. Grantor intends this trust to provide Beneficiary with goods and services to meet Beneficiary's special needs, which are needs that are not provided for by any government programs.

2. Special needs include but are not limited to: out-of-pocket medical and dental expenses; medical equipment not provided by Medicaid or similar programs; eyeglasses; exercise equipment; annual independent checkups; transportation; vehicle maintenance; vehicle insurance premiums; life insurance premiums; physical rehabilitation services not covered by Medicaid or similar programs; essential dietary needs; materials for hobbies; tickets for recreational or cultural events; musical instruments; cosmetics; home furnishings; home improvements; computer or electronic equipment; Internet service, cable television; telephones; televisions; radios; cameras; trips; vacations; visits to friends; entertainment; membership in book, health, record, video, or other clubs; newspaper and magazine subscriptions; athletic training or competitions; personal care attendant or escort; vocational rehabilitation or habilitation; professional services; costs of attending or participating in meetings, conferences, seminars, or training sessions; and tuition and expenses connected with all types of technical degree programs and higher education.

ARTICLE 4. TRUSTEES

1. The following persons or entities shall serve, in the order listed, as trustee(s) of this special needs trust:

   Trustee(s): Gloria C. Escobar and Richard Sanchez

   First Successor Trustee(s): Jaime L. Sanchez

   Second Successor Trustee(s): Lola S. Sanchez

2. If any person or entity named as a trustee or cotrustee is unable to serve, the trust shall be managed by the remaining cotrustees or successor cotrustees.

3. All cotrustees shall act: [X] jointly [ ] independently.

4. Cotrustees shall cooperate with each other to carry out the trust purpose set out in Article 2, to prevent harmful and costly duplication of activities, and to avoid unnecessary delay in making disbursements to Beneficiary.

5. If no successor trustee named here is available to serve, the trust protector named in this trust may name a trustee to manage the special needs trust. If there is no trust protector, the personal representative of Grantor's estate may name a trustee to manage this special needs trust. If there is no personal representative, the successor trustee of Grantor's revocable living trust, if any, may name a trustee to manage this trust. In the event there is no successor trustee of Grantor's revocable living trust, then, on petition of any interested person, a court of competent jurisdiction shall designate the successor trustee. In no event shall a court obtain jurisdiction over this trust by exercise of this provision.

6. All references to trustee in this trust document include each cotrustee named in this Article.

7. Any trustee may resign at any time. The resigning trustee shall give written notarized notice of the resignation to Beneficiary, Beneficiary's legal guardian or conservator, and all persons and entities named in the trust as successor trustees or remainder beneficiaries.

8. If a remainder beneficiary is also named as a trustee or successor trustee, Grantor is aware of the potential conflict of interest and intends for the trustee or successor trustee to serve as provided for in this Declaration of Trust.

ARTICLE 5. POWERS OF SUCCESSOR TRUSTEES

All authority and powers, including discretionary powers, conferred upon a trustee or cotrustee shall pass to all successor trustees.

ARTICLE 6. TRUST PROTECTOR

1. The function of the trust protector is to assist, if needed, in protecting the interests of Beneficiary and in achieving the objectives and intent of this trust agreement.

2. The following persons or entities shall serve, in the order listed, as trust protector of this special needs trust:

   Trust Protector: Stephen Brust
   First Successor: Roger Zelazny
   Second Successor: Patrick Rothfuss

3. The trust protector shall have the authority to remove any trustee with or without cause and appoint a trustee under this agreement. Whenever the office of trustee is vacant and no successor trustee is effectively named, the trust protector shall appoint an individual or a corporate fiduciary to serve as trustee familiar with the administration of special needs trusts.

   A trust protector may not appoint himself or herself as a trustee and a trust protector may not simultaneously serve as both trust protector and trustee. This is in keeping with the intent and purpose that the trust protector's only interest will be to protect the financial resources governed by this agreement and the intent that the assets of this trust agreement not be considered income or resources for all needs-based and entitlement benefits from any government agency.

4. The trust protector may amend any provision of this agreement to:

   (a) Add or modify terms of the trust so that the trust will protect the financial resources governed by this agreement and to comply with the intent of this trust that trust assets shall not be considered income or resources for all needs-based and entitlement public benefits from any government agency for which the trust beneficiary is eligible;

   (b) Alter the administrative and investment powers of trustee to comply with any changes in the law;

(c) Reflect tax or other legal changes that affect trust administration; and

(d) Correct ambiguities, including scrivener errors that might otherwise require court construction or reformation.

Notwithstanding the foregoing, our trust protector shall not amend this agreement in any manner that would limit or alter the rights of Beneficiary in any trust assets held by the trust before the amendment, unless the purpose of the amendment is to modify an existing provision in the trust that defeats the trust's intent of preserving public benefits.

An amendment made by the trust protector in good faith shall be conclusive on all persons interested in the trust and the trust protector shall not be liable for the consequences of any amendment or for not having amended the trust. An amendment to this agreement shall be made in a written instrument signed by the trust protector. The trust protector shall deliver a copy of the amendment to the trust beneficiary, the trust beneficiary's legal representative, and the currently serving trustee.

5. The books and records of this trust agreement, including all documentation, inventories, and accountings, shall be open and available for inspection by the trust protector at all reasonable times.

6. Any trust protector (including successors) shall have the right to appoint a successor trust protector in writing. Such appointment shall take effect on the death, resignation, or incapacity of the appointing trust protector. If there are successor trust protectors named in this agreement, the appointment of a successor trust protector under this subsection shall take effect only if and when all trust protectors named fail to qualify or cease to act.

7. A trust protector may resign by giving notice to Beneficiary and to the trustee then serving. Such resignation shall take effect on the date set forth in the notice, which shall not be earlier than 30 days after the date of delivery of the notice of resignation, unless an earlier effective date shall be agreed to by the trustee.

ARTICLE 7. CONTRIBUTIONS TO THE TRUST

Trustee shall accept contributions to the trust from any person or entity. However, Trustee shall not accept any assets that are owned by Beneficiary, including public assistance, Social Security benefits, or any other earned or unearned income.

ARTICLE 8. USE OF PRINCIPAL AND INCOME

Income earned from trust property shall be retained in the trust to be used for trust purposes. When making disbursements for Beneficiary's benefit, Trustee shall keep adequate records to show that current and accumulated trust income is used first, and then trust principal.

ARTICLE 9. TRUSTEE'S DUTY TO COOPERATE IN SEEKING GOVERNMENT BENEFITS

Trustee shall cooperate with Beneficiary by providing information that is necessary for Beneficiary to obtain or maintain eligibility for needs-based public benefits and entitlement programs, including, but not limited to, Social Security payments, Supplemental Security Income, Social Security Disability Insurance, Veterans Administration benefits, HUD housing benefits, Medicare, and Medicaid. However, Trustee shall not be responsible to the Beneficiary to obtain or maintain Beneficiary's eligibility for these programs.

ARTICLE 10. TRUSTEE'S DISCRETION OVER DISBURSEMENTS

Trustee shall have complete discretion in how the trust property is used, provided that the property is used only for the purpose of helping Beneficiary by providing Beneficiary with goods and services that supplement those provided by SSI, Medicaid, or similar programs, and never for a purpose that will eliminate Beneficiary's eligibility for those programs unless it is in the best interests of Beneficiary to do so. All actions of Trustee shall be directed toward carrying out the primary purpose of this trust to supplement Beneficiary's public benefits. Trustee's discretion to carry out this purpose is absolute. Hence, while Trustee is to be guided by the needs of Beneficiary, as determined by Trustee, in Trustee's sole and absolute discretion, Trustee is not obliged to make any specific distributions under the terms of this trust. Because Trustee shall be solely responsible for determining what discretionary distributions may be made from this trust, Beneficiary does not have access to principal or income of the trust or authority to direct distributions from the trust for any purpose.

ARTICLE 11. TRUSTEE'S DUTY TO FILE TAX RETURNS AND MAKE REPORTS

1. Trustee shall prepare and file all required trust tax returns.

2. Trustee shall provide to Beneficiary, or Beneficiary's legal guardian, conservator, representative payee, or agent, if any, all information necessary for the reports required by a government agency as a condition of the Beneficiary's continued eligibility for SSI, Medicaid, and other similar benefits.

3. Trustee shall annually provide Beneficiary, Beneficiary's legal guardian, conservator, representative payee, or agent, if any, and the remainder beneficiaries named in Article 13, with written information about trust activity, including an accounting of current trust assets, income earned by the trust, contributions from outside sources made to the trust, disbursements made to meet Beneficiary's special needs, and an accounting of all purchases by Trustee.

4. Upon request, Trustee shall provide the persons named in Section 3 of this article with copies of the trust's annual income tax returns.

ARTICLE 12. TERMINATION OF THE TRUST

1. Trustee shall terminate this trust if:

   • in his or her sole discretion, the Trustee determines that the value of the trust property makes it impractical to administer the trust, or

   • in his or her sole discretion, Trustee determines that changes in Beneficiary's disability make a special needs trust unnecessary, or

   • Beneficiary dies.

2. If Trustee terminates the trust for any reason other than Beneficiary's death, upon termination of the trust, and after all debts and taxes legally owed by the trust have been paid, Trustee shall distribute the trust property and accumulated income to Beneficiary or Beneficiary's legal guardian, conservator, representative payee, or agent, if any, unless such distribution would deprive Beneficiary of needed government benefits. In that event, Trustee shall distribute as much of the property as possible to Beneficiary consistent with maintaining the benefits and distribute the rest of the property to the remainder beneficiaries named in Article 13.

3. If Trustee terminates the trust because of Beneficiary's death, the trust property and accumulated income shall be distributed to the remainder beneficiaries as set out in Article 13 after all debts and taxes legally owed by the trust have been paid.

4. Any termination of the trust shall be in writing and notarized. Trustee shall provide copies of the termination to Beneficiary, Beneficiary's legal guardian or conservator, and all persons and entities named in the trust as successor trustees or remainder beneficiaries.

ARTICLE 13. REMAINDER BENEFICIARIES

1. If Trustee terminates this special needs trust, and there are trust assets that Trustee does not distribute to Beneficiary under the terms of Article 12, Trustee shall distribute the remaining trust principal and accumulated income, after all debts and taxes legally owed by the trust have been paid, to Lola S. Sanchez.

2. If the remainder beneficiary or beneficiaries named in Section 1 of this article fails or fail to survive Beneficiary by 30 days, Trustee shall distribute the property to Maria S. Sanchez.

3. If the remainder beneficiary or beneficiaries named in Section 2 of this article fails or fail to survive Beneficiary by 30 days, Trustee shall distribute property to Beneficiary's heirs at law, per stirpes.

4. While administering this special needs trust, Trustee shall in all cases exercise discretion in accordance with Article 10 and without regard to the interests of any remainder beneficiary named in this article.

5. If, when a remainder beneficiary inherits property under this article, he or she is not yet 18 years old, or, in the opinion of Trustee, is unable to prudently manage the property to be distributed and is under the age of 21, Trustee shall either (a) retain that beneficiary's share as a custodian under the Uniform Transfers to Minors Act of Kentucky, or (b) name another person to serve as custodian for the property under that act and distribute the property to that custodian. The custodianship shall end when the remainder beneficiary turns 21 unless the law requires it to end at age 18. When the custodianship ends, the custodian shall distribute any remaining custodial property to the beneficiary.

ARTICLE 14. TRUSTEE POWERS

Trustee shall, in addition to the powers given by law, have the following powers applicable to all property held in trust, whether principal or income, and exercisable without order of any court that has jurisdiction over Beneficiary:

1. To retain any property transferred to this trust, and to make such investments and reinvestments and in such proportions as Trustee considers beneficial and prudent in light of the trust purposes set out in Article 2, provided that the Trustee's investment decisions shall be guided by the Prudent Investor Act as enacted by the state where this trust is administered, or if it has not been so enacted, by the Uniform Prudent Investor Act as originally published by the National Conference of Commissioners on Uniform State Laws.

2. To contribute to a qualified ABLE account under Section 529A of the Internal Revenue Code on Beneficiary's behalf. All such contributions must be made in cash and may not cause the annual aggregate contribution limit (from all contributors) imposed by Section 529A(b)(2)(B) to be exceeded, and shall not cause the aggregate excess contribution limit imposed by Section 529A(b)(6) to be exceeded.

3. To (1) participate in any merger or reorganization affecting securities held hereunder at any time; (2) deposit stock under voting agreements; (3) exercise any option to subscribe for stocks, bonds, or debentures; and (4) grant proxies, discretionary or otherwise, to vote shares of stock.

4. To manage, operate, or repair real estate or other property and to lease real estate and other property upon such terms and for such period as Trustee deems advisable.

5. To buy or sell (and to grant options for the sale of) any real or personal property at public or private sale for such prices and upon such terms as Trustee thinks proper.

6. To purchase, maintain, improve, or replace a residence, or any interest in it, where Beneficiary may reside, including any portion of the residence that may be owned by a family member.

7. To permit any person to reside at any real property held in this trust at which Beneficiary is residing, on such terms as Trustee deems proper, for the purpose of providing care, supervision, or simple companionship to Beneficiary.

8. To seek court permission to amend the trust only if necessary to fulfill the trust purposes set out in Article 2.

9. To make loans, but not gifts, for Beneficiary's benefit, provided the loans do not interfere with the trust purposes set out in Article 2.

10. To pay premiums to provide supplementary health insurance for Beneficiary or life insurance policies that may be owned or acquired by the trust. If Trustee is also the insured of any life insurance policy owned by the trust, then Trustee may exercise all rights and incidents of ownership with respect to such policy only in a fiduciary capacity, including the power to change the beneficiary, to surrender or cancel the policy, to assign the policy, to revoke any assignment, to pledge a policy for a loan, or to obtain a loan against the surrender value of the policy from the insurer.

11. To start or defend such litigation with respect to the trust or any property of the trust as Trustee deems advisable, at the expense of the trust.

12. To carry, at the expense of the trust, insurance of such kinds and in such amounts as Trustee deems advisable both to protect the trust property against any damage or loss and to protect Trustee against liability with respect to third persons.

13. To prepare and file returns and arrange for payment with respect to all local, state, federal, and foreign taxes incident to this trust, to prepare all necessary fiduciary income tax returns, and to make all necessary and appropriate elections.

14. To prepare and, if necessary, file all reports required of providers of government benefits received by Beneficiary, and to prepare and distribute annual reports of trust activity to Beneficiary and any named remainder beneficiaries.

15. Upon termination of the trust, to pay all debts and taxes determined by the trustee to be legally owed by the trust.

16. To hire attorneys, accountants, investment advisers, financial advisers, tax preparation services, and any other experts should Trustee, in Trustee's unfettered discretion, determine such expertise to be necessary for proper management of the trust.

17. To appoint one or more persons or agencies to serve as successor trustee in case no other trustees or successor trustees named in this trust are available to serve. Such appointment shall be made in writing and notarized. Trustee shall provide copies of the appointment to Beneficiary, Beneficiary's legal guardian or conservator, and all persons and entities named in the trust as successor trustees or remainder beneficiaries.

ARTICLE 15. TRUSTEE COMPENSATION

Trustee shall be entitled to reasonable compensation, from trust assets, commensurate with the services actually performed, and to reimbursement for expenses properly incurred. Trustee shall determine what compensation is reasonable by referring to the fees charged for similar services in the community where Trustee is serving.

ARTICLE 16. SPENDTHRIFT PROVISIONS

1. Beneficiary has no right or power, whether alone or in conjunction with others in whatever capacity, to amend, revoke, or terminate this special needs trust. No interest in the income or principal of this trust may be anticipated, assigned, encumbered, or subject to any creditor's claim or legal process.

2. Because trust funds will be conserved and maintained for Beneficiary's special needs, no part of the income or principal shall be construed as part of Beneficiary's "estate" or be subject to the claims of voluntary or involuntary creditors for the provision of care and services (including residential care) to or for Beneficiary by any city, county, or state government; the federal government; or any public or private agency except as otherwise provided in this trust instrument.

ARTICLE 17. BOND

Unless required by a court of competent jurisdiction or the trust protector, Trustee and successor trustees are not required to post a bond.

ARTICLE 18. PHOTOCOPIES

All photocopies of this Declaration of Trust shall carry the same legal weight as the original.

ARTICLE 19. TRUSTEE NOT LIABLE FOR GOOD-FAITH ACTIONS

A trustee of any kind nominated by this document shall not be liable to any beneficiary for the trustee's acts or omissions, except in cases of willful misconduct, bad faith, or gross negligence.

CERTIFICATION BY GRANTOR

I certify that I have read this Declaration of Trust and that it correctly states the terms and conditions under which the trust property is to be held, managed, and disposed of by the trustee, and I approve the Declaration of Trust.

Dated: _____ June 15, 20xx _____

Gloria C. Escobar

Gloria C. Escobar, Grantor and Trustee

CERTIFICATION OF TRUSTEE(S)

I certify that I have read The Bessie Escobar Special Needs Trust and, having been appointed as Trustee by Grantor, I agree to serve as Trustee and to manage the trust property under the trust's terms and conditions.

Dated: _____ June 15, 20xx _____

Richard Sanchez

Richard Sanchez, Trustee

[Certificate of acknowledgment attached]

Finalizing and Funding Your Special Needs Trust

I f you have finished drafting your trust, congratulations! Now you have just a few more steps to finish it up. First, you'll take your trust to a notary, sign it, and have it notarized. Then you'll apply to the IRS for a taxpayer ID number, set up a trust bank account, and modify your estate plan to transfer money into the trust at your death. This chapter discusses each of these final steps.

Making Your Trust Legal

Your signature and the certificate of acknowledgment provided by a notary public make your special needs trust legal. Getting your trust notarized will be a straightforward task. Here are some tips.

Make Your Final Changes

Before you take your trust document to the notary, check it over carefully to make sure everything is as you want it to be. Here are some things to go over:

- Do you understand all of the clauses and why they're there?
- Are all of the names spelled correctly?
- Are the clauses numbered sequentially?
- Have you deleted all extraneous instructional text?

It's important that you double-check every part of the trust, because after you sign it and have it notarized, it becomes irrevocable. In other words, you can't make any changes to it other than to name a new successor trustee to replace one who becomes unable to serve.

Take Your Trust Document to the Notary

When you are satisfied with your document, take it to a notary public or another official qualified to make legal acknowledgments. (In some states, lawyers or judges can also perform notary tasks.) You and your initial cotrustee, if you have one, will sign the trust in front of the notary. The notary will check your IDs to make sure you are who you say you are, so bring your driver's license or your passport. The notary will then complete an "acknowledgment" that certifies that you were the one(s) who signed the trust. The notary will make that form official with his or her signature and a stamp or seal. When it's finished, attach the certificate to your trust.

To find a notary public, you can look online or in the yellow pages. Most title companies and banks also have notaries on site. Some UPS stores also have notaries on site. Fees for notary services are often set by state law and are usually less than $10 per signature. For an extra fee, you might also be able to find a mobile notary who will come to you. Since the COVID-19 pandemic, several states have allowed "virtual" notarization, where the notary and the document signers participate in an online meeting (audio and video).

When you have signed your document and attached the notary's certificate of acknowledgement, your special needs trust is legal and final.

What If You Want to Change Your Special Needs Trust?

You generally are not allowed to legally amend an irrevocable trust without permission from a court, except for those few exceptions you might have set forth in the document for the trust protector. If other changes need to be made, the person serving as trustee (presumably you, while you are alive) can terminate the trust under certain conditions. For example, the trust allows the trustee to terminate the trust for lack of adequate funding. After terminating the trust, you can create a new trust with a new taxpayer ID number that incorporates the changes you wish to make. If, acting as trustee, you do terminate the trust, make sure you notify the beneficiary, all successor trustees, all remainder beneficiaries, the beneficiary's guardian or conservator, and any affected agencies, such as SSI and Medicaid. If possible, also retrieve all copies of the terminated trust you have distributed.

> ! CAUTION
>
> **Florida requires witnesses.** Florida requires that you sign your trust in front of two witnesses. Use the special Florida Witness Statement, provided to you as a downloadable eForm. (See Appendix C.) Bring the witnesses with you to the notary. You will all sign the document there together. Trustees, successor trustees, or trust protectors of the trust may be witnesses, but the beneficiary of the trust may not.

Copies

After you sign your special needs trust and have it notarized, you should make copies to distribute to all the people who should know about it. For example, you might want to give copies to the people you have named as successor trustees, guardians or conservators of the beneficiary, remainder beneficiaries, and relevant agencies like SSA.

Keep the original in a safe place, perhaps with your estate planning documents. Some people keep these important documents in a safe at home or a safe deposit box at a bank. Make sure the successor trustees know where you keep the original in case someone needs to see it when you are no longer available.

Taxes

The trustee must file a federal income tax return (Form 1041) for the trust if the trust generates more than $600 (for tax year 2020) of gross income or any taxable income during the taxable year. Income generated by the trust is taxed at a special high tax rate for trusts. However, if income earned by the trust is used for the beneficiary's benefit, it can be claimed by the beneficiary and taxed at the beneficiary's rate which is commonly a lower rate even though the beneficiary never actually receives the income. So, when making disbursements from the trust for your loved one's benefit, use trust income before using the principal.

Form **SS-4** (Rev. December 2019) Department of the Treasury Internal Revenue Service	**Application for Employer Identification Number** (For use by employers, corporations, partnerships, trusts, estates, churches, government agencies, Indian tribal entities, certain individuals, and others.) ▶ Go to *www.irs.gov/FormSS4* for instructions and the latest information. ▶ See separate instructions for each line. ▶ Keep a copy for your records.	OMB No. 1545-0003 EIN

Type or print clearly.

1	Legal name of entity (or individual) for whom the EIN is being requested

2	Trade name of business (if different from name on line 1)	3	Executor, administrator, trustee, "care of" name

4a	Mailing address (room, apt., suite no. and street, or P.O. box)	5a	Street address (if different) (Don't enter a P.O. box).

4b	City, state, and ZIP code (if foreign, see instructions)	5b	City, state, and ZIP code (if foreign, see instructions)

6	County and state where principal business is located

7a	Name of responsible party	7b	SSN, ITIN, or EIN

8a	Is this application for a limited liability company (LLC) (or a foreign equivalent)? . . . . ☐ Yes ☐ No	8b	If 8a is "Yes," enter the number of LLC members . . . . . . ▶

8c	If 8a is "Yes," was the LLC organized in the United States? . . . . ☐ Yes ☐ No

9a	**Type of entity** (check only one box). **Caution:** If 8a is "Yes," see the instructions for the correct box to check.

☐ Sole proprietor (SSN) _____
☐ Partnership
☐ Corporation (enter form number to be filed) ▶ _____
☐ Personal service corporation
☐ Church or church-controlled organization
☐ Other nonprofit organization (specify) ▶ _____
☐ Other (specify) ▶

☐ Estate (SSN of decedent) _____
☐ Plan administrator (TIN) _____
☐ Trust (TIN of grantor) _____
☐ Military/National Guard   ☐ State/local government
☐ Farmers' cooperative   ☐ Federal government
☐ REMIC   ☐ Indian tribal governments/enterprises
Group Exemption Number (GEN) if any ▶ _____

9b	If a corporation, name the state or foreign country (if applicable) where incorporated	State	Foreign country

10	**Reason for applying** (check only one box) ☐ Started new business (specify type) ▶ _____ ☐ Hired employees (Check the box and see line 13.) ☐ Compliance with IRS withholding regulations ☐ Other (specify) ▶	☐ Banking purpose (specify purpose) ▶ _____ ☐ Changed type of organization (specify new type) ▶ _____ ☐ Purchased going business ☐ Created a trust (specify type) ▶ _____ ☐ Created a pension plan (specify type) ▶ _____

11	Date business started or acquired (month, day, year). See instructions.	12	Closing month of accounting year
13	Highest number of employees expected in the next 12 months (enter -0- if none). If no employees expected, skip line 14.	14	If you expect your employment tax liability to be $1,000 or less in a full calendar year **and** want to file Form 944 annually instead of Forms 941 quarterly, check here. (Your employment tax liability generally will be $1,000 or less if you expect to pay $5,000 or less in total wages.) If you don't check this box, you must file Form 941 for every quarter. ☐

Agricultural	Household	Other

15	First date wages or annuities were paid (month, day, year). **Note:** If applicant is a withholding agent, enter date income will first be paid to nonresident alien (month, day, year) . . . . ▶

16	Check **one** box that best describes the principal activity of your business. ☐ Health care & social assistance ☐ Wholesale-agent/broker ☐ Construction ☐ Rental & leasing ☐ Transportation & warehousing ☐ Accommodation & food service ☐ Wholesale-other ☐ Retail ☐ Real estate ☐ Manufacturing ☐ Finance & insurance ☐ Other (specify) ▶

17	Indicate principal line of merchandise sold, specific construction work done, products produced, or services provided.

18	Has the applicant entity shown on line 1 ever applied for and received an EIN? ☐ Yes ☐ No If "Yes," write previous EIN here ▶

Third Party Designee	Complete this section **only** if you want to authorize the named individual to receive the entity's EIN and answer questions about the completion of this form.		
	Designee's name		Designee's telephone number (include area code)
	Address and ZIP code		Designee's fax number (include area code)

Under penalties of perjury, I declare that I have examined this application, and to the best of my knowledge and belief, it is true, correct, and complete.

Name and title (type or print clearly) ▶		Applicant's telephone number (include area code)
Signature ▶	Date ▶	Applicant's fax number (include area code)

For Privacy Act and Paperwork Reduction Act Notice, see separate instructions.   Cat. No. 16055N   Form **SS-4** (Rev. 12-2019)

Tips for SS-4

Be sure to read the instructions that accompany Form SS-4. Here are our instructions, which assume that you are the initial trustee. If you're not, substitute the trustee's information for yours (except on Line 7; see below).

SS-4 Line Number	What to Write
Line 1—Legal name of entity (or individual) for whom the EIN is being requested.	Name of the trust, usually "The [*Name of Beneficiary*] Special Needs Trust."
Line 2—Trade name of business.	Leave blank.
Line 3—Executor, administrator, trustee, "care of" name.	Your name, as initial trustee.
Lines 4a–b—Mailing address.	Your mailing address, as initial trustee.
Lines 5a–b—Street address.	Your street address, as initial trustee, if different from Line 4. Otherwise leave blank.
Line 6—County and state where principal is located.	The county and state where the trust bank account will be located.
Lines 7a–b—Name of responsible party.	Your name and Social Security number.
Lines 8a–c	Mark "No" in 8a; leave 8b and 8c blank.
Lines 9a–b—Type of entity.	Check "other" and enter "Special needs trust" and your SSN on the line. Leave 9b blank.
Line 10—Reason for applying.	Mark "Created a trust" and write "special needs trust" on the line.
Line 11—Date business started or acquired.	Date the trust was notarized.
Line 12—Closing month of accounting year.	Write "December."
Line 13—Highest number of employees expected in the next 12 months.	Write "0."
Line 14—Employment tax.	Mark "No."
Line 15—First date wages or annuities were paid.	Write "Not Applicable."
Line 16	Mark "Other" and write "Special Needs Trust."
Line 17	Write "Special needs trust services."
Line 18	Check "No" unless you've applied before for an EIN. If you have, write in your previous EIN.
Third Party Designee. Fill out this section only if someone other than the grantor is doing the paperwork and should be contacted if the IRS has any questions.	
Name and Signature. Print your name, then sign and date on the line below. Write your phone number and fax number (if you have one).	

The trustee may also have to file state tax returns. Look for state-specific tax information on the state tax board's website or consult with a local tax professional.

See Appendix A (Letter to Trustee) for more information on filing trust taxes. If you have concerns about filing tax returns or about how trust income taxes work, see a tax professional who is knowledgeable about special needs trusts.

Obtaining an Employer Identification Number

Your special needs trust must have a taxpayer ID number. The IRS refers to this number as an Employer Identification Number (EIN) even though in your case it has nothing to do with employers.

You can get your number immediately by applying by phone or online at www.irs.gov. If you send the form through the mail or by fax, it might take you several weeks to get your EIN. The IRS will send you an official hard copy of your EIN after it processes your application. Make sure to keep this EIN confirmation with the trust document. Follow the tips above on how to complete the form.

Opening the Trust's Deposit Account

Once you have obtained your EIN and have the actual document from the IRS, you can open a deposit account for the trust at a financial institution.

Financial institutions typically require a document called a Certificate of Trust in order to get the account open. This is a short two to three page document summarizing the parts of the trust that the institution needs to know about in order to set up the account. Using a Certificate of Trust rather than giving the institution the entire trust document protects you and the trust beneficiary's privacy, because it allows you to set up the account without giving the institution sensitive personal information that it does not need. See Appendix C for a sample Certificate of Trust.

Take the document from the IRS showing your EIN and a copy of the Certificate of Trust to your institution of choice (bank, credit union, or brokerage firm) and tell an officer you want to open an account for the trust. Some financial institutions have their own Certificate of Trust that they prefer you to use. If that is the case, use the institution's form.

If you do not have a Certificate of Trust, the institution will probably want to see a full copy of the trust. Call your financial institution and make an appointment, if possible. During that call, ask what your financial institution requires to set up an account for a trust and make sure to bring the required documents, along with your photo identification.

Make a Small Initial Deposit

Depository institutions differ in the amounts they require to open and maintain trust accounts—usually in the low hundreds. You'll probably benefit from depositing the minimum, at least at first. The main reason to open a bank account now is to create a place to route property when you die. There is no particular reason to keep lots of money in the trust's bank account while you are alive. On the other hand, you might need to put money in the trust's bank account for other reasons. For example, you may choose to use this account to receive the beneficiary's gifts from other benefactors, or to minimize the assets in your estate if you're concerned about eventual estate tax.

> ！ CAUTION
>
> **Keep the beneficiary's funds separate from trust funds.** Never put the beneficiary's own funds in this special needs trust account. Doing so would put the beneficiary's SSI or Medicaid benefits at risk, because it might prompt those programs to treat all trust assets as a resource available to the beneficiary. If you want to shelter your loved one's own savings or other property in a special needs trust, see a lawyer. Do not use the trust in this book.

Keep in mind, however, that the less you deposit, the less you'll have to worry about taxes. As long as the trust produces less than $600 a year in income, you won't have to file a federal tax return. So you might want to keep the deposit less than the amount it would take to produce that amount of interest (roughly $12,000, at a 5% rate of return).

Notifying Appropriate Agencies

If you have deposited funds into the trust and the beneficiary of the trust receives need-based benefits through programs such as SSI and Medicaid, contact the office that runs that program and tell them about the trust. They will probably want you to send them a copy of the trust document so they can make sure it really is a third-party trust and that the trust property is not available to the beneficiary as a countable resource. They may also ask for proof of funding. A trust bank account statement or a copy of the check you used to deposit funds into this account will suffice as proof of funding. (See Chapter 3.)

If you have chosen not to deposit any funds into the trust at this time, there is no need to notify the public benefits agencies of this trust. SSA has specifically stated that they want to see special needs trusts only when they have funds in them. Remember that if you choose to fund this trust later during your lifetime, you should notify the appropriate agencies at that time.

Incorporating the Trust Into Your Estate Plan

To protect your loved one's benefits after you die, you'll need to leave property as a gift to the trust, not directly to your loved one. You must do this through your will, living trust, life insurance, deposit account, securities, or another estate planning tool.

If you die without legally specifying who should receive your property, the probate court will distribute it following "intestacy" laws. These laws give property to the deceased's closest relatives. Property passing to your loved one through intestate laws (rather than going directly to the special needs trust) will be owned by him or her. Medicare and SSI will consider that property your loved one's resource, seriously jeopardizing eligibility for benefits.

Avoid this problem by leaving property to the special needs trust through a will or revocable living trust, or by designating the trust as the beneficiary to inherit a deposit account, insurance policy, or securities.

Using a Living Trust or Will to Fund the Special Needs Trust

If you use a will or revocable living trust to provide for the beneficiary of your special needs trust, in the will, name the trustee of the special needs trust as the beneficiary of the property you want to leave.

> **EXAMPLE:** Carlos wants to provide for his three children in his will. One child, Jose, has a disability and will likely need SSI and Medicaid for the rest of his life. Carlos leaves two-thirds of his property directly to the other children and leaves the last third to Jose through the special needs trust. Carlos uses this language: "I leave one-third of my property (subject to this will) to the Trustee of the Jose Esparza Special Needs Trust created on January 20, 20xx." When Carlos dies, that third will go to whoever is serving as trustee at that time and will be placed in the trust's bank.

Funding a Trust Through a Beneficiary Designation

You can also leave money or property to a special needs trust through a beneficiary designation, used with a life insurance policy, deposit account, retirement account, or securities. Many people use insurance policies to fund their special needs trusts.

Because these types of assets involve a beneficiary designation, they pass to your loved ones outside of your will or revocable living trust. This means that in order for it to pass to the special needs trust, you must fill out the beneficiary designation correctly (the insurance company, bank, or broker will have a form that they can send you).

Name the trustee of the special needs trust as the policy beneficiary. You don't need to name the actual person, because you don't know who that will be. Rather, you name the "Trustee" of the trust. The proceeds will go to the person who holds that position when the time comes.

> **EXAMPLE:** Shirley creates a special needs trust for her son Richard, naming herself as trustee and her daughter Nan and nephew Ken as successor cotrustees. She designates the "Trustee of the Richard Jones Special Needs Trust" as the beneficiary of her $25,000 life insurance policy. When Shirley dies, Ken is unable to serve as trustee because of illness, so Nan receives the benefits as sole trustee of the trust. The money is held in the special needs trust, managed by Nan.

You can do the same with a bank account, certificate of deposit (CD), money market account, or stock brokerage account. Simply name the "Trustee" of the trust on the account's payable-on-death beneficiary designation form, which you can get from the company that administers the account.

Leaving retirement accounts to a special needs trust is very complex and requires special language in the trust (see Chapter 3), which the trust in this book does not include. If you plan to leave a retirement account to your loved one with a disability, you must speak to an attorney.

CAUTION

Do not name your loved one on the beneficiary designation form —name the trustee! Making this mistake could seriously jeopardize your loved one's public benefits after your death. Leaving the money directly would mean that your loved one would need to either spend the assets down until reaching the resource threshold for public benefits, or hire an attorney to put it into a different type of special needs trust, during which time, your loved one would be without the public benefits needed for daily and medical needs.

Leaving Property to a Pooled Trust

If you decide you want to join a pooled trust (discussed in Chapter 6), use your will, revocable living trust, insurance policy, or beneficiary designation to route property to the pooled trust.

Fortunately, most pooled trusts will tell you exactly how to leave property to the trust through your will, revocable living trust, or beneficiary designation. If they don't, they can usually put you in touch with a lawyer who can help you draft the right language. Here are some general instructions to give you an idea about the process.

If You Sign Up With a Pooled Trust Now

If you sign up with a pooled trust during your life and want to fund it with property you leave at your death, name the trustee of the pooled trust to receive any property you want to go to your loved one. This will authorize the successor trustee of your revocable living trust or the executor of your will to distribute the property to the pooled trust. For this to work, you'll need to know the identity of the trustee of the pooled trust. Some pooled trusts will want you to name the nonprofit organization in charge of the pooled trust and others will want you to name a bank or an individual who coordinates with a bank.

> **EXAMPLE:** Michael's daughter Annie has a developmental disability and receives SSI benefits. Michael signs a joinder agreement with a local pooled trust operated by The Arc. He plans to fund the trust when he dies by leaving money through his revocable living trust.
>
> Michael finds out that the trustee of the pooled trust is Bank of America, but that the pooled trust wants him to use the name of an individual cotrustee instead of the bank. So he names "John C. Parcival, Trustee of The Arc of Ohio Pooled Trust" to receive property left by Michael to Annie in his living trust.

Here is how this would appear in a revocable living trust document:

V. BENEFICIARIES

All trust property left to Anne L. Casey shall be given to John C. Parcival, Trustee of The Arc of Ohio Pooled Trust, to be used for Anne L. Casey's benefit under the joinder agreement signed by Grantor on January 3, 20xx.

As with all estate planning documents, review your living trust regularly to make sure it continues to reflect your wishes. As part of your review, confirm the name of the pooled trust and its trustee. These may change over time, and if the clause is outdated when you die, it will likely complicate your loved one's ability to join the pooled trust.

If You Don't Sign Up Now

If you want to use a pooled trust but can't find a suitable one that's available to you, create a special needs trust now to be used as a backup and direct the executor of your will or the successor trustee of your living trust to look for a suitable pooled trust after your death. (See Chapter 6.) With luck, by then there will be a pooled trust that will work for your loved one.

If this option sounds right for you, here is the language you can insert into your will or revocable living trust.

PART ___. [*NAME OF BENEFICIARY*] SPECIAL NEEDS TRUST

[*Testator/Grantor*] has created a special needs trust on [*date trust was notarized*] in the name of [*name of beneficiary*]. However, [*Testator/Grantor*] directs the [*executor/trustee*], before placing property in that trust, to explore the possibility of joining a pooled trust for the purpose of managing all property left to [*name of beneficiary*]. If after such exploration a suitable pooled trust is found, the [*executor/trustee*] shall join the trust and transfer property to that trust. If no suitable pooled trust is located and joined, all [*property left through this will/trust property*] left to [*name of beneficiary*] shall be placed in the [*name of beneficiary*] Special Needs Trust and managed according to its terms.

Preparing a Letter of Intent

A special needs trust can be an excellent tool to protect eligibility for public benefits and to provide financial support to a beneficiary. However, the trust itself doesn't provide much information about a beneficiary's needs or about how trust money should be spent. Without more information, a trustee who is taking over for a parent or another long-term caregiver might be left with little understanding about the beneficiary's disability, day-to-day needs, advocacy requirements, or how the trustee should spend trust funds.

A "letter of intent" (sometimes called a "memorandum of intent") is the best way to fill in the gaps that the special needs trust document doesn't cover. In the letter, you can explain your loved one's current needs, describe the care that he or she might need in the future, and lay out your wishes for how the trustee should spend trust funds. A letter of intent is not a required document—if you decide not to prepare one, the trust is still valid. But a letter of intent does provide an opportunity to leave critical information about your loved one to future caregivers. In fact, successor trustees might look at a letter of intent more frequently than the trust document itself, because it more fully addresses the financial and personal decisions caregivers have to make on a daily basis.

Preparing a letter of intent is a good idea even if the person who serves as successor trustee is the beneficiary's parent, sibling, other close relative, or friend who already has a deep understanding of the beneficiary's likes, dislikes, proclivities, habits, needs, and desires. If your successor trustee dies or becomes unavailable, your letter of intent helps ensure that whoever takes over will have a good understanding about how to proceed. Also, time can cloud or confuse memory, so if you have any specific wishes that should endure over years or even decades, writing them down in a letter can keep your wishes from fading with time.

The passage of time can also change the life circumstances of the person with a disability. It is important to review the letter of intent from time to time, to ensure the letter still fits the beneficiary's needs. An easy way to remember to review and update the letter of intent is to take it out each year on the beneficiary's birthday. You might need to update contact information, new therapies, new hobbies the beneficiary has taken up, or other changes.

Letters of intent are not legally binding. They offer trustees guidance and information, but a trustee is not required by law to follow a letter of intent's suggestions. Trustees are free to use their judgment to make decisions for the best interest of the beneficiary, even if those decisions contradict the beneficiary's preferences, or the preferences of the beneficiary's parent or previous caregiver. If you decide to write a letter of intent and find that you want future trustees to be legally bound to make certain decisions on behalf of your loved one, see a special needs planning attorney for help. (See Chapter 11.)

How a Letter of Intent Helps

A letter of intent documents the information that is often lost when a main caregiver (often a parent and trustee of the special needs trust) dies or can no longer care for a trust beneficiary. The main caregiver for a person with special needs is often also that person's lifelong advocate and decision maker, so when that caregiver becomes unavailable, critical information about caring for the person with special needs can be lost. Writing a letter of intent provides need-to-know information about caring for the person with special needs, so that a successor trustee can step in to make informed decisions.

When you write a letter of intent, you can include whatever information you feel would be relevant for a successor trustee to know about your loved one. The letter might include serious information, like a medical allergy or required treatment. Or it could be as simple as listing the beneficiary's favorite foods. It also might list which family members and friends should be allowed to visit and which should be avoided. Even when beneficiaries have the capacity to make their own decisions, a parent might still want to express some preference and limitations. Ultimately, the content of the letter is up to you. See "What to Include in Your Letter," below for more content suggestions.

In addition to information about the beneficiary, a letter of intent can provide guidance and instructions to a successor trustee about how to use the trust money. The trustee is often working with limited resources, and the trustee might be faced with difficult decisions about what to provide or not provide to the beneficiary to meet his or her daily needs. The trustee could also face questions about whether to make large disbursements for specific expenses (like a new therapy that shows promise) or whether the funds should be kept in the trust for later needs. A letter of intent can help a trustee make these tough decisions when the letter shares what the beneficiary's parent or former caretaker would do.

Tips for Writing a Letter of Intent

- Parents, brothers, sisters, other family members, and especially your loved one with special needs can contribute to the letter.
- The contents of the letter should reflect your wishes, without laying out demands. Future circumstances might make it difficult for others to carry out strict instructions. You must trust that those carrying out your plan will try to adhere to your expectations.
- Gear the preferences in the letter toward enhancing your loved one's independence and growth.
- Put your loved one's needs first; try to prioritize your loved one's needs over the convenience of others.
- Write the letter in your own personal style, avoiding technical language when possible. Use the letter to communicate your heartfelt desires.
- While a letter of intent is not legally binding, its contents should not contradict your trust. Provide a copy of your letter to your attorney (if you have one), so that he or she can check to make sure that it is consistent with the terms of your trust.

EXAMPLE 1: Julie is a 30-year-old with a rare genetic disorder that does not allow her to speak or communicate. Her mother recently died and Julie lives in a board and care facility. Her mother set up a special needs trust that exceeds $200,000. Julie's cousin Brian was named trustee of her trust because he is around Julie's age. Brian lives several states away and has not spent a lot of time with Julie. Upon funding the trust, several family members confront Brian about paying for them to come and visit Julie. Julie's board and care facility is demanding that Brian pay them for therapies that Julie is receiving, and are seeking to raise her monthly payment by a $1,000. Further, another family member is asking Brian to fund a $40,000 therapy that could give Julie a chance to communicate.

Brian wants to do a good job, but he does not know where to turn. The trust document does not include instructions on how to spend trust funds, but Julie's mother also wrote a letter of intent. In it, she explains that Julie should not visit the relatives who are demanding compensation (or have them visit her), as they have said hurtful things to the mother about Julie's condition and they have never helped with Julie's care. The letter goes on to explain that Julie's board and care is notorious for seeking payment for services it does not render. She has had to fight them over this many times, and she included the name of an attorney she has used to fight the facility. The letter of intent ends with a description of the various therapies they had tried for Julie over the years. Included in that list was the therapy proposed by the other family member, and it was unsuccessful.

Armed with this knowledge, Brian refuses to pay for the relatives to visit, rejects the distribution for the therapy, and hires the attorney to advocate on Julie's behalf with the board and care facility. Without the letter of intent, he would not have known the proper course to take. He could have made a misstep or spent weeks, if not months, to learn this information on his own.

EXAMPLE 2: Johnny, a 28-year-old former athlete with paraplegia, wants to climb the famed El Capitan monolith in Yosemite National Park. The cost, including paying a highly skilled fellow climber and renting lots of special equipment, will exceed $50,000.

Johnny's special needs trust currently contains assets worth $150,000, which were placed in the trust from Johnny's mother's will. Matthew, the person serving as trustee, has computed a rough budget of $10,000 a year. Matthew is concerned at spending one-third of Johnny's trust fund—and five times the annual budget—on one event, especially because Johnny might live another 50 years and will undoubtedly have many special needs over that period of time. Matthew is undecided on how best to handle Johnny's request.

Fortunately, Johnny's mother left a letter of intent. In it, she describes how she wants to support Johnny's lifelong dream to climb El Capitan, and that she would fully support spending money to do so. Matthew agrees to the distribution.

In this example, Johnny's mother could also have said that she wants to preserve the money in this trust for his lifetime needs, and that she would not support spending substantial amounts of money on one trip. Had she done so, Matthew might have made a different decision. However, in either case, Matthew has full discretion to make whatever decision he feels is in Johnny's best interest—even if such a decision directly contradicts the statements made in a letter of intent. That said, a trustee does have responsibility to comply with the intent of the people who established the trust. So, if the trustee refuses to follow an instruction in a letter of intent, he or she must have a good explanation as to why it is in the beneficiary's best interest to do so.

Before You Write Your Letter

Drafting a letter of intent can be difficult. It takes time, it might bring up difficult memories, and information can change quickly. Take your time, and keep in mind that there is no right way or wrong way to prepare one; it is just important to have one.

There is no set number of pages you should write, nor is there an exhaustive or exact list of topics to cover. For some people, it's enough just to put together one page of names and addresses of the people who have knowledge of their loved one. At the other end of the spectrum, other people might write 50 pages covering every aspect of their loved one's life.

> **TIP**
> **Try keeping a daily record of your loved one's needs.** If you're having trouble figuring out what to include in your letter, try keeping a daily diary of your loved one's needs for a few weeks or months. Doing so will likely provide a thorough record of what a future trustee might need to know, and it might be less overwhelming than trying to think of everything in one sitting.

What to Include in Your Letter

Below is a list of some topics you can cover in your letter. Read it as a way to spark ideas about what to include in a letter that reflects your loved one's needs and circumstances. To view an example of a completed letter of intent, see Appendix B. You might wish to include:

- **Basic information.** Include basic information about your loved one. For example, his or her full name, date and place of birth, and Social Security number, as well as the name and date of the special needs trust.
- **Contact information for close friends and family.** Provide the names of and contact information for relatives who have a good relationship with the trust beneficiary. Describe how often the beneficiary sees them and what the visits are like.
- **Agencies.** List any agencies that relatives, trustees, and guardians should contact for advice and help. For example, include the local chapter of The ARC, law firms, case managers, care providers, physicians, and therapists.

- **Financial information.** List financial information that might be of use. This could include any government benefits the beneficiary receives or may be eligible to receive, and any arrangements with a corporate trustee, a care manager, or another entity needed for continued care. Include the name and address, plus any special instructions.

- **Employment.** Note the jobs or volunteer positions your loved one has held. Also note any potential for employment, and the types of employment your loved one might like.

- **Education.** List specific courses and teachers that bear on the beneficiary's present abilities. Reflect on what types of educational opportunities might be possible in the future.

- **Living arrangements.** Describe the beneficiary's current living situation, and perhaps describe the living situation you anticipate for the future. For example, you can describe the type of living situation (live with a relative, or in a small group home, or an apartment with support), any preferences about location (such as the exact location or type of location), and any unique features (nonsmoking, religious adherence) that are relevant.

- **Day-to-day routines.** List favorite foods, daily and weekly appointments, and regular recreational activities.

- **Programs and services.** Provide schedule and contact information about school programs, day programs, sports programs, habilitation programs, or other programs and activities in which your loved one regularly participates. Also list any therapies or medical interventions that are needed, or might be needed, such as job training, speech therapy, or behavioral evaluations.

- **General medical history.** Explain your loved one's disability, how he or she has coped, and what you expect in the future.

- **Current medical care.** Describe your loved one's routine medical care and offer your opinions about whether it is appropriate or could be improved. List the contact information for doctors and other health care providers, including physical or occupational therapists.

- **Health insurance.** List any health insurance that should be maintained, including addresses, phone numbers, and insurance policy number. Make a copy of any insurance cards and attach them to the letter.

- **Personal preferences.** Provide some information about your loved one's personal interests and inclinations. For example, you could describe favorite clothes or personal care products, likes and dislikes about food, chores, and other routine daily activities, or favorite personal items (like an iPad, a pet, or a blanket). Also describe any personal habits that it would be important for someone else to know about.

- **Recreation.** List any favorite recreation and other leisure activities, including their frequency and the level of independence your loved one experiences while doing them.

- **Social environment.** Describe relationships with friends and acquaintances, including how often your loved one likes to visit with them.

- **Religious proclivities.** Offer a religious history, including contact information for any religious leaders with whom the beneficiary has a relationship.

- **Abilities.** Provide information about your loved one's level of independence for getting around the community. For example, explain any ability to ride public transportation, independence in shopping, and ability to go out alone. Describe your loved one's ability to handle money, as well as his or her ability to read, write, communicate, and comprehend communications from others. If your loved one is nonverbal, describe how he or she communicates desires or replies to others.

- **Preferences for funeral arrangements.** Give some thought to what you want to happen when the beneficiary dies. Do you have a preference about what kind of funeral to have, or whether you'd want a burial or cremation? How much money do you want the trustee to spend on funeral arrangements?

- **Beneficiary's estate planning or legal documents.** If your loved one has prepared his or her own estate planning documents, it might be a good idea to provide information about those documents, along with information about who is serving as the person's agent for financial or health care decisions. Also, if the person has a guardianship or conservatorship, identify the case name, county of origin, case number, and who is the legal representative.
- **Other relevant information.** Describe any aspects of your loved one's disability that you feel are particularly important to understand. For example, provide details if your loved one needs a structured environment, needs to be kept away from food, or becomes upset at loud noises.

After You Write Your Letter

When you've finished your letter, give a copy to anyone who might be responsible for decisions about the beneficiary, including the successor trustee. Or, attach the letter to the original special needs trust document so that it will be easily available to the successor trustee when the time comes.

To make sure that the letter is up to date and reflects your loved one's current reality, schedule a regular time to review and update it. For example, you could review the letter on your loved one's birthday each year. Is there a new primary care physician, a new address, a new therapy? Things change and your letter of intent should keep up. Remember to provide updates to anyone who has a copy. ●

Where to Get More Help

I n the course of using this book, you might find yourself in need of some expert advice, or at least some additional information. This chapter steers you to resources available online or in the library and offers some tips on working with professionals.

> **TIP**
>
> **The Internet is a great resource.** Getting answers can be as simple as using a search engine to look up "special needs trust" or other words that describe your questions, such as "Illinois pooled trust," or "SSI eligibility standards." You'll quickly get a lot of hits. Be patient and discerning and you likely will find what you need.

Robert Berring, a well-known law professor, always advises that the first step in all research is: Talk to a human being who knows something about the subject. The humans you will want to talk to about your special needs trust are:

- lawyers who specialize in special needs planning law, elder law, or Medicaid issues and who can give you individualized advice, and
- financial planners with a background in assisting persons with disabilities, who can help you figure out how much property you'll need to put in the trust and how to set up a sensible budget.

Lawyers

You can't beat a knowledgeable lawyer for good legal advice. In fact, licensed lawyers are the only people permitted to give legal advice. Other professionals, such as financial planners, insurance agents, Social Security Administration (SSA) personnel, and paralegals, might incidentally dole out information related to special needs trusts as part of their overall services. Lawyers, however, are the only people you can go to for legal advice tailored to your individual situation.

When to See a Lawyer

First and foremost, you'll want to talk to a lawyer if you feel uncomfortable about doing this important task yourself.

Even if you are comfortable with drafting your own trust, it's important to keep in mind that special needs trusts are intended to last for many years. Questions might arise that weren't anticipated in this book, perhaps occasioned by big changes in the SSI and Medicaid rules. Having a relationship with a lawyer whose job it is to keep track of new legislation might save you and your loved one with special needs a lot of grief due to loss of public benefits and potential fines down the line.

Finally, this book tries to cover the situations that most people encounter, but it doesn't contain details that might be important to you if your situation is unusual. For example, if two of your children have disabilities and you want to provide for them in a single special needs trust, you'll need help beyond this book. On the other hand, if you create a separate trust for each child, then there is no problem. The point is, if you have questions that aren't answered between these covers, a lawyer can help.

Asking a Lawyer to Review a Trust You've Drafted

If you want to draft your own special needs trust but just need some additional information, ideally you should be able to have a short consultation with a special needs trust lawyer, pay a reasonable fee, and get all your questions answered. Even better, for an additional fee, the lawyer would review your trust, make helpful suggestions, and give you the peace of mind that comes from having a knowledgeable professional looking over your shoulder. Unfortunately, these scenarios are unlikely for two reasons:

- Many special needs trust lawyers think people shouldn't create special needs trusts themselves because of the complexity and ever-changing rules and regulations on public benefits.

- Lawyers might be concerned that if they give you piecemeal advice or services, and down the road something goes wrong that had nothing to do with the lawyer's review, you or your heirs will still sue for malpractice.

Additionally, most states' laws specify that when lawyers have reviewed one part of a document, this creates responsibility for the entire document. If something is wrong with a part of the document that the lawyer did not review, the attorney can still be sued for malpractice.

It's also difficult for lawyers to analyze someone else's trust document—even one created by another lawyer. They much prefer to simply use the one with which they are familiar.

This being said, an experienced special needs lawyer might be willing to go over the trust document from this book and give you advice.

For experienced special needs planning attorneys, the trust in this book should not be too difficult to review and give you advice on. In searching for a lawyer who will do this work, we recommend that you find one who has experience in drafting special needs trusts (not all estate planning attorneys will have that experience) and, if a lawyer agrees to provide this advice, that the fees for doing so are put in writing.

How to Find Special Needs Trust Lawyers

The world is full of lawyers—but finding one who has the expertise you need and a manner you like can take some shopping around.

General Estate Planning Lawyers

If you are already working with an estate planning lawyer—perhaps for your will or revocable living trust—that lawyer will most likely be able to help you or refer you to a special needs trust specialist. Be careful though—many estate planning lawyers will try and draft these trusts themselves even if they don't have the necessary experience. This can result in an inexperienced lawyer drafting the wrong type of special needs trust, or inadvertently including provisions that can affect public benefits eligibility for your loved one. Use this book to educate yourself so that you can ask questions to see if your lawyer has the expertise to understand how to plan for your loved one with special needs.

Special Needs Planning Attorneys

The best way to find an attorney who specializes in this area is to go to the website for the Academy of Special Needs Planners. This is a national organization of attorneys devoted to doing planning for persons with disabilities. The organization has attorneys in just about every state with multiple attorneys in most states. You can search for an attorney in your state by going to www.specialneedsanswers.com/USA-special-needs-planners.

You might also try to get a recommendation from someone in your own informal network of friends and acquaintances. You undoubtedly know people with a family member who has the same or similar disability as your loved one—they might have already found a lawyer who could help you

You can also check in with any local or national group that concerns itself with a particular disabled population. There are hundreds of groups that focus on specific disabilities, such as spina bifida, paraplegia, cystic fibrosis, and autism. Chances are these groups work with lawyers who are adept at special needs trusts. Often, these lawyers have a child or relative of their own with a disability and have both practical and legal insights to offer.

Organizations that create pooled trusts (discussed in Chapter 6) can be an excellent place to obtain a referral. Go to the website of the Academy of Special Needs Planners at http://specialneedsanswers.com/pooled-trust to get contact information for pooled trusts in your state.

- **Nolo's Lawyer Directory.** Nolo has an easy-to-use online directory of lawyers, organized by location and area of expertise. You can find the directory and its comprehensive profiles at www.nolo.com/lawyers.
- **Lawyers.com.** At Lawyers.com you'll find a user-friendly search tool that allows you to tailor results by area of law and geography. You can also search for attorneys by name. Attorney profiles prominently display contact information, list topics of expertise, and show ratings—by both clients and other legal professionals.
- **Martindale.com.** Martindale.com offers an advanced search option that allows you to sort not only by practice area and location, but also by criteria like law school. Whether you look for lawyers by name or expertise, you'll find listings with detailed background information, peer and client ratings, and even profile visibility.

What to Look for in a Lawyer

First and foremost, you want a lawyer who has experience in drafting special needs trusts and to whom you feel comfortable asking questions.

In many parts of the country, you might have little choice of special needs trust lawyers. If so, as the old song goes, "Love the one you're with." But if you have several lawyers to pick from, here are a few questions to consider after an initial meeting:

- Does the lawyer seem interested in helping you resolve your specific questions and issues?
- Is the lawyer respectful of your self-help efforts?
- Does the lawyer seem confident of having the skills and knowledge to do the job well?
- Does the lawyer understand the disability and state benefits that your loved one with special needs is receiving?
- Are you willing and able to pay the lawyer's fee?
- Does the lawyer carry professional liability insurance?
- Perhaps most important, is the chemistry right? Do you feel reassured that you'll get exactly the services you need, no more and no less?

Paralegals

Social Security regulations explicitly authorize nonlawyer paralegals to represent clients in administrative proceedings dealing with benefit disputes. So, if you have questions about SSI and your state's Medicaid income and resource rules, a paralegal can be a good resource.

You can find paralegals in your area by searching online or using the yellow pages. In your area they might be called "document preparers" or "legal document assistants." Look for a paralegal who specializes in SSI and Medicaid matters, and compare fees.

Paralegals who work in the Social Security area are largely unregulated. If you want recourse in case you get bum advice, hire a paralegal who carries "errors and omissions" insurance—many do. Of course you might have to pay more if your paralegal is insured, but it can be worth it.

If you need information about customizing your special needs trust or your options for a different type of trust—for instance, one that takes effect at your death—you'll need to see a lawyer. Paralegals are limited to advice and information about Social Security matters. While paralegals are often critical team members in special needs planning law firms, they are prohibited from giving legal advice.

Certified Financial Planners

Special needs trusts can involve financial planning over a long period of time. Financial planners are people with accounting, investment, and insurance knowledge who can help you compute how much money you will need to accomplish your general estate planning goals and adequately fund your special needs trust.

Financial planners are not licensed professionals, but a central board certifies them. (For information about the certification process, visit www.cfp.net.)

Financial planners can provide a wealth of information on:

- how much money the special needs trust will need to accomplish your goals for your loved one

- a budget for the trustee who will manage the trust, and
- the best sources of funding for the trust, including advice on insurance options.

Just like attorneys, not all financial planners understand the unique financial requirements of a person with special needs. Make sure that the financial planner you select understands the financial needs that your loved one will have. Be sure to ask all of them how many times they have planned for a person with a disability and how they will incorporate public benefits into their planning. If they cannot answer these questions to your satisfaction, find another planner.

To find a local certified financial planner, visit these websites (or enter "certified financial planner" and your city's name into your favorite search engine):

- www.fpanet.org
- www.paladinregistry.com, or
- www.wiseradvisor.com.

Also some large financial institutions have planners who specialize in this area of financial planning:

- MassMutual has a program called Special*Care*, dedicated to special needs financial planning. The program provides information, specialists, and financial solutions to families with dependents of any age who have a disability. To get started, visit the company's website, www.massmutual.com/specialneeds.
- Merrill Lynch & Co. has set up a program that focuses on financial planning for special needs families and has a training program for its brokers. Call 800-260-2919 or visit the company's website at https://fa.ml.com/california/modesto/snt.

! **CAUTION**

Financial planners aren't always disinterested advisers. Many financial planners are affiliated with one or more insurance companies. Their advice might be sound, but they also have interest in selling insurance at rates that might not be in your best interest. Especially when you are exploring insurance options, make sure you ask the right questions. See Chapter 3.

SSA and Medicaid Personnel

A special needs trust is designed to preserve your loved one's SSI and Medicaid benefits. If you need more information about those benefits than this book provides, ask someone at your local SSA office. You might get lucky and get your question answered. However, even SSA and Medicaid personnel don't always know the rules, so be sure to get a second opinion before following their advice.

If a program near where you live delivers legal services to the poor, you might visit it and see what materials it has. You might find written resources explaining various aspects of the SSI and Medicaid programs, and the staff might be able to answer your questions.

Keeping Up to Date

Many years can pass between the time you create the trust and the time when it is fully funded (probably at your death). For example, if you are in your 40s or 50s when you create a special needs trust, at least 30 or 40 years will probably go by before you die. During that time, things that might happen include:

- SSI and Medicaid rules change in ways that require you to revoke or amend the trust.
- SSI and Medicaid rules change and make your loved one ineligible for benefits—which would eliminate the need for a special needs trust.
- Your loved one develops additional needs that you want to specifically provide for in the trust.
- Your loved one is no longer disabled and can inherit the property outright.

Obviously, you need to stay on top of such developments.

Subscribe to the Authors' Monthly Online Newsletter

Authors Kevin Urbatsch and Jessica Farinas Jones send out a monthly online newsletter called the "Special Needs News." The newsletter provides updates on public benefits and issues that involve persons with disabilities. To receive the newsletter, go to www.urblaw.com and follow the instructions for signing up.

Disability Groups' Newsletters and Websites

One excellent way to keep up to date on changes is to become active with a group that cares about disabilities and check its newsletters and website. Such an organization will pick up on any changes in government regulations. Some groups are listed below. You can also get information from groups that focus on a specific condition, such as autism or Down syndrome.

Getting Information About Disability Benefits and Laws

- Academy of Special Needs Planners, www.specialneedsplanners.com
- *Exceptional Parent* magazine, www.eparent.com
- Federal government agencies that provide services to persons with disabilities, www.disability.gov
- National Alliance on Mental Illness (NAMI), www.nami.org, and
- The Arc, www.thearc.org.

Federal Statutes and Regulations

If you want to be connected directly to the source of SSI and Medicaid regulation changes, you can read the government regulations themselves. Some of the language is dense, but the regulations can be helpful if you are willing to take some time to read and digest them. Most of them are in Volume 20 of the Code of Federal Regulations (C.F.R.), Section 416. Online sources are listed below.

Topic of Regulation or Statute	Citation	Website
Regulations issued by the Social Security Administration	20 C.F.R. §§ 416.101–416.2227	www.gpo.gov/fdsys
SSI resource rules	20 C.F.R. §§ 416.1210–416.1238	www.gpo.gov/fdsys
SSI in general	20 C.F.R. §§ 416.101–416.2227	www.gpo.gov/fdsys
Medicaid	42 C.F.R. §§ 430–456.657	www.gpo.gov/fdsys
Medicaid eligibility	42 C.F.R. §§ 435.700–435.740	www.gpo.gov/fdsys
Guidelines relied on by workers at the Social Security and local district offices	POMS (*Program Operations Manual System*)	http://policy.ssa.gov
State rules for Medicaid		www.medicaid.gov
How local SSI and Medicaid offices must treat special needs trusts	42 U.S.C. § 1396r-5 (Medicare Catastrophic Coverage Act of 1998), 42 U.S.C. § 1396p(d)(4) (A–C)(a–e)	www.ssa.gov

The particular areas of interest to you at all these sites are:
- how the SSI and Medicaid programs view special needs trusts funded by third parties
- what property the SSI and Medicaid programs consider the recipient's countable resources for eligibility purposes
- what the SSI and Medicaid programs consider to be income, and
- what the SSI and Medicaid programs consider to be income in-kind, including in-kind support and maintenance (ISM).

CAUTION
Help with legal research. Legal research, like other types of specialized research, has its own logic and terminology. Finding appropriate cases, knowing how to read them, and knowing how to find out whether a case you find is still good law are beyond the scope of this book. But Nolo can help you: *Legal Research: How to Find & Understand the Law*, by The Editors of Nolo (Nolo) will get you where you need to go.

Books

Needless to say, a fair number of books discuss persons with special needs. Most deal with raising children with special needs and address the entire subject, from cradle to grave. Special needs trusts are but one subject of many.

To find these books, simply go to a good bookstore and look in the special needs or parenting sections. Or try an online bookstore and search for "special needs." You might be surprised at how many titles appear.

A few books provide a more detailed discussion of special needs trusts, both self-settled and third-party trusts. Many of them were written for lawyers, and you're most likely to find them in a law library. Law libraries accessible to the general public typically are located in courthouses, civic center buildings, or public law schools.

All law libraries have reference librarians, who are generally most helpful and willing to get you started. Just ask for materials on special needs trusts and you'll probably be given more than you can comfortably deal with.

RESOURCE
Learn about administering a special needs trust. *Administering the California Special Needs Trust*, by Kevin Urbatsch and Michele Fuller (iUniverse), explains to trustees how to administer a special needs trust. You can find this book through Amazon.com or Barnes and Noble.

Glossary

Achieving a Better Life Experience (ABLE) account. An ABLE account is a tax-advantaged savings account available to individuals diagnosed with disabilities before age 26. The ABLE account is exempt for up to $100,000 for SSI recipients and allows a person with a disability to manage their own funds.

Affordable Care Act (ACA). A federal program that ensures health care for all Americans. Many persons with disabilities will qualify for subsidies if their income is under 400% of the Federal Poverty Level (FPL), or they may qualify for expanded Medicaid if their income is under 138% of FPL.

Antitransfer laws. Laws that penalize people who, in order to become eligible for means-tested benefits, such as SSI and Medicaid, have transferred their assets to others for less than fair market value.

Asset. Anything of value, including cash, promissory notes, tangible and intangible personal property, and real estate.

Beneficial interest. A type of property ownership held by people who are expected to benefit from trust assets in some way but who currently have no legal claim to them. The beneficiary of a special needs trust has a beneficial interest in the trust assets.

Beneficiary. Any person or entity entitled to inherit or receive property under a will or trust. The person for whom a special needs trust is created and whose needs will be paid for under the terms of the trust is the trust beneficiary.

Beneficiary designation. A document in which the owner of a deposit account, retirement account, brokerage account, or life insurance policy names a beneficiary to receive any funds left in the account at the owner's death.

Burial policy. An insurance policy that covers the cost of disposing of a person's remains.

Certificate of Trust. A brief document containing essential information about a trust, which financial institutions use to set up a bank account for a trust.

Code of Federal Regulations (C.F.R.). A set of publications containing regulations issued by federal agencies and organized by subject. Regulations for the SSI program are found in 20 C.F.R. §§ 416.101 and following.

Community trust. See "pooled trust."

Conditional SSI payments. Temporary SSI payments made on the condition that the recipient get rid of certain assets in an appropriate manner. They are made if an applicant for SSI has too many assets to qualify for that program.

Conservator (sometimes called a guardian). A person appointed by a court to make personal and/or financial decisions for another person (the conservatee or ward) who is not able to make them.

Conservatorship (sometimes called a guardianship). The relationship between a conservator and conservatee.

Corporate trustee. A bank or another financial institution that provides trustee services for various types of trusts. Many special needs trusts expected to be funded with $250,000 or more have a corporate trustee, instead of a family member, manage trust assets.

Corpus. A Latin term for the assets held in a trust.

Cotrustee. One of two or more persons or institutions named to manage trust assets together.

Countable resource. Property that the SSI and Medicaid programs consider available to an applicant or a recipient when determining that person's eligibility for benefits. Assets held in a properly drafted third-party special needs trust are not countable assets.

Custodianship. An arrangement created under a state law called the Uniform Transfers to Minors Act, under which a person may name an adult (the custodian) to manage property left to a minor until the minor turns an age between 18 and 25, depending on the state.

Direct inheritance. Property left outright to someone. SSI and Medicaid benefits might be reduced or eliminated if a recipient receives a direct inheritance, since the inheritance will be counted as income in the month received and as a resource in the following months. Property left to a special needs trust is not counted as a direct inheritance.

Disability. In general, a physical, sensory, psychiatric, learning, or intellectual impairment that affects daily living activities. Disabilities can be either temporary or permanent; they can arise from illness or injury or be present from birth. For the purpose of obtaining SSI and Medicaid, a disability is a mental or physical condition that leaves someone permanently unable to "do any substantial gainful activity."

Disabled. Having a disability. Many people with disabling conditions prefer to be identified according to their specific disability, such as "a person with paraplegia" or "a person with cerebral palsy."

Disbursements. Payments of trust funds by the trustee. In a special needs trust, the trustee typically makes disbursements to pay for the beneficiary's needs that aren't covered by SSI or Medicaid, such as a companion, school tuition, books, or hobby equipment.

Earned income. Wages paid by an employer or income from self-employment. Earned income can result in a reduced SSI payment.

Elder law. Legal issues typically faced by the elderly, including government benefits, nursing home care, and elder abuse.

Estate planning. Creating documents necessary to carry out your wishes for what should happen to your property and minor children after your death. Often, estate planning involves strategies designed to minimize probate fees so that more is left for inheritors.

Estate tax. Federal and state taxes imposed on the value of a person's net worth at death. For deaths in 2021, federal estate taxes apply only to estates with a net worth greater than $11.7 million, but some states tax smaller estates. For married couples, this threshold is doubled, meaning the net worth for 2021 can go up to $23.4 million.

Executor. The person named in a will to carry out the will's provisions, including filing the will in the proper court, inventorying the deceased person's property, paying debts and taxes, and distributing the remaining property to the beneficiaries named in the will. Called personal representative in some states.

Exempt asset. See "noncountable resource."

Federal benefit rate. The share of the SSI grant paid by the federal government. Many states add a supplementary grant to the federal benefit rate.

Federal poverty level (FPL). An annual guideline issued by the U.S. Department of Health and Human Services, used to determine who receives federal aid or subsidies. The Affordable Care Act uses the FPL to determine who qualifies for subsidies and who should have access to expanded Medicaid.

Fiduciary. A person who owes a special duty of trust to another person or entity. In a special needs trust, the trustee owes a fiduciary duty to the beneficiary of the trust to strictly comply with the trust's terms and to manage the trust solely for the beneficiary's benefit.

Financial planner. A person skilled in assessing people's financial needs and the various options for meeting them, including various types of insurance and investments. Many financial planners are certified by a central trade organization, but governments don't license them.

First-party special needs trust. A special needs trust funded with property belonging to the beneficiary, such as a direct inheritance, recovery in a personal injury lawsuit, or gift.

Food. Ordinary food—that is, food that isn't necessary because of special medical needs—needed by a beneficiary of a special needs trust should be paid for by SSI. If the trustee of a special needs trust pays for the beneficiary's food, the SSA considers the amount paid as income to the beneficiary and deducts it from the grant, up to a certain amount.

Funding a trust. Putting property in trust by assigning the property to the trust or changing title documents to reflect the trust's ownership. Technically, the trustee owns the trust property, subject to the trust's terms and the trustee's fiduciary duty.

Furniture and personal effects. As defined by the SSA, just about any property typically used in a home. Furniture and personal effects are not counted as resources for the purpose of determining a person's eligibility for SSI and Medicaid.

Gift. Property permanently transferred to someone without receiving anything in return. Property transferred to an irrevocable living trust while the giver is alive is considered a gift because the property can't be taken back. However, property transferred to a revocable living trust is not a gift, because the giver does not give up control over it and can revoke the trust at any time. Finally, property left at death under a will or living trust is commonly called a gift.

Gift tax. A federal tax on gifts (cash or assets) that are worth over $15,000 made by one person to a single recipient in one calendar year. The tax is not payable when the gift is made, but rather when the person giving the gift dies. Those who die in 2021 can make taxable gifts (during life and at death) that total up to $11.7 million per individual before owing gift tax. These exemption amounts will increase with inflation.

Good faith. The honest belief that one's actions are correct and appropriate. Some special needs trusts provide that trustees are not liable for losses caused by actions taken in good faith. Others do not excuse any actions that cause harm to a beneficiary, even if made in good faith.

Grantor. Someone who creates a trust. Also called settlor or trustor.

Group home. For purposes of the Medicaid program, a home in which two or more SSI recipients live and receive food and shelter for one overall price.

Guardian (sometimes called a conservator). A person appointed by a court to handle the personal and financial affairs of a child, or of an adult who has been judged to be unable to handle these matters alone. In many states, the term conservator is used when the incompetent person is an adult.

Independent trustee. A trustee who is not related to the beneficiary of the trust and does not stand to inherit any property under the trust. Independent trustees are preferred when family members are likely to disagree over management of the trust. However, independent trustees' fees are usually higher than those charged by a family member.

Inheritance. Property received as a result of another person's death. Typically, a person receives an inheritance under the terms of a will, revocable living trust, or state law. (Property belonging to people who die without a will is distributed in probate according to the state's laws of intestate succession.)

In-kind income. See "in-kind support and maintenance."

In-kind support and maintenance (ISM). Shelter or food provided to an SSI recipient. The SSA considers the value of ISM as income. It will reduce an SSI recipient's monthly grant, dollar for dollar, by the total value of the ISM the beneficiary received in a month, up to a certain amount. Also called "in-kind income."

Inter vivos trust. A trust created by a person during their lifetime (inter vivos is Latin for "between the living"). The most popular form of inter vivos trust is the revocable living trust. However, an inter vivos trust can also be irrevocable—for example, when living grantors create special needs trusts that they immediately put into effect.

Joinder agreement. The written contract between a person who contributes funds to a pooled trust on behalf of a disabled loved one and the nonprofit organization operating the pooled trust. The joinder agreement "joins" the beneficiary's funds with the other funds in the pooled trust.

Letter of intent (sometimes called a memorandum of intent). A term commonly used to describe a letter in which the creator of a special needs trust provides personal details about the trust beneficiary for the guidance of future trustees of the trust.

Living trust. A trust created during the grantor's lifetime, usually to avoid probate. The grantor is usually the trustee while the grantor is still alive; then the successor trustee takes over and distributes the trust property to beneficiaries named in the trust document

Long-term care. Nursing home care that lasts more than two months. Nursing home care typically is paid for by long-term care insurance, or by Medicaid if the patient meets strict income and resource limitations.

Master trust. A special needs trust under which a nonprofit organization operates a pooled trust on behalf of many individual beneficiaries.

Medicaid. A health care delivery program intended to serve people with limited income and resources. State and federal funds pay for Medicaid. States administer the program and (under federal rules) determine who is eligible for benefits.

Medically needy. People whose income is too high for regular Medicaid eligibility, but who are eligible for benefits if they contribute part of their income (called their share of cost) toward their medical care.

Medicare. A health care delivery system available to people who qualify because of age or disability and work history. Medicare eligibility does not depend on a person's income or resources. People who qualify for Medicare might still need Medicaid to pay for prescriptions and long-term care, and many people with limited income and resources receive benefits under both programs.

Negligence. Failure to act in a way in which a reasonable and prudent person would act under similar circumstances.

Noncountable resource. Property that is not considered a resource by the SSI and Medicaid programs for purposes of determining program eligibility.

OBRA. The federal Omnibus Budget Reconciliation Act, a law that, among other things, describes the circumstances under which property in a special needs trust will be considered the trust beneficiary's resource for the purpose of determining eligibility for SSI and Medicaid. (42 U.S.C. §§ 1395 and following.)

Payback provision. A provision in a special needs trust requiring that, after the beneficiary dies, the trustee must use any property left in the trust to reimburse Medicaid for benefits the beneficiary received. Special needs trusts containing property originally belonging to the beneficiary (first-party trusts) must have a payback provision to avoid having the property considered the beneficiary's resource for program eligibility purposes. Third-party trusts, like the one in this book, do not have a payback provision.

Per stirpes. A Latin term which describes a method of distributing the assets of someone who has died so that each branch of the family receives an equal share of the estate.

Personal representative. See "executor."

Plan for Achieving Self-Support (PASS). A plan (approved by SSI) that allows an SSI recipient to own otherwise countable resources as part of an effort to become self-supporting.

POMS. *Program Operations Manual System*, a set of guidelines issued by the Social Security Administration to help lower-level employees interpret the federal statutes and regulations that govern the SSI and Medicaid programs.

Pooled trust. A special needs trust operated by a nonprofit organization for the benefit of several beneficiaries. Assets are jointly managed and invested. SSI does not consider pooled trust funds donated by a third party for a beneficiary to be a resource available to the beneficiary.

Presumed maximum value (PMV). The presumed value of food or shelter provided to an SSI recipient by a third party. The PMV is the amount of the federal portion of the SSI grant plus $20. In 2021, this amount is $284.66. The recipient can prove that the value is, in fact, less.

Principal. Property held in trust. Income generated by the trust principal is considered income in the year received and principal if retained in the trust after that time. Also called "trust corpus."

Principal residence. A person's home and the land on which it is situated. SSI does not consider a person's principal residence a resource, regardless of its value.

Probate. A court proceeding in which the probate judge establishes the authenticity of a will (if any) and appoints the person (the executor or administrator) who will be responsible for handling the deceased person's estate. The executor or administrator pays the deceased person's debts and taxes, identifies the people who will inherit the deceased person's property, and distributes the property to them. Probate happens only when someone petitions the court to open a probate proceeding, and affects only property that hasn't been disposed of in some other way—for example, through a trust.

Prudent Investor Act. A law containing investment principles articulated by a group of nationally respected judges and law professors. Most states apply these principles to trustees in the absence of contrary investment instructions in the trust document. As a whole, the law requires trustees to make commonsense investment decisions that will best serve the purposes of the trust.

Remainder beneficiary. A person or an institution named in a special needs trust to receive trust property that remains in the trust at the death of the disabled beneficiary.

Representative payee. A person authorized by a government agency, such as the Social Security Administration, to receive benefits such as SSI payments on behalf of a recipient who is not competent to handle his or her own money.

Resource. For purposes of determining SSI eligibility, any property that the SSI program considers available to the applicant. See "countable resource" and "noncountable resource."

Revocable living trust. See "living trust." The term "revocable" refers to the ability of the person who sets up the trust to amend or revoke it.

Section 8 housing (also known as the Housing Choice Voucher Program). A federal rent subsidy program under which landlords accept low-income tenants. Tenants pay 30% of their income as rent, and the agency pays the rest.

SECURE Act. A law that became effective on January 1, 2020, which changed how retirement accounts are inherited after the account owner's death. Under the act, most beneficiaries of an inherited retirement account will be forced to receive the money within ten years, which could lead to a high income tax to the receiving individual. Persons with disabilities and their special needs trusts, however, can avoid this ten-year deadline and stretch out distributions over the individual's lifetime. In order to receive this stretch-out, the special needs trust must contain special language. *The trust in this book does not contain this special language. Readers should consult counsel if this issue pertains to them.*

Self-settled special needs trust. A special needs trust established by the person with a disability and funded with the person's own assets, such as a direct inheritance, recovery in a personal injury lawsuit, or gift.

Settlor. Someone who creates a trust; another term for "grantor."

Shelter. For SSI purposes, any item commonly associated with housing, such as rent, heat, utilities, and mortgage payments. Disbursements from special needs trusts for shelter are considered in-kind support and maintenance (ISM) and are deducted from the SSI grant up to a certain amount.

Sheltered workshop. A place of employment designed and managed to accommodate the needs of people with disabilities.

Social Security Act. A collection of federal statutes that govern a variety of federal programs, including Social Security retirement and disability benefits, Medicare, SSI, and Medicaid.

Social Security Administration (SSA). The agency charged with administering the programs created under the Social Security Act, including SSI and Medicaid.

Special needs. All needs of a disabled person for goods and services other than food and shelter, which SSI deems to be provided in the SSI grant itself.

Special needs trust. A trust designed to hold and disburse property for the benefit of an SSI recipient, without the SSI and Medicaid programs' considering the trust property or disbursements to be a resource or income. To accomplish this purpose, the trust typically gives the trustee sole discretion over trust disbursements and bars the trustee from making disbursements that would impair the beneficiary's eligibility for SSI and Medicaid. In addition, the trust must bar creditors from going after trust assets. A special needs trust funded with the beneficiary's own property (a first-party special needs trust) is subject to additional restrictions.

Spend down. A process in which a person spends resources on immediate needs, when that person would like to apply for certain Medicaid benefits but has resources over the resource limit. When the applicant's resources are sufficiently reduced, he or she will qualify for Medicaid.

Spendthrift provisions. Clauses in a trust aimed at protecting the trust property from the beneficiary's creditors or allowing the beneficiary to use the trust property as collateral for a loan. All special needs trusts contain spendthrift provisions.

SSDI. Social Security Disability Insurance. This federal program provides monthly cash payments to disabled persons who qualify because they have paid enough Social Security taxes. There are no resource or income ceilings.

SSI. Supplemental Security Income, a federal program that provides cash payments to persons of limited income and resources who are disabled (according to federal standards), over age 65, or blind. SSI is the main form of government support for people who aren't eligible for Social Security retirement or disability benefits and who meet the program's income and resources requirements.

Successor trustee. A person named in a trust to take over as trustee when the first trustee dies or is otherwise unable to serve. In a revocable living trust, the first trustee is the person who sets up the trust (the grantor). The successor trustee is the person who carries out the provisions of the trust after the grantor's death.

Supplemental needs trust. Another name for a special needs trust.

Support trust. A type of trust that allows the trustee to make disbursements for the beneficiary's general support as well as other needs. A support trust does not qualify as a special needs trust for the purpose of sheltering trust property from consideration as a resource by SSI and Medicaid.

Term life insurance. A type of life insurance that pays out the face value of the policy at the policy owner's death but that does not have an investment or savings feature. Term life insurance is often used to fund a special needs trust.

Testamentary trust. A trust created as part of a will or revocable living trust that goes into effect at the grantor's death.

Testator. Someone who makes a will.

Third-party special needs trust. A special needs trust funded exclusively with property given by people other than the beneficiary. The trust in this book is a third-party trust. Compare "first-party special needs trust," which contains property originally belonging to the beneficiary.

Transfer of assets. The act of getting rid of property for less than its fair market value in order to become eligible for SSI or long-term care benefits under Medicaid.

Trust. An arrangement under which a person called a trustee has a duty to manage certain property in a way that benefits a beneficiary. Trusts are created for many different purposes. See "special needs trust" and "living trust."

Trust administration. A trustee's management of trust property according to the trust's terms and for the benefit of the beneficiaries.

Trust protector. A person given limited authority to review a trustee's actions. Depending on the terms of the trust, a trust protector could have the authority to remove and replace a trustee, review trust records, and make minor modifications to the trust document. A group of trust protectors appointed and working together is sometimes called a "trust advisory committee."

Trustee. A person named in a trust instrument, or chosen by an existing trustee, to manage the trust under the terms of the trust document. The trustee must be loyal to the trust and avoid conflicts of interest with the trust beneficiaries. In a special needs trust, the trustee has a duty to manage the trust so that the beneficiary's special needs will be met without jeopardizing the beneficiary's eligibility for SSI and Medicaid.

Trustee powers. Specific grants of authority given to a trustee by the trust document in addition to, or in place of, authority granted by state law.

Unearned income. For SSI purposes, all income that does not result from employment.

Uniform Transfers to Minors Act. A law that provides a method for transferring property to minors and arranging for an adult, called a custodian, to manage the property until the child is older. (Not available in South Carolina.)

Whole life insurance. A type of life insurance that builds up equity in the policy owner's name and pays out a predetermined amount—when the insured person dies—to beneficiaries designated by the policy owner. Compare "term life insurance."

Will. A legal document in which someone leaves property and names a guardian to raise any surviving minor children after death. ●

Letter to Trustee

This appendix contains a wealth of information that you can put together for the people you choose as trustees. It explains the responsibilities the trustee will assume when he or she takes over the administration of the trust.

Read this appendix and think about any modifications you might want to make. For example, you will probably want to personalize the introductory letter and you might want to add notes about specific topics (such as investments or properties). Then, you can use the electronic version of this appendix to make your changes and print out copies for your trustees. For help accessing and using the downloadable e-forms, see Appendix C.

Letter to Trustee

Dear _____ :

Thank you for agreeing to be the trustee of a special needs trust for [*name of beneficiary*]. Here you will find some basic information about how that special needs trust works and what you will be expected to know and do as trustee.

You won't have to handle the trustee's job alone if the trust names a successor cotrustree to serve with you. In that event, the trust document will also tell you whether you can act independently or whether you and the other cotrustee(s) must agree to any actions taken on behalf of the trust. You should do your best to cooperate with other cotrustees to fulfill the purposes of the trust.

If you have questions that aren't answered here, the terms of the actual trust document are the final authority. The trust document was created using *Special Needs Trusts: Protect Your Child's Financial Future*, by Kevin Urbatsch and Jessica Farinas Jones (Nolo). You might want to look at that book for explanations of the various trust provisions. (If your trust document was drafted by an attorney, contact that attorney for specific instructions; don't rely on these instructions.)

You might also to want to review the book *Administering the California Special Needs Trust*, by Kevin Urbatsch and Michele Fuller (iUniverse). This book—written for trustees—covers nearly every situation that might arise during the administration of a special needs trust.

Again, sincere thanks for taking on this responsibility.

Managing a Special Needs Trust

This trust was created because the beneficiary is receiving—or will receive—benefits under the Supplemental Security Income (SSI) and Medicaid programs because of a disability. Both programs are generally available only to people with limited income and resources. The trust is designed to enhance the beneficiary's quality of life without interfering with SSI and Medicaid benefits.

As trustee, you have complete discretion over disbursements. The beneficiary has no legal control over trust property. As a result, the SSI and Medicaid programs don't consider trust assets to be a resource available to the beneficiary, and trust assets don't interfere with the beneficiary's eligibility for those programs.

An Overview

You are responsible for:
- communicating with the beneficiary
- investing trust assets prudently
- spending trust money to meet the beneficiary's special needs in a way that minimally interferes with his or her SSI and Medicaid benefits
- keeping good records
- preparing reports and notices required by SSI, Medicaid, and other interested parties identified in the trust document, and
- filing trust tax returns.

Each of these duties has a learning curve. You can get expert help with all of them, as discussed below.

Communicating With the Beneficiary

The core purpose of the special needs trust is to enhance the beneficiary's quality of life. This means you'll need to be sensitive to the beneficiary's special needs and have a basic understanding of how those needs can best be met. In some cases, there will be another person in the beneficiary's life—an advocate, a conservator, or a guardian—whose job it is to look out for the beneficiary. But in other situations, you will be the primary person the beneficiary depends on for help. If the beneficiary is unable to act independently, you might be called on to function as a surrogate parent.

If you are already well acquainted with the beneficiary—perhaps you are a sibling or another close relative—you will know what to do. But if you do not have much of a prior acquaintance with the beneficiary, you will need a lot of information. Ideally the person creating the special needs trust—the grantor—will have prepared a "letter of intent" that informs you about such things as the beneficiary's family and medical history, education, employment, living situation, social life, routines, and religion. If not, you should try to find these things out by talking to others who are familiar with the beneficiary.

Your Fiduciary Duty

As trustee, you are a "fiduciary"—someone who occupies a special position of trust. And because you have been entrusted with someone else's money, you have a "fiduciary duty" to faithfully implement the trust's terms. This means you'll need to give the trust document a very close reading and make sure you understand what you can and cannot do. For example, no matter how much you want to make a particular disbursement, you can't if doing so would result in the beneficiary's losing SSI and Medicaid.

You must administer the trust for the beneficiary's benefit. If a conflict of interest arises, your first duty is to the beneficiary. For example, if you are also the remainder beneficiary—the person who will receive any money left in the trust when the beneficiary dies—there is a conflict of interest between your duty to spend money to benefit the beneficiary and a natural desire to conserve the trust money in case you inherit it. This conflict doesn't legally prevent you from being trustee, but it does require that you put your own interests aside and administer the trust in the interests of the beneficiary.

Others can benefit indirectly from your acts as trustee, as long as your primary purpose is to benefit the beneficiary. For example, you could use trust funds to buy the beneficiary a car even if a friend or relative might use it on occasion.

Spending Trust Money to Meet the Beneficiary's Needs

All spending decisions are up to you. When you use trust property to benefit the beneficiary, you must make sure your disbursements don't cause the beneficiary to exceed the SSI income and resource limits. The trust prohibits you from making disbursements that would cause the beneficiary to lose SSI and Medicaid benefits unless it is in the beneficiary's best interest to make such disbursements.

SSI and Medicaid Eligibility Rules

SSI and Medicaid are available only to people who have limited resources and income. In most states, someone who qualifies for SSI also qualifies for Medicaid.

To avoid running afoul of SSI resource and income limits, follow these guidelines:

- **Never give the beneficiary cash.** A beneficiary who receives too much income will lose SSI benefits—and so Medicaid—at least temporarily. Except for the first $20 a month, all unearned income that is reported to SSI is deducted dollar for dollar from the SSI grant. And if you give too much income to the beneficiary, the SSI grant will be terminated for that month, along with Medicaid benefits.
- **Make payments from the trust directly to the provider of the goods or services for the benefit of the beneficiary.** The reason? Payments directly to the beneficiary count as income (regardless of what it's spent for), but payments to a third party for the beneficiary's benefit do not.

- **Don't use trust funds to pay for food or shelter unless you know it won't cause the beneficiary to lose SSI benefits.** (See below.)
- **Don't buy the beneficiary items that would put him or her over the SSI resource limit of $2,000 in assets.** (Many items, however, aren't counted toward the limit. See below.)

Exceptions to the rule that SSI eligibility equals Medicaid eligibility. In nine states, Medicaid eligibility is determined independently of SSI eligibility. These states are Connecticut, Hawaii, Illinois, Minnesota, Missouri, New Hampshire, North Dakota, Oklahoma, and Virginia. If the beneficiary lives in one of these states, you'll need to contact the state Medicaid office to get an exact fix on the effect of resources and

---

Some Things Special Needs Trusts Can Pay For

There are an enormous number of things that a special needs trust can pay for because the primary intent behind such a trust is to enhance the quality of life of a person with a disability. However, some care needs to be taken so a disbursement will not interfere with the beneficiary's public benefits. Below is a list of some (but by no means all) items and services that can be purchased that will not interfere with public benefits.

Automobile (car, van)	Conferences
Accounting services	Cosmetics
Acupuncture/acupressure	Courses or classes (academic or
Appliances (TV, VCR, DVD player,	recreational), including books
stereo, microwave, stove,	and supplies
refrigerator, washer/dryer)	Curtains, blinds, and drapes
Bottled water or water service	Dental work not covered by
Bus pass/public transportation costs	Medicaid, including anesthesia
Camera, film, recorder and tapes,	Dry cleaning and laundry services
development of film or photo files	Education expenses including
Clothing	tuition and related costs
Clubs and club dues (record clubs,	Elective surgery
book clubs, health clubs, service	Eyeglasses
clubs, zoo, advocacy groups,	Funeral expenses
museums)	Furniture, home furnishings
Computer hardware, software,	Gasoline and maintenance for
programs, and Internet service	automobile

Some Things Special Needs Trusts Can Pay For (continued)

Haircuts and salon services

Hobby supplies

Holiday decorations, parties, dinner dances, holiday cards

Home alarm, monitoring, and response systems

Home improvements, repairs, and maintenance (not covered by Medicaid), including tools to perform home improvements, repairs, and maintenance by homeowner

Home purchase (to the extent not covered by benefits)

House cleaning and maid services

Insurance (for automobile, home, or possessions)

Legal fees

Linens and towels

Magazine and newspaper subscriptions

Massage

Musical instruments (including lessons and music)

Nonfood grocery items (laundry soap, bleach, fabric softener, deodorant, dish soap, hand and body soap, personal hygiene products, paper towels, napkins, Kleenex, toilet paper, and household cleaning products)

Over-the-counter medications (including vitamins and herbs)

Personal assistance services not covered by Medicaid

Pets, pet supplies, and veterinary services

Physician specialists not covered by Medicaid

Pornography (as long as production and viewing is legal)

Private counseling if not covered by Medicaid

Repair services (for appliances, automobile, bicycle, household, or fitness equipment)

Snow removal, landscaping, and gardening (lawn) services

Sporting goods, equipment, uniforms, and team pictures

Stationery, stamps, and cards

Storage units

Taxicabs (and ride-sharing services such as Lyft and Uber)

Telephone service and equipment, including cell phone or pager

Therapy (physical, occupational, or speech) not covered by Medicaid

Tickets to concerts or sporting events (for beneficiary and an accompanying companion, if necessary)

Transportation (automobile, motorcycle, bicycle, moped, gas, bus passes, insurance, vehicle license fees, or car repairs)

Tuition and other educational expenses

Utility bills (satellite TV, cable TV, telephone—but not gas, water, or electricity)

Vacation (including paying for a personal assistant to accompany the beneficiary if necessary)

income on Medicaid eligibility. Medicaid eligibility standards in these states are roughly similar to those in the other states but, where there are variances, the rules tend to be a tad stricter. In these states, you will want to find a good contact person in the Medicaid department, or a private Medicaid specialist, to answer your questions.

SSI and Medicaid Resource Rules: The $2,000 Limit

The beneficiary can own the following assets and still be eligible for SSI:
- a primary residence, regardless of its value
- one vehicle of any value
- furniture and personal effects (such things as clothing, jewelry, recreation equipment, games and crafts, books, magazines, videotapes, telephone and answering machine, TV, radio, VCR, DVD, computers, musical instruments, and stereo)
- a total of $2,000 worth of any other kind of asset, including a bank account
- any property necessary for a plan (approved by the SSI program) of self-support (such as office equipment), and
- a life insurance policy and/or burial policy worth equal to or less than $1,500.

Trust funds are not, for purposes of SSI eligibility, counted as a resource available to the beneficiary. The beneficiary's special needs trust is called a third-party trust because the trust money in it never belonged to the beneficiary. It's important to keep it that way. So never put any of the beneficiary's own property into the trust. Doing so could jeopardize the beneficiary's eligibility for SSI and Medicaid.

Payments for Food and Shelter

If you never give the beneficiary cash, you probably won't have a problem with the SSI income limits. But you can also jeopardize SSI benefits by providing the beneficiary with food or shelter.

That's because trust money used to pay for food or shelter is counted as income to the beneficiary. It has a special name: "in-kind income" or "in-kind support and maintenance" (ISM).

SSI is intended to pay for food and shelter. If you use trust funds to give the beneficiary these items, the SSI grant will be reduced. The value of the food and shelter the trust pays for in a given month will be deducted, dollar for dollar, from the SSI grant—up to a maximum deduction of one-third of the federal portion of the grant, plus $20. In 2021, the maximum deduction is $284.66 per month. This cap will change every year, so you'll want to keep up to date.

If the SSI grant is wiped out completely by this deduction, Medicaid benefits will be lost as well. So, to avoid even a temporary loss of Medicaid eligibility, make sure that ISM doesn't exceed the SSI grant. In most states, the beneficiary's SSI grant is more than the $284.66 cap, so you don't have to worry.

For example, depending on where the beneficiary lives and the amount of money in the trust, you might reasonably pay $1,000 a month for the beneficiary's rent, causing a reduction of only $284.66 in the SSI grant. Not a bad deal. But if the SSI grant were less than $284.66, paying that rent would disqualify the beneficiary for SSI and therefore for Medicaid.

What is "shelter"? Expenses related to the beneficiary's residence count as shelter expenditures and can cause a reduction in the SSI grant under the ISM rule.

Items that count as shelter and trigger an ISM reduction	Items that don't count as shelter
• mortgage payments • rent • real estate taxes • gas • electricity • water • sewer • homeowners' insurance required by lender • condo charges that include the above items	• telephone • cable or satellite TV • premiums for personal property insurance • laundry and cleaning supplies • staff salaries • capital improvements to the home • repairs to the home

(416 C.F.R. § 1130(b); POMS SI 00835.465D)

If you are a tad nervous by now, here are two comforting thoughts to keep in mind:

- ISM payments count as income only in the month they're received. So, if you blow it and give the beneficiary too much income of whatever type, SSI and Medicaid will be restored the next month, provided the resource limit isn't violated.

- Even if the beneficiary is kicked off SSI because of too much income, there might be a way of reestablishing Medicaid eligibility if the trust pays the Medicaid program a certain amount every month as a share of cost.

Setting and Sticking to a Budget

Once you know the ground rules for keeping the beneficiary eligible for SSI and Medicaid, you'll want to decide how much the trust can reasonably spend every year on the beneficiary's special needs without bankrupting the trust. A ballpark budget would be based on four variables:

- value of the trust property
- the beneficiary's life expectancy
- the beneficiary's likely special needs, and
- how the trust property is invested.

You know, roughly, the value of the trust property. You can also obtain a rough life expectancy from actuarial tables and, if necessary, the beneficiary's doctors.

The information about the beneficiary's likely special needs will come from your personal knowledge or conversations with the beneficiary's family and friends. Also read any written information about the beneficiary that accompanies the trust document.

If you have financial skills, you might be able to sort this out yourself. But it would certainly be reasonable for you to hire a financial planner to help you arrive at a tentative initial budget.

One of the most difficult aspects of managing the trust can be sticking to your budget even if the beneficiary protests. For example, if the trust's budget is roughly $2,000 a year, and the beneficiary wants something that would cost the trust $10,000, should you honor the request or deny it? There is no easy answer. You'll have to use your best judgment. Whatever you decide, do your best to explain your decision to the beneficiary. Also, do your best to document the disbursement request and the reasoning behind your decision to either pay for the expense or not. If the beneficiary, the SSA, a trust protector, a public benefits agency, or anyone else challenges your reasonable decisions, having a documented history of your actions, made at the time, will corroborate your later explanations.

Investing Trust Assets

Your trust requires that you follow the investment guidelines set out in a law called the Prudent Investor Act. So, when investing trust assets, you must:

- balance risk against return
- diversify investments
- consider the purpose of the trust, and
- evaluate the investment portfolio as a whole.

Because the purpose of the trust is to supplement an SSI grant, your investments will normally be conservative and favor liquidity over long-term growth. However, if you invest too conservatively, investment income will not keep up with inflation. It will be important to find a balance that will produce sufficient income at a low risk. A mix of money market funds, index funds, equity funds, and bonds would be a typical investment portfolio for a special needs trust.

A closer look at these rules follows. A financial planner or another investment expert will be well versed in these requirements.

Balance risk against return. The Prudent Investor Act allows high-risk investments only if there is the reasonable possibility of a high return.

Diversify investments. To reduce risk, the act requires you to diversify investments. For example, if all of the trust property were invested in high-risk volatile stocks or in a low-risk savings account, the investment would not be diversified. Similarly, putting all the property in equity stocks, rather than part in stocks and part in bonds or other government securities, would fail the diversification test.

Consider the purpose of the trust. The purpose of the trust is to pay for the beneficiary's special needs for as long as possible without jeopardizing eligibility for SSI and Medicaid. The purpose is definitely not to build the value of the trust assets beyond what the beneficiary will need. Although all special needs trusts have essentially the same purpose, that doesn't mean that one investment strategy is right for all special needs trusts. You must take into account:

- the type of assets in the trust
- their value
- the beneficiary's life expectancy, and
- the projected cost of the beneficiary's special needs.

For example, a typical investment strategy might be to keep some cash in the bank to meet immediate needs and invest the rest in diversified mutual funds, keep a house that the beneficiary lives in, and sell trust assets that the beneficiary isn't interested in and that don't generate income—jewelry or a car, for example.

Evaluate the portfolio as a whole. Every investment decision is looked at as it relates to how all the other trust assets are being invested. And to plan a coherent investment strategy for all trust assets, you are allowed to look at all kinds of circumstances, including the economic climate, taxes, and unique nature of some assets.

Discussed below are some of the factors the Prudent Investor Act allows you to consider.

General economic conditions. If economic conditions are good, it makes more sense to invest in a growth stock than if economic conditions are bad. Put differently, optimistic investing should be justified by marketplace conditions.

Possible inflation or deflation. In inflationary times, it makes more sense to invest in real estate than in bonds. Similarly, inflation renders the value of money in a bank account stagnant, but investing in securities gives the trust property a chance to grow with the rest of the economy.

Tax consequences. As tax laws change, so should the types of investment you make. For instance, if the tax laws someday removed the capital gains tax on appreciation in real estate, it might make a lot of sense to invest some trust funds in real estate, as opposed to an investment that is subject to capital gains tax.

The expected total return. When making investment decisions, you'll want to consider the income that the trust assets are likely to generate and the expected appreciation of the value of tangible assets, such as real estate or art collections.

The beneficiary's other resources. If the beneficiary already owns a house (which is not considered a resource under SSI/Medicaid rules), investing trust funds in something other than real estate might make sense. But if the beneficiary needs adequate shelter, and the trust has enough cash for his or her special needs, it makes sense to buy a house.

Need for liquidity. A special needs trust always needs liquid assets that can be used to pay for expenses not covered by government benefits. So, you must put a priority on investments that provide enough cash to pay for the beneficiary's special needs. It's not the trustee's goal to have trust property appreciate in value in a way that will benefit only the remainder beneficiary.

An asset's special value. If some of the trust property consists of family heirlooms, furnishings, or personal effects that are important to the disabled beneficiary, it might make sense to hold on to them, even if it would benefit the trust economically to sell them and invest the proceeds.

Handling Taxes

You'll need to file annual federal and state tax returns. The trust has a taxpayer ID that you will use for all your transactions with trust funds.

Trust income is taxed at a much higher rate than personal income. If the trust income is kept in the trust, this higher rate will apply. But if you spend the income on behalf of the beneficiary (but don't give it directly to the beneficiary), the income can be taxed at the beneficiary's lower personal rate and still not be considered income to the beneficiary for the purpose of SSI and Medicaid eligibility. To accomplish this result, the trust's records should match the trust income against the trust expenditures.

If you are also the beneficiary's guardian, don't mix the beneficiary's income with trust property. For instance, if, in addition to your role as trustee, you are authorized by the Social Security Administration to receive the beneficiary's grant on his or her behalf (termed a representative payee), you'll want to maintain one bank account for the beneficiary's public benefits payments and another for the trust assets. This separation is necessary to keep the special needs trust from interfering with the beneficiary's SSI and Medicaid benefits.

Unless you are a tax expert, you'll be wise to work with one to set up your record-keeping system and to prepare and file the trust tax returns.

Making Reports

You'll need to keep careful records of all trust transactions so that you can make required reports.

Reports to SSI and Medicaid. SSI and Medicaid recipients are required to file monthly reports on any changes in their income, assets, or living arrangements and annual reports on trust activity. As long as you keep accurate books of trust activity, the beneficiary (or you, or the beneficiary's representative payee, guardian, or conservator) will have an easy time of meeting the beneficiary's reporting obligations.

Keep yourself informed about SSI and Medicaid. The SSI and Medicaid laws governing resources and income are subject to change. Because you must avoid trust disbursements that jeopardize the beneficiary's eligibility, you'll want to become and stay familiar with some key rules. You can find them online. There are two sets of rules for SSI:

- Regulations issued by the Social Security Administration and published in Volume 20 of the Code of Federal Regulations (C.F.R.), starting with Section 416.101 and ending with Section 2227. The income rules are found in Section 1100 and the resource rules in Section 1200. These regulations are available online at www.ssa.gov.

- Guidelines relied on by workers at the Social Security and local district offices are referred to as *POMS* (*Program Operations Manual System*). You can find information about *POMS* at http://policy.ssa.gov.

Each state issues its own Medicaid rules. Find them at www.cms.gov.

Terminating the Trust

Someday, you'll need to wrap up the trust. The trust document gives you the authority to terminate the trust in the following cases:

- The beneficiary dies.
- The beneficiary is no longer disabled.
- The funds in the trust are exhausted.
- SSI or Medicaid regulations change to make the trust a liability.

If the beneficiary dies, you must distribute any remaining trust assets to the people named as "remainder beneficiaries" in the trust document (Article 13).

If the beneficiary is no longer disabled, then you will distribute the trust funds outright to the beneficiary. If the funds are about to run out, there is no reason to continue the trust. Simply close any existing accounts and file a tax return indicating that the trust has been terminated. Check with the IRS to see whether other forms are necessary.

If SSI or Medicaid regulations change so that maintaining the trust would knock the beneficiary off those programs, the trust allows the trust protector to amend the trust to make it comply with current regulations.

If the regulations change so that there are no longer any resource limits for SSI or Medicaid, you will distribute the property to the beneficiary outright.

Before you terminate the trust, you are responsible for making sure that any debts and taxes owed by the trust are paid out of remaining trust assets. Specifically, you are required to:

- pay any legitimate debts that the trust still owes, such as legal or tax preparation fees
- file final federal and state income tax returns for the trust
- prepare what's known as a final account, showing a zero balance in the trust account

- pay any administrative expenses incurred in winding up the trust, such as attorneys' fees, and
- pay the beneficiary's funeral costs if there are no other sources.

If there is not enough money in the trust to take care of all these expenses, get some legal advice on setting priorities.

Getting Help

Most trustees need expert help from time to time. You can pay a reasonable amount, from trust funds, to hire such help. Here are some examples.

Kind of Help You Need	Where to Get It
Bookkeeping and tax preparation	Accountants, tax preparers
Investment advice	On the Internet Brokers Financial planners Books
Help with SSI and Medicaid rules	On the Internet Nonlawyer Medicaid experts Elder law lawyers Special needs planning lawyers

Here are a few books that might help you:

- *Special Needs Trust: Planning, Drafting and Administration,* by numerous California lawyers and edited by Kevin Urbatsch (CEB). This book is written for lawyers but it is the most comprehensive book covering administration issues for third-party special needs trusts.
- *Administering the California Special Needs Trust,* by Kevin Urbatsch and Michele Fuller (iUniverse). This book is written for the administrator of a California special needs trust and goes into depth on all aspects of special needs trust administration. Much of it can be applied throughout the country.

- *The Trustee's Legal Companion,* by Liza Hanks and Carol Elias Zolla (Nolo), provides key information about trustee duties. Although it's aimed at trustees for "living trusts," you'll find it helpful for some duties involved in administering a special needs trust, too. The book describes how to handle paperwork and keep beneficiaries informed and when to call in professionals if necessary.

Lawyers. You might find it necessary to get legal advice about your duties or the operation of the trust. Most lawyers who handle special needs trusts call themselves "special needs planning" or "elder law" attorneys. Because special needs trusts require knowledge of SSI and Medicaid rules, special needs trusts have become a specialty for these lawyers.

Two places to find special needs planning attorneys are:

- the Academy of Special Needs Planners website, www.specialneedsanswers.com, which lets you search for lawyers by state, and
- the National Academy of Elder Law Attorneys website, www.naela.org, which lets you search for lawyers by zip code or city.

Certified financial planners. Financial planners are people with accounting, investment, or insurance backgrounds who are adept with the numbers necessary to compute how much money you will need over time to accomplish a particular result. They are not licensed professionals, but a central board certifies them. They can provide a wealth of information on a feasible budget.

To find a certified financial planner in your area, enter "certified financial planner" and your city into your favorite search engine or visit these websites:

- www.fpanet.org
- www.paladinregistry.com, and
- www.wiseradvisor.com.

Documenting the Authority of Successor Trustees

The trustee must be able to show authority to invest or spend trust assets on the beneficiary's behalf. While the grantor serves as trustee, that person's signature on the trust document proves his or her authority to manage it. However, when a successor trustee—whose signature was not required on the face of the trust—takes over, it becomes more complicated to prove that authority. Successor trustees will need a paper trail that documents why each unavailable trustee cannot serve and who has taken his or her place. As trustee, you might also need to document your resignation or your appointment of a new successor trustee. The following sections show you how.

Assuming the Duties of Trustee

If the trust named you as a successor trustee, you will need to put together documents to show that all previous trustees are unavailable and that you have agreed to assume the position. For example, if the previous trustee died, you might need to produce that person's death certificate to show that he or she can no longer serve. If the previous trustee resigns or becomes incapacitated, you will need a letter of resignation or a doctor's letter attesting to the incapacity. If you are not the first successor, but the third or fourth successor trustee, you'll have to show that all trustees in line to serve ahead of you are unavailable.

In addition to showing that the trustee authorized to serve before you has become unavailable to serve, you must document that you have willingly assumed the trustee's role. An easy way to do this is to sign an affidavit to that effect and have it notarized. You can write the affidavit yourself and then sign it in front of a notary. An example affidavit is shown below—you can copy it, selecting and adding the appropriate terms and names to fit your situation.

After you've had the affidavit notarized, distribute copies to the beneficiary, the beneficiary's legal guardian or conservator, all successor trustees, and all remainder beneficiaries.

AFFIDAVIT OF ASSUMPTION OF DUTIES BY SUCCESSOR TRUSTEE

State of _____ County of _____

[*Successor trustee's name*], of legal age, first being duly sworn, declares:

On [*date*], [*name of grantor*] created The [*name of beneficiary*] Special
Needs Trust.

The [*name of beneficiary*] Special Needs Trust names me, [*name of successor
trustee*], as successor trustee to serve as [ ] trustee [ ] cotrustee if [*name(s)
of trustee or trustees*] [is/are] unavailable to serve.

On [*date*], [*name of unavailable trustee*] [died/resigned/was declared
incapacitated by a licensed medical doctor] and is therefore unavailable
to serve as trustee.

Attached to this Affidavit is [a death certificate for/a notice of resignation by/a
doctor's letter attesting to the incapacity of] [*name of unavailable trustee*].

[*Repeat these two clauses as necessary for each unavailable trustee named
in the trust.*]

I hereby accept the office of trustee of The [*name of beneficiary*] Special
Needs Trust and now act as trustee of that trust.

Dated: _____

Signed: _____
            [*Name of successor trustee*], Successor Trustee

[*Attach a certificate of acknowledgment.*]

Resigning as Trustee

If you need to resign your duties as trustee, you should do it in writing. Create a Notice of Resignation, have it notarized, and distribute it to the beneficiary, the beneficiary's legal guardian or conservator, all successor trustees, and all remainder beneficiaries. Here's an example of a Notice of Resignation.

NOTICE OF RESIGNATION

I, [*name of resigning trustee*], current trustee of The [*name of beneficiary*] Special Needs Trust, dated [*date trust executed*], resign my position as trustee, effective immediately.

Dated: _____

Signed: _____

       [*Name of trustee*], Trustee

[*Attach a certificate of acknowledgment.*]

Appointing a New Trustee

The trust document authorizes the trust protector to appoint a successor trustee if there is no named successor trustee available to serve. If, as trustee, you find it necessary to appoint a successor trustee to replace yourself, you should create an Appointment of Trustee. Have it signed by the trust protector, notarized, and distribute it to the beneficiary, the beneficiary's legal guardian or conservator, all successor trustees, and all remainder beneficiaries. Here is an example of that document.

APPOINTMENT OF TRUSTEE

I, [*trust protector's name*], trust protector of The [*beneficiary's name*] Special Needs Trust, dated [*date trust executed*], appoint [*name of person or entity being appointed*] as trustee, effective immediately. This appointment is made under the authority granted to the trustee in Article 6 of the trust document.

Dated: _____

Signed: _____

[*Name of current trust protector*], Trust Protector

[*Attach a certificate of acknowledgment.*]

Sample Letter of Intent

This appendix contains two sample letters and forms, which will make life easier for trustees as they assume and carry out their duties as a trustee. You can use the "Letter of Intent" as a model to provide your trustee with personal and intimate information about your loved one—information that will assist the trustee in making the best possible decisions about how the trust assets can be managed and spent for your loved one's benefit. Of course, every letter of this type will be different than another and should be tailored to each family's situation and experience. However, this example might stimulate your thinking about the letter you will want to write about your own loved one.

Also included in this appendix is a sample "Certificate of Trust," which summarizes key features of the trust. If you want to open a bank account for the trust, you'll need to provide the bank with certain information, which is contained in the certificate. Without a certificate, you will likely need to give the financial institution a full copy of the trust. If you use a certificate, sign it in front of a notary.

For your convenience, copies of the sample letter of intent and certificate of trust are available as downloadable e-forms. (See Appendix C.)

Sample Letter of Intent

May 6, 20xx

To the Trustee of the Special Needs Trust for Paul Sanchez:

We appreciate your future efforts on behalf of our beloved Paul and hope that you delight in him and his uniqueness as we have. We hope the following information will be helpful.

Family History

Paul has three older siblings who have always been affectionately involved in his life. We feel it is significant that each brother and his sister approached us individually years ago to ask to be his guardian if anything were to happen to us.

David Sanchez, 41 (wife Rebecca Chang, daughter Tiena Mei Sanchez, 2), 3211 Bayview Avenue, Alameda, CA 94501, 510-555-4567. Paul spends weekends with David and his family about once every six weeks and has phone contacts between visits. David often helps Paul find special DVDs he wants.

Mark Sanchez, 40 (wife Sonja Sanchez, sons Benjamin, 3, and Thomas, 1, and a child expected in a few months), 2445 Oak Avenue South, Minneapolis, MN 55405, 612-555-3219. Paul visits Mark and his family perhaps twice a year and has occasional phone conversations with Mark. Because Mark is a physician, we feel it is wise to consult him about any medical problems that Paul might have before making final treatment decisions.

Juliet Sanchez, 35 (partner Juliana Sorenstram, daughter Annika, 2, son Marcus, nine months), 815 Marcos Court, Santa Rosa, CA 95404, 707-555-9876. Juliet was a constant companion to Paul throughout his childhood, unbidden, a veritable "second mommy." Juliet and Paul share frequent phone calls. Paul spends the weekend with Juliet and her family about once per month. Among other helpful acts, Juliet is comfortable with Paul's personal needs, like helping him buy new shoes that accommodate his unusually small but wide feet, or even clipping toenails if she notices a need.

(Uncle) Steve Sanchez (wife Catherine Sanchez), P.O. Box 1750, Lakeport, CA 95453, 707-555-7895. Uncle Steve and Aunt Catherine have taken a warm and cheerful interest in Paul from his birth. One of Paul's first words was "Nunc" for "uncle." If Paul were ever to have any needs of a legal nature, we feel it would be wise to discuss them with Steve, who is an attorney.

(Cousin) Nicole Davis, 40, 1290 Eighth Street, San Francisco, CA 94122, 415-555-4369. Nicole spends time with Paul, usually at family celebrations, several times per year.

Other relatives with whom he has cordial but less frequent dealings are **Anne Davis and Richard Ross** and **Carol and Mickey Forlani** (aunts and their spouses), **Ken Sanchez and Sara Sanchez** (uncle and his wife), **Rubin Sanchez** (cousin), **Megan Sanchez** (cousin), **Dionne Davis** (cousin), and **Walter and Olivia Forlani** (cousin and wife).

General Medical History

Paul was born on July 31, 1985; he has Down syndrome. As a young child, he enjoyed good health but needed consistent medical attention for frequent ear infections, sore throats, and colds that regularly morphed into sinus infections. Fortunately, he had no cardiac problems, an issue for half the children with Down syndrome. He had pneumonia two times as a child. We find that yearly flu shots and pneumonia immunization as directed by his physician are important preventive measures.

His dentition was irregular and late. His skin is very fair and he sunburns easily. He continues to need to use sunscreen daily and to wear dark glasses outdoors. He has dry skin; flaking on his face or scalp is treated with Aquanil HC, an over-the-counter preparation.

When he was about 12 he had a difficult episode lasting many days of fearfully thinking he was changing into an animal. The episode faded, but as the years passed, occasionally other fears dominated his waking hours, basically unpleasant thoughts that he could not banish from his mind.

When he was 17, his father (a psychiatrist) realized that Paul had a form of obsessive-compulsive disorder. Treated with Zoloft, the uncomfortable symptoms disappeared at once. He continues to take Zoloft.

As a teenager he underwent a hernia operation.

At 22, he became very ill when he was thrown abruptly from a supportive school program (work experience for a couple of hours a day and a few more hours spent learning to make his way in the community) into an eight-hour workday with a brand-new 1½-hour bus ride on either end of the already exhausting regimen. Whatever sort of illness he had resulted in a painful mouth and gum infection. He already was having some problems with his gums, and the illness greatly exacerbated them. Then began serious dental work: gum grafts that were unsuccessful, rigorous training in dental hygiene and oral rinses with Periogard, and extractions of a number of teeth. He does not wear a prosthesis because it would have to be attached to teeth that are already loosening and would hasten their loss. He now alternates appointments for cleaning and checkups between his dentist and periodontist every two months. (Contact information below.)

In his mid-20s he developed low thyroid, and now takes Levoxyl to normalize his thyroid levels. Nevertheless, he tires easily and needs significantly more rest than average. He uses Beconase inhalant to prevent sinus infections. Paul has had a lifelong tendency toward constipation. He takes mineral oil nightly to control the problem.

Paul has a high pain tolerance. If he says something is painful, it is advisable to obtain medical assistance. He might have difficulty in localizing or explaining what is happening to him physically. For example, he might say, "My throat hurts," when he is nauseated. His internist is Kent Yasuda, M.D.

None of these health issues is particularly alarming, but like most people with Down syndrome, Paul benefits greatly from regular, consistent medical and dental care.

Paul has a tendency to put on weight. We try to advise him and monitor his eating habits, but with limited success. We worry that this tendency might cause health problems eventually.

Paul has severe obstructive sleep apnea and must always sleep—naps included—with his CPAP (continuous positive air pressure) mask in place.

Some additional caveats: People with Down syndrome have a severe hypersensitivity to atropine, a substance that can be used in eye examinations and sometimes following a surgery. Doctors treating Paul should be reminded of this. People with Down syndrome have more problems with anesthesia because of "sloppy airways" due to their low muscle tone; surgery should not be lightly undertaken. Some people with Down syndrome develop weakness in their spinal cord due to atlanto-axial subluxation; Paul did not have the condition when he had spinal X-rays as a child, but it can develop later in life.

Paul handles the regimen of health measures and medicines described above on his own. He benefits from regular reminders, lists, and discussion. Often when asked, for example, if he is remembering to take his Beconase, he will say, "Oh, that's right, I forgot."

Paul had therapy and counseling for several years after some traumatic events. He enjoyed the support and benefited greatly from therapy. If he seems troubled, we would like him to have this opportunity again. It would be best to investigate which therapists are comfortable, experienced, and interested in working with Paul.

Current Medical/Dental Providers

We have always kept Paul on our medical insurance; at this time he uses Medicare and has a supplemental insurance plan from the County Health Plan. He has no dental insurance. We feel adequate medical and dental care are a priority and prefer to have Paul cared for by specialists who have treated other people with Down syndrome and are familiar with the medical needs that can accompany the syndrome.

Kent Yasuda, MD, internist, 4710 Yolanda Avenue, Santa Rosa, CA 95403; 123-555-8764

Robert Jeffords, DDS, dentist, 40 North Main Street, Santa Rosa, CA 95403; 123-555-4567

Richard Smithson, DDS, periodontist, 1416 Mountain View Lane, Santa Rosa, CA 95403; 123-555-6589

Education

Paul was "mainstreamed," as the practice of attending regular school classes was termed when he was a boy, until he was 17 years old. He was extremely well liked by other students, with many friendships extending to the present. He was usually supported academically by the Resource Room Specialist. He reads at about a fourth- or fifth-grade level, and writes perhaps like a third-grader. Paul can add a little and used to be able to subtract.

He developed a talent for writing unique poems. They are quite wonderful. If asked, he will write one for any occasion.

Paul's speech is often difficult to understand; his missing teeth compound the problem. Patience is sometimes required. His thought processes are much more advanced than one would expect listening to his articulation.

At 17, he began attending Special Education classes to prepare him for practical issues like work experience, bus riding, and money management. It was also an opportunity for him to have classmates who were true peers. He finished school at 22 years of age. During those years he enjoyed attending classes at Santa Rosa Junior College, and continues to talk of wishing for such an opportunity again. He lives in walking distance of SRJC, but the logistics of working during the day, doing chores with housemates when he returns home after a lengthy bus ride, and his fatigue have militated against taking more courses. He does delight in thinking of any meeting or class as a "graduate school class."

Employment

Paul has been in supported employment in the community since he was 22. He is with an enclave of several workers with a supervisor on site. We feel this situation is preferable to working alone since he takes a number of weeks of vacation, some without pay; this custom might be difficult if a business was depending only on Paul for certain services. During these approximately four weeks per year, spread out, he travels and celebrates family occasions, as when cousins visit from Sweden. We also feel it is beneficial for him to have peers who are work colleagues. It is possible that as he grows older, Paul might need a different work situation—less stressful perhaps, or perhaps with transportation provided. Time will tell.

Currently he is at Dynamat, a technology company in Rohnert Park. He does assembly work. He is accurate and quite slow compared to the average worker. His supervisor, Tom De Leon, is ideal for Paul. Paul has a tendency to become too easily offended by other people, especially authorities. Mr. De Leon is limitlessly pleasant and respectful with Paul.

The organization that currently supports Paul's employment is **North Coast Industries**, 123-555-9641. He takes part in the occasional social events, such as The Human Race in May and a dinner dance during the year. Generally speaking, Paul needs transportation to these and any social events. He is capable of riding the bus only on routes on which he has been trained. He rides the city and county buses to his workplace. North Coast Regional Center sends him his bus passes monthly.

At times, there have been recurrent issues of Paul's not going to work when he was not ill. We feel it is important for him to be out in the world working during the week, like everyone else. We find that giving him an allowance of spending money contingent on his going to work daily is effective. He receives $30 per week in spending money if he goes to work every day. If he does not go one day, he receives only $5 per day. So, if he stayed home one day, he would receive only $20 allowance that week. Naturally if he is ill or has a conflicting engagement like a medical appointment, his allowance is not docked.

It is common for Paul to ventilate frequently about mild negatives in his life, and not comment on the positives. Therefore, it is best to pay attention, evaluate, and not react too quickly when he complains about work, his supervisor, or coworkers.

Lately, he has been expressing a desire to work at Agilent Technologies, where his sister is employed, and which is near Arcangel House. Perhaps at some point he might try that, since there is a North Coast Industries work group located there that does assembly work.

In the past, Paul had jobs that involved too much heavy labor for him. For example, one job required him to lift many flats of soft drinks. He vastly prefers lighter work, more complex work, too.

Current Living Situation

Our opinion is that Paul currently needs an arrangement between an overly protective group home, where he probably would not have his own room, and living in an apartment by himself with little oversight and companionship. In our county, a continuum of alternatives was not available. Personally, we were very happy living with Paul, but for many years he had been saying, "I want to move out. I want to be independent."

When he was 25, Jane Ford, a lifelong friend and advocate for Paul, called to say, "You know that project we are always talking about for Paul? I'm ready to do it." What a surprise! Jane bought a house, 4567 Arcangel Avenue, in Santa Rosa, perfectly located near shops, markets, Santa Rosa Junior College, the Recreation Center, and buses. It is even across the street from a workshop for more involved people with special needs, so there are speed bumps in the street for safety. And wonderfully, the house is only two miles from our home and his sister Juliet's home. After living at Arcangel House for five weeks, Paul came home to celebrate Passover with all of us. He pointed to the place on the kitchen doorjamb where we have never painted over the dates and heights of our children. "Dad, you've got to measure me again. I'm tall now."

After a few years, Jane Ford wished to sell the house; we bought it so that the situation, which by then we knew worked so well for Paul and his housemates, could continue. The house has three bedrooms, two baths, and a modest garage apartment. Paul lives there with two other people his age who happen to have different special needs, but function roughly about like Paul. Paul has a voucher from HUD from the City of Santa Rosa, which means that he pays up to one third of his income (including Social Security) for rent. The housing authority pays the difference. Right now, his rent is $500, of which he pays around $200.

He and his housemates are supported by a person, currently Cheryl Frost, who lives rent free in the garage apartment. She earns money by being the three housemates' IHSS (In-Home Supportive Services) worker. She helps organize housekeeping chores among the housemates, cooks their evening meal, and generally stays in tune with how their lives are going. **Oaks of**

Hebron (123-555-5927) is an organization that supports the housemates too, by assigning a Community Support Facilitator (CSF) who is available to Paul, and who visits him weekly, helps him pay bills or straighten out problems with the buses—generally is available to help solve problems as they arise. The CSF also can take him to medical or dental appointments. It has been our practice to be at such appointments also, and we usually drive Paul home afterwards.

In Paul's situation, the caregivers can purchase food at the Food Bank, so Paul pays only $150 per month for food. We like to supplement this weekly by buying him melon (cut into chunks), cottage cheese, eight cans of tomato juice, and a bag of romaine lettuce. We do so because he needs low-calorie alternatives to help him control his weight, and because he needs fruit and vegetables in some quantity to help with his chronic constipation.

As is his wont, Paul often complains about aspects of his living situation. We find it best to listen and let him express his feelings, even though we usually judge that his living situation, or job situation, or relationship situation is probably optimal. Paul is not apt to tell us about the positive aspects of his life, for some idiosyncratic reason. He might say he "wants to live in the apartments in Rohnert Park." These are individual apartments for people with special needs with no one permanently on site if a need arises. We do not feel that this situation is safe for Paul over the long haul. We feel he needs more support, especially since he has always had and continues to have difficulty saying "no" to any suggestions by others, which could lead obviously to dangerous situations.

It is possible that Paul might need a more supportive environment, probably a group home, as he grows older. If he were to develop a condition such as diabetes, we would definitely want him to live in a group home where his increased medical needs could be met.

Day-to-Day Routines

Paul is quite self-sufficient. He rises and prepares himself for his workday independently. He fixes his own breakfast, packs a lunch, and walks to the bus stop by 7:30 a.m. He takes the bus to work and begins work at 8:30 or so. He wears a fanny pack with identification, bus passes, cell phone, and dark glasses. He has a backpack with his lunch and other necessaries like his treasured iphone with its Beatles songs.

Because Paul fatigues more readily than the average person, we have had his workday shortened. He walks to the bus stop to catch a bus home around 2 p.m. He arrives home, walking from the bus stop around 3 p.m. He then does assigned household chores, like sweeping and mopping the floors. Whoever is living in the garage apartment prepares dinner for the household and the four of them share the meal.

Paul is accustomed to calling us each evening at around 7 p.m. This is his own idea, though we admit we find it pleasant. He likes to recount a little about his day and his thoughts. It is perhaps a ten-minute chat. We feel happy that his living "on his own" has not lessened the affectionate connection that we have with him.

In the evening, he listens to his music collection or looks at a video or DVD. He and his fiancee Annie share a phone call.

He does his own laundry weekly. Paul likes to wear all clean clothes daily.

He is well groomed. He needs occasional reminders about what to do about, say, flaking scalp.

On weekends, he often visits a family member or his fiancee. He might attend a movie or a party, perhaps with housemates. He doesn't mind being in his home (Arcangel House) on weekends; actually he likes it. On Sundays, he likes to be there shortly after midday to make a transition to the upcoming workweek.

Paul has a longtime interest in and detailed knowledge of the Beatles, especially John Lennon. He likes to purchase tapes, books, videos, and DVDs, plus the occasional T-shirt about the Beatles or other topics. He likes to pore over books about the Beatles. He used to write poetry, and will do so now if encouraged.

He needs to exercise, but tires quickly on long walks or lap swimming. Something is better than nothing, we feel. He does better if the exercise is incorporated in his day—for example, walking to and from the bus stops.

Paul enjoys most foods. He always has, even as a small child.

Social Environment

Paul has always been a well-liked person. He dated frequently as a teenager. He is in a romantic relationship with **Princess** (called **"Annie"**) **Priest** (Eddington Hall Apartments, Rohnert Park; 123-555-7693). We strongly feel that their relationship should be celebrated, but we do not believe that the couple should live together or marry. Paul and Annie seem to get along best when they spend most of a weekend together. Longer contact results in quarreling. Paul spends part of a weekend with Annie about two times per month. We regard Annie as a daughter-in-law; she attends most family celebrations.

As stated above, Paul has frequent and loving contacts with his brothers and sister and their families. He has developed skills in relating to his young nephews and nieces.

Lejf Jensen is a few years younger than Paul; they have been lifelong friends. They continue to see each other socially several times per year. Usually they do an activity together and share a meal somewhere. Lejf is currently a disc jockey at "Four More," a trendy radio station in San Francisco; he also works as a substitute special education teacher.

Matt Conrack is a friend since elementary school. Paul visited him in New York last year, where he was in graduate school. Again, they have cordial social contacts several times per year—usually an outing and a meal together.

Pat and Cassie Garcia, brother and sister, were neighborhood playmates when they were all toddlers together. They remain interested in Paul and sometimes contact and visit him.

Any of these friends would probably need help in setting up a social contact with Paul. If Paul received a phone message, he would not be able to call the person back on his own (although he can do so with family members who are in the speed dial of his phone).

Currently, it seems difficult for Paul to mix socializing and working. Activities that take place during the workweek are too much for him. He thinks of social activities as taking place on the weekend.

Paul usually says "no" if asked if he wants to do something, especially something social. This is a knee-jerk first reaction to most suggestions of any kind, and should not be taken too seriously. We try to help him keep his social life going by encouraging, sometimes almost insisting, that he take part in a social activity. Maybe one or two per weekend. He is often tired after two or three hours at a social event, and it is reasonable for him to return home then if he wishes to.

We believe it is important for him to interact with friends who also have special needs. He and Annie often double-date with Brent North and Julia South, who live in the same apartments as Annie. Her apartment is located near many restaurants and a cineplex, allowing them to choose independently.

In recent years, Paul (and usually Annie) have been delightedly participating in wonderful, low-cost travels arranged by Jane Ford, an old friend, and her organization. This year, he is traveling to the Grand Canyon next month, and will cruise the Inside Passage of Alaska in the fall. Many of the same people are present on each trip. The group also went Christmas shopping in San Francisco this year. Paul considers it "his club." We hope this opportunity will continue.

There are others in the community who understand Paul and his needs from long years of contact and experience. They would be available to consult.

Sue Lake, MA, special education teacher (4672 Alejandro Drive, Santa Rosa, CA 95404; 123-555-4691), was his infant teacher and has remained in close contact with us. A great deal of problem-solving around issues that have arisen for Paul has included Sue's views.

Nancy Fernandez (9420 Glencannon Drive, Santa Rosa, CA 95405; 123-555-9321) is a longtime friend as well as the mother of Lejf Jensen. She is a special education teacher too. Again, problem-solving for Paul usually includes her suggestions.

Nancy Barlotti, RN, (679 Purrington Road, Petaluma, CA 94952; 123-555-0368), is a fellow parent of a person with special needs very different from Paul's and a former coworker in Early Intervention. Her perspective on Paul is wise.

Jane Ford, MSW, (123-456-7890) who originally bought Arcangel House where Paul lives, and who runs the trips for him and others, has known Paul all his life. Her views on any issues would be helpful.

Travel

Sometimes Paul flies to visit friends or relatives. He travels with a family member or on his own. When he flies alone, we buy what the airlines call their "unaccompanied minor program." This means that a staff person on board is assigned to be available to Paul if he needs help, or if the plane must change its itinerary due to weather or another exigency. Paul will be released only to the person whose name is given before Paul boards the plane. Under the program, whoever takes him to the airport or comes to pick him up is allowed through security to the gate. When he flies with a family member, we pay the family member the same amount of money for any supervision that might be helpful to Paul.

Religious Proclivities

As an interfaith family, we have always observed and celebrated both Jewish and Christian holidays. Very occasionally Paul attends First Methodist Church with me. He also participates with Oaks of Hebron personnel in occasional religious activities.

Preferences for Funeral Arrangements: We find it difficult to address this topic for one of our children, but here goes: We would like Paul to participate in organ donation, but are not sure if that is possible if a person has a different number of chromosomes from the average, as is the case with Paul's form of Down syndrome.

Arrangements should be whatever the surviving family deems appropriate. Perhaps a memorial service in a Methodist church or Jewish temple with spoken tributes from those of us who have loved him so, as well as thoughts from a clergyman. Certainly any service should include lots of Beatles music. We would very much like to have him laid to rest near us, his parents; we fervently hope he will never be far from us. Probably cremation is suitable. An informal family celebration of his life, with Beatles music and a buffet, might follow the service.

Other Relevant Information

Paul has a talent for choosing gifts for family and friends, as well as for planning parties.

Paul loves to have the opportunity to "be in charge" or be given a responsibility. For example, he was happy when he could volunteer at the Recreation Center, serving soft drinks. Sometimes when he travels with a small group, he is in charge of keeping track of the suitcases, or of calling everyone for dinner.

Paul is unfailingly punctual (far better than his mother); he organizes his belongings neatly; he remembers all appointments and engagements, and keeps an accurate calendar. He has an excellent memory for people, and for details about them like their birthdays (or even "half-birthdays").

He understands which amounts are more or less as far as money, but needs significant guidance in managing finances. Paul does not have a conservator, so it is necessary to obtain his cooperation through explanation and discussion regarding both medical treatment and financial management.

Paul cannot say something that is untrue, for example to manipulate a person or situation; he doesn't understand the concept. It might be important to know, however, that if he is asked a direct question, such as "Why did you do that?" he will probably interpret it as a demand for an answer. His response then will be his best guess, but he does not use niceties of expression like, "Well, it might have been because...." His answer will sound like a statement, because that is the syntax he understands how to use. This statement might not be accurate, but simply his effort at pleasing with a required response. Also, if he is worried about something, he might state it as a fact. He might say, "My supervisor said I have to get a new job," when what he really means is, "My supervisor reprimanded me today and I am worried that if he is mad at me maybe he won't want me to work here."

Paul is a lifelong client of **North Coast Regional Center**. A specific Client Program Coordinator, currently Dorothy Merriwhether, is assigned to him and available to discuss and help solve issues that arise.

If Paul disapproves of a comment or an opinion we express, he might hang up the phone or storm off angrily. After about ten minutes, he will return to discuss the matter calmly and without anger. He is reasonable and ultimately open to support in the form of suggestions presented in a friendly manner.

We hope you find this account helpful. Paul's welfare has been a priority for our family all his life. We are now entrusting his welfare to you.

Sincerely,

Lois and Bob Sanchez

Certificate of Trust

Paul Sanchez Special Needs Trust

The currently acting Trustee of the Paul Sanchez Special Needs Trust dated, May 6, 20XX, declares as follows:

1. The Grantors of the trust are Lois and Bob Sanchez.

2. The trust is irrevocable and presently exists.

3. The currently acting Trustee of the trust is:
   John Sanchez
   Address: 123 Main Street, City, State, 12345
   Telephone: (123) 456-7890
   Email: john@email.com

4. The Trustee may conduct business of behalf of the trust without the consent of any other person or entity.

5. The tax identification number of the trust is 12-3456789.

6. Assets held in the trust may be titled in any manner that identifies the Trustee and the name and date of the trust, for example:
   John Sanchez, Trustee of the Paul Sanchez Special Needs Trust, dated May 6, 20XX

7. The powers of the Trustee include the power to acquire, sell, assign, convey, pledge, encumber, lease, borrow, manage, and deal with real and personal property interests of all kinds, including accounts at financial institutions.

8. Excerpts from the trust agreement that establish the trust, designate the Trustee, and set forth the powers of the Trustee will be provided upon request.

The statements made above are accurate and the trust has not been revoked or amended in any way that would cause the representations in this Certificate of Trust to be incorrect. The currently acting Trustee of the trust that is identified above is a signatory to this Certificate of Trust.

Dated: June 9, 20XX _____
                              John Sanchez, Trustee

[Attach a certificate of acknowledgment.]

Using the eForms

This book comes with electronic forms that you can access through its Web page:
www.nolo.com/back-of-book/SPNT.html

Using the RTFs

The electronic version of the special needs trust is in rich text format (RTF). You can open, edit, save, and print the RTF files using most word processing programs such as Microsoft *Word*, Windows *WordPad*, and recent versions of *WordPerfect*.

Here are some general instructions about editing RTF forms in your word processing program. Chapter 8 provides detailed instructions about how to complete your special needs trust. Editing functions include:

- **Underlines.** Underlines indicate where to enter information. After filling in the needed text, delete the underline. In most word processing programs, you can do this by highlighting the underlined portion and typing CTRL-U.

- **Bracketed and italicized text.** Bracketed and italicized text indicates instructions. Be sure to remove all instructional text before you finalize your document.

- **Optional text.** Optional text gives you the choice to include or exclude it. Delete any optional text you don't want to use. Renumber numbered items, if necessary.

- **Alternative text.** Alternative text gives you the choice between two or more text options. Delete those options you don't want to use. Renumber numbered items, if necessary.

- **Signature lines.** Signature lines should appear on a page with at least some text from the document itself.

Every word processing program uses different commands to open, format, save, and print documents, so refer to your software's help documents for help using your program. Nolo cannot provide technical support for questions about how to use your computer or your software.

> **CAUTION**
> In accordance with U.S. copyright laws, the forms provided by this book are for your personal use only.

List of Forms

The following files are available for download at:
www.nolo.com/back-of-book/SPNT.html

Form Name	File Name
Special Needs Trust	SpecialNeedsTrust.rtf
Sample Letter of Intent	SampleLetterIntent.rtf
Letter to Trustee	LettertoTrustee.rtf
Florida Witness Statement	FLWitnessStatement.rtf
Questions to Ask a Potential Professional Trustee	QuestionsTrustee.pdf

Index